Subbureaucratic
Government in China
in Ming Times

Instituttet for
sammenlignende
kulturforskning.

The Institute for
Comparative Research
in Human Culture,
Oslo.

Serie B: Skrifter
LXIV

Leif Littrup
Subbureaucratic Government in China in Ming Times
A Study of Shandong Province in the Sixteenth Century

INSTITUTTET FOR SAMMENLIGNENDE KULTURFORSKNING

LEIF LITTRUP

Subbureaucratic Government in China in Ming Times

A Study of Shandong Province
in the Sixteenth Century

Universitetsforlaget
Oslo – Bergen – Tromsø

© Instituttet for sammenlignende kulturforskning 1981
(The Institute for Comparative Research in Human Culture)
Oslo, Norway.

ISBN 82-00-09531-2
ISSN 0332-6217
UNIVERSITETSFORLAGET

Distribution offices:
NORWAY
Universitetsforlaget
Box 2977 Tøyen
Oslo 6

UNITED KINGDOM
Global Book Resources Ltd.
109 Great Russel Street
London WC1B 3NA

UNITED STATES and CANADA
Columbia University Press
136 South Broadway
Irvington-on-Hudson
New York 10533

Printed in Norway by
Tangen-Trykk, Drammen

Contents

To my parents

Acknowledgements

During my seven years in secondary school Aage Fasmer Blomberg made the past come to life both as history and as story-telling. Now in his seventies he still publishes scholarly works on the local history of my native region.

The Institute of History at the University of Copenhagen is a formidable place to learn the craft of the historian, and the East Asian Institute a good place to learn Chinese. Søren Egerod's inspired and inspiring introduction to the Classical Chinese language laid a sound foundation for my work with Chinese sources, and later he has untiringly supported my historical studies.

In a reply to a written request Charles O. Hucker suggested that I translate chapter 20 of the *Da-Ming Huidian* for my *cand.mag.* dissertation. This was the beginning of my interest in Chinese local administration.

I pursued this interest further when I got the opportunity to study in the Department of Far Eastern History, Australian National University, Canberra, in the years 1974–1977. The first draft of the present work was finished as a thesis in the congenial and stimulating environment of that department. Igor de Rachewiltz took time off from his research on Yuan history to guide me through the intricacies of a research apprenticeship. I can only hope that this book does not fall too short of his rigorous standards for scholarship. With Wu Chi-hua and Merrilyn Fitzpatrick I had many stimulating discussions on Ming history. May Wang was a reliable adviser on textual problems, and Andrew Fraser undertook the laborious task of editing and correcting the first version of my English writing. As examiners Wolfgang Franke, Tilemann Grimm, Michel Cartier and Liu Ts'un-yen read through the first draft and suggested a few improvements.

The staff of the Asian Studies Collection, Menzies Library, A.N.U. did amirable work in procuring material. Iwami Hiroshi and Naitō Shigenobu made available a microfilm copy of the *Shandong Jinghuilu*, and Wolfgang Franke, Joanna F. Handlin, and Ray Huang gave prompt replies to my queries about sources. Norma Chin and Marianne Klem have at various stages typed parts of the manuscript, Winifred Mumford drew the map, and Huy-dong Shin wrote the characters.

My wife, Lisbeth Littrup, followed me around the world, but only temporarily suppressed her own career. In Canberra we raised our two infant children, and she found time to pass her *cand.mag.* degree at the University of Copenhagen, using the Royal Danish Embassy in Canberra as an examination hall. She also became a highly esteemed tutor in Southeast Asian studies at A.N.U., and after our return to Denmark she has started her own career as a *gymnasium* teacher. In Canberra Ines de Rachewiltz gave us generous assistance while our family settled in that beautiful city.

My research has been funded first by the Australian taxpayers through a scholarship at A.N.U., and later by a grant from the Carlsberg Foundation and a fellowship at the University of Copenhagen. Instituttet for sammenlignende kulturforskning has now honoured me by including the book in their publications series.

I am grateful to the above-mentioned persons and institutions for their generous support. However, now that I present the book they are all behind the scenes. On stage the supporting parts are the works of scholars I have not yet had the opportunity to meet and learn from. Their parts are revealed in the notes, and I hope that I have been loyal in presenting their results and opinions. The leading parts are the historical sources from Shandong Province. The interpretation of these parts and the direction of the actors to give a coherent performance has indeed been a very solitary struggle, so I can truly say that the responsibility for any omission or commission remains with the author.

Copenhagen, March 1981.   L.L.

JINAN PREFECTURE

BEIZHILI

Haifeng •
• Zhanhua
Leling
• Yangxin
Binzhou •
○ Wuding
Lijin •
Dezhou •
• Deping
Putai •
▲ Lingxian
• Shanghe
Pingyuan
○ Linyi
Qingcheng •
○
• Qidong
• Xincheng
○ Jiyang
Changshan ○
Yucheng ●
Zouping ○
DONGCHANG
○ Qihe
Zhangqiu ○
● Licheng
Zichuan •

QINGZHOU

● Changqing

● I
● Feicheng
◉ II
● Taian
Laiwu ▲
○ III
Xintai ▲
• Zero A
YANZHOU
▲ Zero B

Location map

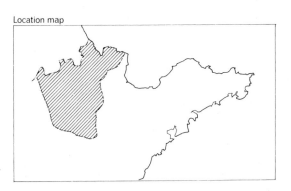

13

MING REIGN PERIODS

Hongwu	1368–1398
Jianwen	1399–1402
Yongle	1403–1424
Hongxi	1425
Xuande	1426–1435
Zhengtong	1436–1449
Jingtai	1450–1456
Tianshun	1457–1464
Chenghua	1465–1487
Hongzhi	1488–1505
Zhengde	1506–1521
Jiajing	1522–1566
Longqing	1567–1572
Wanli	1573–1619
Taichang	1620
Tianqi	1621–1627
Chongzhen	1628–1644

I. Introduction

The years 1380 and 1381 were turning points in the history of the Ming dynasty. During these two years measures with long range implications were taken to curtail the power of the bureaucracy, both at the top and at the bottom of the administrative ladder. In 1380 the Hongwu emperor abolished the Secretariat and the Chief Councillors, in whose hands ministerial authority had been concentrated. He also abolished the Chief Military Commission and the Censorate, but the removal of the Secretariat was no doubt the most important act, since the civil bureaucracy lost its official leaders. In 1381 the whole empire was ordered to adopt the *lijia* organization. With follow-up measures over the next seventeen years a subbureaucratic government system was rapidly introduced, which for a long time impeded the development of the yamen administration under the district magistrates. Much of the subsequent history of Ming administration is the story of how officialdom expanded its power and field of operations without unacceptable infringements on the decisions made by founding emperor of the dynasty, Zhu Yuanzhang.

The abolition of the Secretariat has been much maligned by later generations as the act that initiated imperial despotism unprecedented in Chinese history. Zhu Yuanzhang did sometimes rule in a way that can only be described as unrestricted despotism; and the bureaucracy was left without formal leadership for the rest of the imperial period. However, few if any of the succeeding emperors exercised the despotism of the Hongwu emperor. The workload on the emperors as the sole co-ordinating organ in the central administration was backbreaking, so they had to find capable people to assist them in their daily work. The Grand Secretaries in the Hanlin Academy became the administrative assistants of the emperors. Many of them played a dominant role in the government, but as members of the Hanlin Academy, where many of them had spent their whole career, they were not automatically the leaders of the civil bureaucracy. Other assistants were eunuchs, who at certain times rose to positions of power and influence over the

15

bureaucracy. Some times this influence could be detrimental to the orderly operations of government business. At other times, particularly when alliances were created between capable Grand Secretaries and eunuchs, their combined leadership could generate positive results. So the central administration of the Ming dynasty should perhaps be characterized as pluralistic with despotic elements, rather than purely despotic.[1] Judgements on the positive or negative effects of the abolition of the Secretariat are bound to be speculative. But except for shorter periods China has remained united and has for long periods enjoyed considerable stability and prosperity.

While the development at the top of the administration has been regarded as a decisive break with a long tradition, the developments at the bottom of the administrative ladder have been considered as part of a long tradition. Administrators and historians have, since the Ming period, assiduously traced the roots of the *lijia* organization and associated institutions through the subbureaucratic government systems of the preceding dynasties back to the institutions of local participatory government described in the Rites of Zhou – or vice versa.[2] The modern historian would do well to keep in mind this favourite pastime of many Chinese scholars, particularly in the process of source evaluation. There is, however, a danger of dwelling too much on a superficial description of the institutions through the ages and seeing continuities where they did not exist. This study is, like many recent studies, an attempt to see the institutions in their contemporary context, with only scarce attention to pre-Ming developments. I make no claim of complete success in this aim, and I am not at all sure whether the references to the past are too few or too many.

A few remarks on the history of the subbureaucratic government institutions are warranted here. From the Rites of Zhou onwards they have usually in principle been organized on the basis of a number of households, often multiples of five or ten. Important developments probably took place in the Northern Wei dynasty. Prior to that time the subbureaucratic government service had the character of honorary officials, but later it was regarded as a corvée service.[3] With a few exceptions this was certainly true in the Ming dynasty.[4]

The Tang dynasty had a subbureaucratic government system based upon one hundred households with a *li*-chief (*lizheng*) to «take charge of registering the population, allotting the tasks in agriculture and sericulture, investigate wrongs and crimes, and press the people for the payment of taxes».[5] The Song dynasty continued the Tang system, but significantly the *li*- chiefs became leaders of larger units, the subdistricts or *xiang*, which in Tang times had been organized from 500 households

16

but later had changed into territorial units. The *li*-chiefs were assisted by household leaders (*huzhang*) for the collection of taxes and elders (*qizhang*) for the maintenance of public order.[6]

A major reform occurred in the closing decades of the eleventh century following the introduction of the *baojia* system under Wang Anshi. This system, based upon units of ten households, was initially created for the suppression of local disorder, but it was rapidly drawn into fiscal work as well. In its final form promulgated in 1095 the *baojia* was to be the subbureaucratic government organization for all services. However, allowance was made to retain the *li*-chiefs if the *baojia* did not have sufficient personnel to perform the fiscal duties. This system was by and large continued in the Southern Song and Jin dynasties with basic units of five households.[7]

A more elaborate if brief description of the subbureaucratic government organization in the Yuan dynasty is useful for this study, since the Yuan reforms were first of all designed to meet the special conditions in North China and left most traces there.[8] During the conquest of North China in the first half of the thirteenth century the Mongols applied a feudalistic system of administration with little regard for the traditional territorial divisions. From around 1250 the government began to strengthen central power and adopted to a large extent the traditional Chinese administrative pattern. In this process regulations were issued in 1269, 1270 and 1286 for the creation of communal villages (*she*). The main purpose of these communal villages was to promote the revival of the agricultural economy in the North by means of water control, reforestation, improvements in agricultural education, and the organization of granaries to prevent shortages in lean years. The implementation of such a program is an indication that agricultural production had been seriously interrupted in previous years.[9] Under these circumstances a subbureaucratic unit that did not interrupt the community life of the villages was found to be the solution. There is evidence that the *she* had existed as a mutual assistance organization during the Jin dynasty, but its adoption during the Yuan dynasty marks the heyday of this type of subbureaucratic government as an official policy on a large scale.

The *she* in the Yuan dunasty were organized on the basis of fifty households. Villages with more than fifty households were not, however, divided but remained under one *she*. If there were more than 100 households, an additional *she*-leader (*shezhang*) was appointed. If the villages were smaller than fifty households, two or more villages formed one *she* if the distance between them was not too great. In such *she* the *she*-leader was, if possible, selected from a centrally located village.

17

Each *she* was ordered to select a person from within the *she* to be *she*-leader. He was to be advanced in years, have an understanding of agriculture, and have at least one adult male (*ding*) in the family. The officials were not allowed to ask the *she*-leader to perform duties outside his own *she*. His main duties were to encourage agriculture, advise the farmers on the crops he judged most suitable for cultivation in the area, and to supervise water control. In his efforts to persuade the farmers to cultivate their land in the proper way he could admonish them. If they did not improve, he was to report them to the officials and the misbehaviour was then publicly exposed.

If a household in the *she* was unable to work the fields, then the other households were ordered to assist so that the land was not disused. If a household lost its plough oxen, then the other households were to assist it to get new ones. The *she*-leader was furthermore in charge of the granary (*yicang*), where the villagers were to deposit grain in years of good harvest and from which grain would be distributed to the inhabitants in lean years. He was also in charge of the village school (*shexue*), where a person well versed in the Classics was to instruct the youngsters in the *Xiaojing* and other elementary books on good behaviour. Finally, the *she*-leader was empowered to settle disputes in the *she* involving marriages, family possessions, land, dwellings, and debts. He was to do this by reasoning with the people concerned.

Initially the *she*-leaders did not have fiscal duties. For tax collection the Yuan dynasty depended upon village chiefs (*lizheng*) and cantonal heads (*zhushou*), whose services were considered a corvée obligation.[10] When the workload of these services became too heavy, they were rotated among the wealthier households each year.[11] Later there were developments towards involving the *she*-leaders in the collection of taxes. The government first tried to avoid this by upgrading the status of the *lizheng*, but in the long run the prestige of the *she*-leaders, who where selected by the villagers themselves, was apparently stronger than that of the *lizheng*. The result was a marked tendency for the *she* to become a unit for tax collection.

From what we know of the subbureaucratic government system of the Tang dynasty there was only one subbureaucratic government organization to take care of fiscal and non-fiscal duties. In early Song there were separate offices for these duties. This may have been a continuation of developments in the Tang, but we do not know. The tendency to have separate organizations or offices was furthered with the creation of the *baojia*, but at the same time we see a tendency in Song, Jin, Yuan, and also in the Qing dynasty,[12] for the institutions created for non-fiscal work to take over most or all of the official fiscal work at village level. The Ming dynasty stands out as exception. It only created one subbureaucratic government organization, the *lijia*, primarily for fiscal duties. Certainly, *li*-elders were appointed to take care of the non-fiscal duties, but they were closely attached to the *lijia* and never commanded a structure of their own. Eventually they too were drawn into petty fiscal work. This emphasis on the creation in Ming of one, and only one, subbureaucratic government system, primarily for fiscal work, may have been crucial for the survival of such a system almost to the end of the dynasty.

GEOGRAPHIC SCOPE

An investigation of the subbureaucratic government system naturally leads the historian to local sources, notably the local gazetteers (*fangzhi*). In the research done so far, mostly by Japanese scholars, a wide selection of the 928 local gazetteers and similar works still extant from the Ming period[13] have been used. The approach followed by this research has been to make selections from scattered districts without regard to developments in their neighbouring districts. This has proved valuable, since districts with more informative sources could be selected, and preliminary solutions have in this way been found to many problems in the history of Ming local administration. To get a deeper understanding of the functioning of the local institutions we now need to relate them more to their immediate sourroundings. With the considerable amount of sources available, such investigations must necessarily be confined to a limited geographical area. This has been the approach of the present work. I do not claim unconditional success but will only suggest that further studies of other aspects of local conditions will have to be made before the results of special studies can be placed in their proper context.

The geographic scope of the investigation was initially limited to Shandong Province (excluding the Liaodong Regional Military Commission).[14] This choice was rather arbitrary. The province was attractive for this kind of research because it did not belong to the economically and culturally richer provinces in the south, which abound in available sources and which have so far been the focal point of most research on local history in Ming times. It was not on the border, with its special military problems, nor in the far south or west, where special circumstances were created by the presence of large numbers of non-Han aborigines under their 'native' administration.[15] Shandong was at the same time important to the government as the main route for traffic between the south and the capital, and further to the northern border defences went through the western part of the province. Finally the availability of the *Shandong Jinghuilu (SDJHL)* as one of the main sources made the province very attractive.

With over one hundred subprefectures and districts even Shandong Province was too large an area if gazetteers from all districts were to be collected and processed, so Jinan Prefecture was chosen for special consideration. This choice was made first of all because late Ming gazetteers were available for thirteen of the thirty subprefectures and districts. Jinan was also largely unaffected by the problems of corvée on the Grand Canal, without being one of the more secluded prefectures in eastern or peninsular Shandong.

The area of Shandong Province was in Ming times almost the same as it is today, i.e. c. 150,000 sq. kilometres with a population in the sixteenth century perhaps in the order of ten million people.[16] Topographically the province is dominated by the mountains that occupy the central part and most of the peninsula. The northern section of the central mountains comprises three parallel ranges with a roughly south-west north-east axis. The highest peak is Mount Tai, standing at 1,524 m, and the average height is 300–500 m. On the northern side they present a steep escarpment, while the southern part is less rugged and has broad river valleys draining into the rivers and waterways to the south.[17] These mountains are surrounded by great alluvial plains, which have been formed first of all by the Yellow River in its shifting courses north and south of the Shandong mountains but also by local rivers.[18] During the Ming dynasty the Yellow River entered the sea south of the peninsula, but the North Shandong Plain was still traversed by a river of magnitude, the Daqing river, which largely followed the bed later coursed by the Yellow River.[19]

The borders between Shandong and its neighbouring provinces were all on the plains, in some parts along the Grand Canal or other waterways. Even if they were only minor obstacles to traffic across the provincial borders, there is probably reason to regard Shandong as a fairly coherent region, geographically, economically and culturally. Many of the important cities were in places where they could serve as administrative and commercial links between the mountains and the plain, and many of the rivers that originated in the province ran their entire course within its borders.[20] This cohesion was further strengthened by the network of roads, since both the official postal roads and perhaps also minor roads were oriented towards traffic inside the province, with only a few connecting roads to other provinces.[21]

Jinan Prefecture was in the northern part of the province. It bordered to the north on the Northern Metropolitan Area (Beizhili) and the sea

(Bohai) and on its other sides to the Qingzhou, Yanzhou, and Dongchang Prefectures of Shandong Province. The northern part of the prefecture was on the alluvial plain, which appears for the most part to have been reasonably fertile. Most complaints about infertility of the land are found in the districts close to the coast, where the land still has a high salinity, which makes it less profitable for food production. Extensive cultivation of cotton began to spread to this area in Ming times,[22] but Zhanhua District reported in 1619 that the production of this commodity was still barely enough to provide the households with their own needs,[23] so this development was still in its infancy. Generally information supplied in the gazetteers about soil conditions should be used with care, since there may have been a tendency for the compilers to complain about infertility to avoid increases in the tax quota of the district. A complete survey of the land in Ming times would require extensive comparisons with later and modern data.

Agriculture was of course dominant in the economic life of the province. Millet and wheat were the most important food crops together with kaoliang, beans and buckwheat. Rice was cultivated in a few areas but generally the water supply was insufficient for this crop. All districts also reported a great variety of fruits; and cotton and cotton products are mentioned as commercial products.[24] In the mountains the situation appears to have been slightly different. The gazetteers for Taian Subprefecture, in its section on products, first mention timber products followed by fruits, herbs and grain and later minerals.[25] In some parts of the province the forests could be so dense that it was difficult to get access to the timber.[26]

In the gazetteers scrutinized I have found no direct reference to conditions of land tenure, but Li Kaixian writes around 1560 that in Zhangqiu District the 'elite' (shifu) own much of the land, and that many of them live in the provincial capital or perhaps in other places outside the district. Given the bias in the writings of Li Kaixian, no judgment on the proportion of land under tenancy can be made from this statement.[27] The forms of tenancy are not desribed, but the general impression of tenancy in China during this period is that in the north, where tenancy was less frequent than in the south, the leases were usually very short, perhaps only one to three years.[28]

The sixteenth century is usually described as a time of a booming economy accompanying the influx of silver from overseas.[29] The boom was also felt in the countryside, since there was a considerable increase in the market sector of the economy. In North China regular periodic markets began to supplement the markets in the district cities.[30] Annual or semi-annual temple fairs also seem to have started in this period.[31]

Yamane Yukio suggests that the number of periodic markets began to increase around 1500.[32] The material from Jinan Prefecture seems to corroborate this. The district cities usually had several markets in different parts of the city or suburbs with markets every day or rotating in a ten-day rotation. Rural markets are also recorded for the market towns (*zhen*, *dian*), in some districts with the market days in the ten-day rotation, usually two days with intervals of five days. In the Zhangqiu gazetteer from 1596 eighteen towns (*zhen*) are listed. One of them never had a market, and in one of the others the market had been abolished because of its proximity to another market. Trading days are recorded for the other sixteen market towns, but in addition ten new markets are listed, also with their trading days.[33] In Pingyuan and Putai districts that list the markets with trading days, the number of markets had doubled by the middle of the seventeenth century.[34] So we may conclude that, although the material is scarce, it does indicate a development of markets in the sixteenth century. Unfortunately a detailed study of the management of the markets[35] and their possible influence on the intervillage community life has not been possible for this study.[36]

But even if prosperity increased, the life of the general population was always a precarious balance between a full stomach and famine. The prefecture was constantly subjected to natural calamities such as floods, drought, locusts, or pests, which endangered the balance between food production and the size of the population. Each district and subprefecture reported such calamities at intervals of only a few years, and few if any of the districts avoided famine at least once during the fifty-year span from 1550 to 1600.

CHRONOLOGICAL SCOPE

As the title indicates, the aim of this work is to describe the subbureaucratic government system of the whole Ming period. Chapter II and parts of chapter V describe the origin of the institutions in early Ming and offer some explanations for the developments after the death of the Hongwu emperor. For the detailed study of Shandong Province a much narrower time-limit was necessary. The period from about 1550 to about 1600 was chosen for several reasons. It had to be in the later part of the dynasty in order to get a reasonable coverage from local gazetteers. This also had the advantage of making it possible to study to what extent and in what form the subbureaucratic government system of the early years of the dynasty was still operating. The starting date around 1550 was chosen rather arbitrarily but has proved to be a fortunate choice, because it largely coincided with the introduction of the first Single Whip taxation reform in Shandong and because the period 1550–1570 is well covered by the *Shandong Jinghuilu*.[37] The closing date of around 1600 was chosen so that the investigation would not have to consider the changes that took place during the years of war and internal upheavals in the first part of the seventeenth century.

A chronological sequence of the developments in the province has been attempted in chapters IV and V, the former covering the period until c. 1570 and the latter the rest of the century. Documents and events have as far as possible been dated to fit them into this sequence, but this has not always been possible. I doubt whether greater chronological accuracy is possible, given the nature of the sources. The chronological approach has been necessary because of the geographical limitations put on the investigation. Events and documents had to be dated to fit them into the developments in the prefecture as a whole. I think that the results obtained here warrant further regional investigations along the same lines, rather than the selective research with little regard for a strict chronological sequence which has dominated much of the early work on Ming institutional history. At the same time the results of this study indicate that such research is best carried out on areas for which important collections of documents and narratives are available in addition to the local gazetteers.

SOURCES

1. Local gazetteers
    The main sources have been the local gazetteers (*fangzhi*) for each district in Jinan Prefecture. The principle behind their selection has been to use the earliest available gazetteer for each subprefecture and district, and when this edition was compiled before 1600 to use the following edition as well. Such double coverage is also provided for some other districts, notably those with an earliest available edition compiled during the first half of the seventeenth century. The earliest available gazetteer dates in a few districts from the nineteenth century, but generally pre-1700 editions have been used. Some editions are marred by textual damage. This may be a matter of missing chapters or pages or a few undecipherable lines or characters – sometimes in the middle of a text which promised interesting information but which was rendered useless in this way.

    Officials and local scholars collaborated in compiling the local gazetteers. Both had an interest in such compilations, since a gazetteer gave prestige to the district. For the official the gazetteer furthermore served as a quick and convenient introduction to the district when he first arrived. The local scholars probably wished to exhibit the glory of the district, particularly its attainments in literary works and cultural artifacts. In their descriptions of economic conditions they may, on the other hand, deliberately have understated the performance of the district in order not to induce higher authorities to increase the tax quota.

The content of the gazetteers is a reflection of the interests of their compilers, and all follow more or less the same pattern. In addition to a historical and topographical description of the subprefecture or district a major part of the gazetteer consists of descriptions of local government and educated people. Public buildings and monuments are listed, usually with a detailed history of their construction and repairs, and the administration of the district is described, together with institutions such as schools and granaries. Names of the district officials are listed as far back as the records allowed, usually including a few illustrious officials from earlier dynasties and a comprehensive list at least from the sixteenth century. Examination graduates are listed often for the whole dynasty, and biographies are included of meritorious officials and local graduates, together with other persons who deserved special attention, such as recluses and virtuous women. Persons from educated families seem to have been predominant in these categories. Some information relevant to this study has been gained from these sources and also from the sections on local customs and products.

The most important part of the gazetteers has been the chapters on taxes and corvée, since they often give some information on the fiscal role of the subbureaucratic government system. Finally most gazetteers have a large section entitled 'Literature', in which important writings of officials and local people are quoted, often *in extenso*. Tablets composed for the inauguration of newly constructed and repaired buildings and monuments, or descriptions of other major construction work such as water control, are predominant in this section. Some tablets give details as to how the finance and manpower for the work was raised, mostly by impositions on the people in the district. They give the impression that such work must have represented a considerable burden in addition to normal taxes and corvée. The 'Literature' sections also contain a few descriptions of taxes and corvée and occasionally of the subbureaucratic government system. Unfortunately most of these descriptions are for the Qing period. The sections also include some administrative documents, sometimes concerning the district itself but every so often documents composed by local men on higher government service outside the province. This raises the question whether documents relating to Jinan

24

can be found in gazetteers of other parts of the empire. This is possible, but for this study neither time nor resources were available for a systematic perusal of home-district gazetteers of Shandong officials. Such work will have to be postponed until more gazetteers are available in reprint and until indexes are published.

2. *Shandong Jinghuilu*

The single most important source has been the *Shandong Jinghuilu*, which was compiled in the provincial administration of Shandong in 1571:10. This work has been used by Liang Fangzhong in the 1930's,[38] and a copy was found in 1958 by Iwami Hiroshi in a private library in Japan. I have used a microfilm copy of the latter. The work has twelve chapters with a total of 928 pages. It is divided into six parts: taxes (Ch. 1–4), equal corvée (Ch. 5–9), *lijia* corvée (Ch. 10), postal services (Ch. 11), horse administration, and salt administration (Ch. 12). Each part is further divided into four sections: tables (*hengtu*) giving the levied figures for each item in each district in 1571, summaries (*zonge*) of these figures, changes (*yinge*) – particularly since 1540 – and finally documents and deliberations (*fulu*) relating to major changes. The preface is fragmentary (together with the last few pages of Ch. 12, the only damaged part), so its authorship cannot be established, but there is sufficient information to show that it was compiled in the provincial administration, perhaps with the administration commissioner as editor-in-chief.[39] The work was probably a forerunner of the later Comprehensive Registers on Taxes and Corvée (*fuyi-quanshu*), and it is known that similar works existed in other provinces during the Jiajing period.[40]

The most important sections for the present study have been the *fulu* sections, particularly the deliberations and documents about the Single Whip. Deliberations are intermingled with decisions by the governors, so it is sometimes difficult to decide whether the policies described were actually carried out. A final conclusion on this problem can only be reached if further details of the administrative procedures in the provincial government can be obtained, and this is very unlikely. My own conclusion at the moment is that most of the proposals and decisions recorded on these sections were in some way reflections of policies carried out in the whole province or at least part of it, since local variations were obviously allowed by the provincial administration either by choice or by necessity.

3. Other important sources

These are the writings of Li Kaixian, Ge Shouli, Yu Shenxing, and Lü Kun. Li Kaixian was born in Zhangqiu District, Jinan Prefecture, in 1502 and obtained his *jinshi* degree in 1529. After a career in the capital he retired in 1541 and spent the rest of his life at home in Zhangqiu writing plays and collecting folklore. The latter interest may have given him the opportunity to learn more about conditions in the district than other persons of similar background. Around 1560 he wrote some essays about conditions in Zhangqiu, but these writings are difficult to use, partly because we do not know the background and partly because of their very strong bias. These essays, which are in the form of questions and answers, can almost be regarded as early examples of propagandistic journalism.[41] I have used them when they related to subbureaucratic government but have avoided making statements about social and economic conditions. I do not regard Li's complaints as unfounded. There is other evidence to support his claim that the situation in the province needed reform. But the careful assessment of his claims which is needed before conclusions can be drawn could not be made on the sources available.

Ge Shouli was from Deping District, Jinan Prefecture, and a *jinshi* graduate from 1529. He was probably the most ardent and outspoken opponent of the introduction of the Single Whip taxation policy in Shandong. His opposition was directed mainly against the levy of corvée on land in place of *ding* and households, since he had seen from administrative experience in Henan how this had created hardship for the primary producers. He spent the years 1556–1567 in retirement and thus had a good opportunity to study at first hand the introduction of the early Single Whip. His interest in this problem can be seen in several letters to provincial officials both in Shandong and Henan, but his main argument is presented in a memorial that obtained imperial approval in 1567, while he was Minister for Revenue.[42] These writings contain important information, but they have been used with some caution because of his strong bias against the Single Whip.

Yu Shenxing was from Donga District, Yanzhou Prefecture. He was born in 1545 and became a *jinshi* graduate in 1568. After a career in the capitals he retired in 1591 and probably spent most of his time at home, editing the prefectural gazetteer, among other tasks. His writings used here are those about the Single Whip in the Wanli period, mostly describing this policy in Donga and the neighbouring Pingyin on the western border of Changqing District. He does, however, also discuss the suitability of the Single Whip for other parts of the province, so I have made use of his arguments, since he seems to have been well informed and, although in favour of the policy, at least to have lacked the fiery bias of Ge Shouli.[43]

In late Ming, Lü Kun was one of the best known officials connected with initiatives with regard to subbureaucratic government. He was born in Ningling District, Henan Province, and became a *jinshi* in 1574. During his career he turned away from the philosophical interest of the scholars and took an interest in the livelihood of the common people and particularly their education. He blamed the social unrest both on the inequitable distribution of wealth and on the lack of communication between the upper and lower social strata, so he tried to use a language that was understood by all.[44] When he was governor of Shanxi from 1592 to 1594, he issued detailed instructions for subbureaucratic government, including regulations for the non-fiscal duties. He had served in Shandong Province from 1587 to 1589 as administration circuit intendant of Jinan, and he reveals in parts of his instruction that he had already adopted similar policies while serving in Shandong.[45] As initiatives in Jinan with regard to the non-fiscal subbureaucratic government organizations can clearly be connected with his stay in the province, I have used his regulations for Shanxi to describe the principles of such institutions as they probably operated in Jinan.

ADMINISTRATION IN SHANDONG PROVINCE

The provincial administration created in the beginning of the dynasty was, like the central administration, organized under several heads, so that no official was in a position to usurp all power in the province. The routine management of provincial affairs was the responsibility of the Provincial Administration Office. The Provincial Surveillance Office maintained general surveillance over local government personnel and had a direct role in reviewing judicial cases. Military administration was under the Regional Military Commission. The commissioners in these three organs formed a deliberative council to deal with important provincial affairs, but from the fifteenth century special Grand Coordinators were sent out from the capital to coordinate administration in certain areas on an *ad hoc* basis. In some provinces these Grand Coordinators developed into permanent provincial governors. Shandong had such a governor from before 1500.[46]

.Some of the ministries and agencies in the capital had representatives in the provinces. The most important was the Regional Inspector from the Censorat. These were relatively young officials of low rank sent out on tours of inspection of certain areas lasting one year. Shandong Province had one inspector each year. They reviewed the administrative performance of officials in the province and seem to have wielded considerable influence. In Shandong the Censorate also had a special salt-control censor,[47] and the Ministries of Revenue and Works had

27

branch offices in connection with the transport on the Grand Canal to control the water level and collect revenue.[48]

The province was divided into several circuits with deputy officials in the provincial administration and surveillance offices appointed as circuit intendants. The circuits had specific functions, and the province was covered by one or more circuits for each function. A list of 1571 for the allocation of door-men to provincial offices gives the following circuits: one Tax Storage Circuit (*liangchudao*), three General Administration Circuits (*fenshoudao*), one Ministry Taxation Circuit (*buliangdao*), all under the Provincial Administration Office. The Provincial Surveillance Office had the following circuits: one for 'troop purification' (*qingjun*), one for education (*tixue*), one for postal services (*yichuan*), three General Surveillance Circuits (*fenxundao*), and six Military Defence Circuits (*bingbeidao*).[49]

More permanent territorial divisions of a province were the prefectures (*fu*), subprefectures (*zhou*), and districts (*xian*). Shandong had six prefectures and 104 subprefectures and districts. Jinan Prefecture had four subprefectures and twenty-six districts. The prefectures exercised a supervisory role over the subprefectures and districts, and the subprefectures also supervised the districts under their jurisdiction. Only eleven of the districts in Jinan came under a subprefecture; the others were directly under the prefecture.[50] The subprefecture differed functionally from the prefecture in that it was directly responsible for an area, acting as a district under prefectural control in addition to its supervisory role.

The subprefectures and districts only had a handful of officials. In districts the regular officials (*zhengguan*) were the magistrate (*zhixian*), the vice-magistrate (*xiancheng*), and the assistant magistrate (*zhubu*), while the docket officer (*dianshi*) was the only chief officer (*shoulingguan*). In the sixteenth century there was even a tendency to abolish the offices of deputy officials, perhaps as a recognition that they did not have any independent role in the district administration.[51] A list of the total complement of yamen personnel is given in the Binzhou gazetteer from 1583. As a subprefecture the numbers may have been relatively high, but they are still worth recording here, since they impress upon us the need for subbureaucratic institutions or other forms of participatory government in the administration of a population of perhaps over 100.000 people. Besides the magistrate (*zhizhou*), the vice-magistrate (*tongzhi*), and two assistant magistrates (*panguan*), Binzhou had one docket officer, twenty-four lesser functionaries (*li*), and only ninety yamen underlings for the menial work in the administration.[52]

SUBBUREAUCRATIC GOVERNMENT IN CHINESE SOCIETY

Subbureaucratic government is the term used in this study for the official system of local government below the level of the district yamen. It was instituted by the government or other levels of the bureaucracy, and the leaders and other officers were selected among the local population. The term used in modern Chinese and Japanese literature is *difang zizhi* (*chihō jichi*), which is best translated as «local self-government». This term only crept into the Japanese language in the 1880's and probably from there into Chinese. In the Republican period the term had «a heterogenous body of ideas attached to it, particularly that of political democracy».[53] Prominent Chinese scholars who have published carefully researched studies in English on the local government institutions of the Qing dynasty have gone to considerable length to refute the existence of local self-government in China.[54]

Their argument is valid insofar as the subbureaucratic government institutions were never completely autonomous. No legal provision ever existed to prevent the emperor and the government from interfering with the work of the subbureaucratic government system, and much of its work was under the direction of the bureaucracy.[55] However the arguments of Hsiao and Ch'ü also seem to have been influenced by the problem of democracy in local self-government.[56] They are probably right in asserting that there was no formal democracy with elected leaders and councils of representatives. Their judgment may in this respect have been influenced by the Chinese discussion in the Republican period and their own experience of American local government.

To me the question of democracy seems hardly relevant to the problem of «local self-government». Such criteria may distort the picture of the situation in pre-modern China, particularly when terms such as «imperial control» or «rural control» are substituted for «local self-government». Such terms may give the impression of a very efficient centralized government structure, which controlled society in every detail, rather than the pluralistic picture of local government which Hsiao and Ch'ü have also painted in their works, and which was probably necessary in a pre-modern bureaucratic empire like China.

If local communities had real power to manage to some extent their own affairs, it may have been due to insufficient administrative capability of the bureaucracy. However, for early Ming John Watt has argued that it was a deliberate policy of the Hongwu emperor to strengthen the subbureaucratic government system and diminish the power of officialdom over rural society.[57] This corresponds with my own interpretation of early Ming administration, and my impression gained from this study is that in the sixteenth century the officers of the subbureaucratic government system were still given considerable powers of discretion in carrying out their duties. However, much more research is probably required before we can decide the question of «local self-government» in Chinese history. So for this study I have chosen what I hope is a neutral term – «subbureaucratic government».

The purpose of the subbureaucratic government system in Chinese history was to fill the vacuum in the administrative hierachy between the lowest level of the bureaucracy and the people. From Qin and Han times the lowest level had been that of the district (*xian*) under the direction of the district magistrate. He was personally responsible for all government business in the district and was in Ming times often called the «father and mother of the people».[58] The number of districts never kept pace with the territorial expansion of the Chinese empire nor with the increase in population.[59] The Ming figure of 1400–1500 districts was not higher than previous dynasties and remained fairly stable throughout the imperial period. This resulted in districts with a population in Ming times of perhaps over half a million inhabitants.[60] Even in the relatively smaller districts of Jinan Prefecture the population in the sixteenth century was several tens of thousands and in some districts probably over 100.000.[61]

The governments were reluctant to provide the district magistrates with sufficient funds to hire qualified personnel to carry out effectively the administration of the district without assistance from the local population. This may have been due to the tradition of conscripting corvée labour from the population, a measure suitable in times when natural economy prevailed, often in beginning of dynasties, but it may also have been a deliberate measure to curtail the power of the district magistrate.

At the same time the government needed a subbureaucratic government organization that gave it access to and some degree of control over the local communities. Skinner has suggested that the peasant communities of China closed themselves to outside influences during the wars of dynastic change, and that the success of new dynasties, particularly conqueror dynasties, depended on their ability to open up these closed communities.[62] In societies with institutional religion the church establishment has no doubt played a role in such processes.[63] It has provided a hierachy of leadership down to the village level, where it actually performed some of the functions of the subbureaucratic government system in China, such as population registration and ideological control. Such hierachies often collaborated with or were under control of the political establishment, but even when this did not

30

happen they no doubt served to counteract the closure of the local community.

The Hongwu emperor may have harboured ideas about creating a state religion. Altars were established at all levels of the administration, even village level, and sacrifices were to be performed to the deities at the same level in the otherworld Pantheon. The form of these sacrifices underscored the diffuse character of Chinese religion. Sacrifices were performed by the officials, and there was never any attempt to set up a separate clerical hierarchy for this state religion. The officials also kept under close surveillance the potential hierarchies of the Buddhist and Taoist faiths.[64]

Studies and tales from nineteenth-century China make it quite clear that religion had an important place in the lives of the individual Chinese and also in their community life. The lists of temples and descriptions of religious ceremonies in the local gazetteers of Jinan prefecture are strong indications that religion was also an important part of daily life in the sixteenth century. But there is not much evidence that religious movements were connected with subbureaucratic government.

The only example is possibly in Wuding Subprefecture. Under the heading *she*, which is often used for the *lijia*, the 1588 edition of the gazetteer describes communities of a Buddhist nature. The people mostly ate vegetables and in cases of illness they did not use medicine but attempted a cure with witchcraft and other invocations of supernatural powers. Most people, but not the educated ones (*shidafu*), belonged to these *she* and each *she* had a leader. On the first and the fifteenth day of the month the members deposited money with the leader, and this money was lent out at interest. At the end of the year the money was returned and used for beneficial work, such as assistance with tax and corvée payments, dowry and funeral expenses. The ceremonies for marriage and funerals were conducted by the *she*. Wang Ye, the military defence circuit intendant from 1543 to 1548, had attempted to bring these customs under official control and had scholars appointed to conduct the four ceremonies of capping of youth, marriage, funerals, and sacrifices, but with no apparent success.[65]

The impression we get from this account is that the *she* were not higly regarded by the officials and educated people. Such unofficial organizations, religious or secular (if such existed), do not appear to have impressed the officials as supplementary administrative organizations. They were rather regarded as a nuisance, something which should be controlled.

Military hierarchies can also provide the rulers with access to and control over local society. The *baojia* of Wang Anshi in the Song dynasty and other forms of militia were possibly established partly to fulfil such functions. But the military hierarchy of the Ming dynasty, like all later dynasties, was firmly under the control of the civil bureaucracy and do not appear to have provided a separate channel for the exercise of power over local communities. Anyway, the local militia was under the command of the district magistrates and intimately connected to the civil subbureaucratic government system, so we can hardly regard it as part of an independent military hierarchy.

Finally the educated 'élite' (gentry) could have provided the rulers with means of access to the local communities. The ésprit de corps and common interests of the examination graduates, officials and potential officials could have given this group sufficient cohesion to serve the same societal functions as the church and military in other societies. It is, however, difficult to imagine the élite as an alternative channel for the exercise of power and control over local communities. In their function as officials they were not an alternative; they were the civil bureaucracy. In their function as local élite the evidence available does not suggest that they were a reliable channel. They were rather more interested in furthering the interest of the local community of their immediate surroundings than in providing an external control over such communities.[66]

The sixteenth century is generally regarded as the time when 'élite' influence over local communities began to accelerate. This coincided with the growing tendency to establish institutionalized lineages which could perpetuate the power of certain families. The sources consulted for this study have not revealed much information on the creation of such lineages in Shandong and their possible influence. They did exist, as Ping-ti Ho has shown,[67] but to trace their rise and influence would require a special study, like Hilary Beattie's on Tongcheng District.[68]

The following pages will, I hope, reveal that throughout the investigation I have kept in mind the possible role of unofficial leadership in local communities. As it stands now, this is a study of the subbureaucratic government system as operated and described by contemporary administrators as a part of the administrative system of the empire. Perhaps we may add with the benefits of hindsight that it is also a study of the subbureaucratic government system at the eve of élite dominance over local communities.

1. The best introduction to early Ming history and institutions is the essay by Charles O. Hucker, *The Ming Dynasty: Its Origins and Evolving Institutions*, (Ann Arbor, 1978). See also Edward L. Farmer, *Early Ming Government. The Evolution of Dual Capitals*, (Cambridge, Mass., 1976), pp. 40 ff., and Charles O. Hucker, «Governmental Organization of the Ming Dynasty», *HJAS* 21 (1958), 1–66. The best political history of the whole Ming dynasty is still the biographies of emperors and leading officials in L. Carrington Goodrich and Chaoying Fang, eds., *Dictionary of Ming Biography, 1368–1644*, (New York & London, 1976) (hereafter, *DMB*), together with Daniel Bryant, «A DMB Chronology», *Ming Studies* 8 (1979), 27–40.

2. A reference to the system of the Rites of Zhou is found in *Putai xianzhi* 1591/5/3. The most detailed historical description found in a local gazetteer is in the essay «Lijia lun» (Discourse on the *lijia*) by Liu Qi included in *Tangyi xianzhi* 1710/2/9-10. General political encyclopedias of the Ming period also included such historical descriptions; see appendix V. The standard Japanese history of subbureaucratic government in China, Wada Sei, ed., *Shina chihō jichi hattatsushi*, (Tokyo, 1939), also begins with the Rites of Zhou.

3. Wada (1939), pp. 13–14.

4. The possible exceptions in Ming were the tax captains (*liangzhang*) and *li*-elders (*lilaoren*), who in early Ming had audiences with the emperor and could be promoted to officials. Liang Fangzhong, *Mingdai liangzhang zhidu*, (Shanghai, 1957), p. 23–24; George Jer-lang Chang, «The Village Elder System of the Early Ming Dynasty», *Ming Studies* 7 (1978), 58.

5. D. C. Twitchet, *Financial Administration under the T'ang Dynasty*, (Cambridge, 1963), p. 218.

6. Brian E. McKnight, *Village and Bureaucracy in Southern Sung China*, (Chicago, 1971), pp. 23, 75.

7. *Ibid.*, pp. 33 ff., Li Jiannong, *Song-Yuan-Ming jingji shigao*, (Beijing, 1957), p. 260.

8. The description of the Yuan dynasty follows Paul Oscar Elmqvist, *Rural Control in Early Modern China*, (Ph. D. thesis, Harvard University, 1963), pp. 107–185. Elmqvist translates the documents on subbureaucratic government institutions for the Song, Yuan and Ming dynasties which are reprinted in Wada (1939).

9. Herbert Franz Schurmann, *Economic Structure of the Yüan Dynasty*, (Cambridge, Mass., 1956), p. 7.

10. *Ibid.*, p. 96.

11. Wada (1939), p. 68.

12. Kung-chuan Hsiao, *Rural China. Imperial Control in the Nineteenth Century*, (Seattle, 1960), pp. 60–62.

13. Wolfgang Franke, *An Introduction to the Sources of Ming History*, (Kuala Lumpur-Singapore, 1968), p. 236.

14. *Da-Ming Huidian* (*DMHD*) 15/28.

15. Hucker (1958), p. 48.

16. The official population figures for Shandong Province were in 1393 5,255,876 and in 1578 5,664,099 persons. *DMHD* 19/2, 13. Late Ming population figures are notoriously wrong. The general estimate is that the population had more than doubled between 1393 and the late sixteenth century. Available population figures for subprefectures and districts in Jinan Prefecture are given in Appendix III. They can be manipulated in many ways. I suggest a population in Jinan Prefecture around 1580 of three millions or more. For a general discussion of Ming population data see Ping-ti Ho, *Studies on the Population of China 1368–1953*, (Cambridge, Mass., 1959), *passim*.

3 – Subbureaucratic government . . .

17. *The Times Atlas of China*, (London, 1974), pp. 32–35.
18. James Thorp, *Geography of the Soils of China*, (Nanking, 1936). p. 171.
19. *Lidai yudi yangetu*, (Taipei, 1975), vol. 30, p. 20.
20. Robert E. Hosack, *Shantung: An Interpretation of a Chinese Province*, (Ph. D. thesis, Duke University, 1951), pp. 128–195.
21. Kōno Mitsuhiro, «Shindai Santōshō no kansei rikujō kōtsūro», *Shirin* 33.3 (1950), 325–326.
22. Nishijima Sadao, «Mindai ni okeru momen no fukyū ni tsuite», *Shigaku Zasshi* 57 (1948), 295.
23. *Zhanhua xianzhi* 1619/3/65.
24. All gazetteers include long lists of local products. The editions of the late sixteenth century usually begin the list of staple crops with millet followed by the other crops in varying order. Rice paddy is recorded in *Binzhou zhi* 1583/2/53. In 1473 the governor began to teach the people to construct irrigated fields with level water in Licheng District. *Licheng xianzhi* 1640/13/46.
25. *Taian zhouzhi* 1603/1/7–8.
26. *Zichuan xianzhi* 1602/10/1.
27. *Li Kaixian ji*, (Preface 1556, Shanghai, 1959 ed.), p. 707.
28. Dwight D. Perkins, *Agricultural Development in China, 1368–1968*, (Chicago, 1969), pp. 89–103.
29. William S. Attwell, «Notes on Silver, Foreign Trade, and the Late Ming Economy», *Ch'ing-shih wen-t'i* 3.8 (1977), 1–8.
30. Many northern districts established city markets in early Ming. See Yamane Yukio, «Min Shinsho no Kahoku no shishu to shinshi.gōmin», in *Nakayama Hachirō kyōjo shōju kinen Min Shin shi ronshū*, (Tokyo, 1977), pp. 304–306.
31. Putai District had an annual fair in the middle of the third month in connection with incense burning at the Yanhuo Tai. *Putai xianzhi* 1592/3/3, 5/8. On Northern Chinese temple fairs in general see C. K. Yang, *Religion in Chinese Society,* (Berkeley and Los Angeles, 1961), pp. 82 ff. and Yamane Yukio, «Kahoku no byōkai», *Shiron* 17 (1967), 1–22.
32. Yamane Yukio, «Min Shin jidai Kahoku ni okeru teikishi», *Shiron* 8 (1960), 494.
33. *Zhangqiu xianzhi* 1598/14/98–99.
34. *Pingyuan xianzhi* 1590/1/10; *Putai xianzhi* 1591/5/8, 1763/2/29.
35. Yamane (1977) gives examples of local peoples' involvement in the establishment and management of markets. As for management he too had problems in finding material from late Ming.
36. For a general introduction to the rural markets and local community life in Late Imperial and Republican China see G. William Skinner, «Marketing and Social Sturcture in Rural China», *JAS* (1964), 3–43.
37. Leif Littrup, «The Early Single Whip in Shandong, 1550–1570», *Papers on Far Eastern History* 15 (1977), 65–67.
38. Liang Fangzhong, «Mingdai yitiaobianfa nianbiao», *Lingnan xuebao* 12.1 (1952), 19.
39. Wang Zongmu was left administration commissioner in Shandong until 1571:10:5. He was the author of a work titled *Dongsheng jingzhilu*. Ray Huang, who wrote the biography of Wang in *DMB* but has seen neither the *SDJHL* nor the *Dongsheng jingzhilu*, strongly suspects that they are essentially identical. *DMB*, pp. 1439–1440; personal communication from Ray Huang dated 4 November 1976.
40. Iwami Hiroshi, «'Santō keikairoku ni tsuite», in *Shimizu hakase tsuitō kinen Mindaishi ronsō*, pp. 197–220.
41. *DMB*, pp. 835–836; Wolfgang Franke, «Material aus Gesammelten Schriften (*piehchi*) als Quellen für Lokalgeschichte. Bemerkungen zu einer untersuchung von Michel Cartier», *Oriens Extremus* 21 (1974), 192–193.

42. Littrup (Single Whip), pp. 81–88, and Ch. III below.
43. *DMB*, pp. 1614–1616, and Ch. V below.
44. Joanna F. Handlin, «Lü Kun Compromises with the People», *Ming Studies* 1 (1975), 82–83.
45. *DMB*, pp. 1006–1010, and Ch. VI below.
46. Hucker (1958), *passim*; *Jinan fuzhi* 1839/25/2–4.
47. Charles O. Hucker, *The Censorial System of Ming China*, (Stanford, 1966), pp. 47 ff; *Jinan fuzhi* 1839/25/12–17.
48. *SDJHL* 7/10–11.
49. *Ibid.*
50. *DMHD* 15/24–28.
51. Ibid. 4/6; John Watt, *The District Magistrate in Late Imperial China*, (New York and London, 1972), pp. 132 ff. This tendency is corroborated in Jinan gazetteers.
52. *Binzhou zhi* 1583/2/56. A useful description of the administrative personnel and their functions in a district is given in Michel Cartier, *Une réforme locale en Chine au XVIᵉ siecle, Hai Rui à Chun'an 1558–1562*, (Paris-La Haye, 1973), pp. 35–55.
53. Philip A Kuhn, «Local Self-Government under the Republic. Problems of Control, Autonomy and Mobilization», in Frederic Wakeman, Jr. and Carolyn Grant, eds., *Conflict and Control in Late Imperial China*, (Berkeley, 1975), pp. 257 ff.
54. Hsiao, *passim;* T'ung-tsu Ch'ü, *Local Government in China under the Ch'ing*, (Cambridge, Mass., 1962), p. 198.
55. Hsiao, p. 263.
56. Ch'ü (1962), p. 198; Hsiao, p. 264.
57. Watt, pp. 114–115.
58. *Ibid.* p. 90.
59. G. William Skinner, «Urban Development in Imperial China», in G. William Skinner, ed., *The City in Late Imperial China*, (Stanford, 1977) pp. 17–21.
60. Shanghai District reported 114,326 households and 532,803 «mouths» in 1391. Ho (1959), p. 12.
61. In 1596 Qidong District reported 141,220 inhabitants while Wuding Subprefecture for 1588 had reported 62.770 males and 69,880 females. These figures may not be correct, but they are probably a good indication of the population. *Qidong xianzhi* 1617/15/4; *Wuding zhouzhi* 1588/5/1.
62. G. William Skinner, «Chinese Peasants and the Closed Community: An Open and Shut Case», *Comparative Studies in Society and History* 13 (1971), 272.
63. The terms 'institutionalized religion» and 'diffused religion' are taken from Yang, p. 294.
64. Romeyn Taylor, «Ming T'ai-tsu and the Gods of the Walls and Moats», *Ming Studies* 4 (1977), 37 ff.
65. The assistant surveillance commissioner is only mentioned by his personal name Ye. A memorial about horse markets from assistant surveillance commissioner Ye is mentioned under 1547. The list of military defence circuit intendants in the Wuding gazetteer has a Wang Ye from Jintan District serving from 1543 to 1548. *Wuding zhouzhi* 1588/7/2–3, 2/3, 10/14.
66. Hsiao, p. 506; Skinner (1971), p. 227.
67. Ping-ti Ho, *The Ladder of Success in Imperial China. Aspects of Social Mobility, 1368–1911*, (New York and London, 1962), pp. 127–137, 165.
68. Hilary J. Beattie, *Land and Lineage in China. A Study of T'ung-ch'eng County, Anhwei, in the Ming and Ch'ing Dynasties*, (Cambridge, 1979), *passim*.

II. Establishment of subbureaucratic government in the Ming dynasty

INTRODUCTION

The subbureaucratic government system of the Ming dynasty originated at a time when the government wanted the local population to participate in the administration of the empire. At that time the government was still in the process of stabilizing the empire after the civil war at the end of the Yuan dynasty in order to safeguard the future of the dynasty. The best guarantee would be an efficient civil and military administration; and a happy population where nobody was exploited by the government or private persons. Population registration was an important part of the government's policy to gain control over all households in the empire, both to secure a fair distribution of taxes and corvée and to ensure that no household illegally usurped power over other households.[1]

This chapter is concerned with the subbureaucratic government system and household registration of the early years of the dynasty. Following a tradition set by Japanese scholars, the relationship between the *lijia* and traditional territorial units is examined for Jinan Prefecture. Some explanations are also offered as to why the *lijia* organization developed as it did, particularly with reference to administrative and political developments following the death of the founding emperor, Zhu Yuanzhang.

The sources are laws and regulations from the central government and the local gazetteers for Jinan Prefecture; but as modern secondary literature is also used extensively, the problem arises whether the themes developed depend too much upon the views that have been expounded by other scholars. This is possible, but the value of the previous research is such that it cannot be disregarded. Also a total disregard would make an investigation of the conditions in sixteenth-century Shandong extremely difficult if not impossible. I hope that too heavy reliance on the views and themes in previous scholarly literature is compensated for in later chapters, which are based almost exclusively on the sources from Shandong Province.

ESTABLISHMENT OF SUBBUREAUCRATIC GOVERNMENT

1. Population registration in early Ming

The Ming dynasty had its origins in the economically important area with high population density around the lower Yangzi river. The administrative changes in population control introduced in the beginning of the dynasty should first of all be regarded as attempts to bring the population in this area under control. As in the Yuan, this control was first exercised along two different lines, the first being population registration for the purpose of conscription of taxes and corvée, and the second being organization of groups of the population for maintaining and expanding ideological control over the people. The latter control is here defined in a broad sense to include the maintenance of public security and encouragement to agriculture. These two lines were merged to a large extent in the dynasty with the introduction of the *lijia* system in 1381. This development in population control coincided with the consolidation of the imperial power over the bureaucracy through the purges of 1380–1381. It has been suggested that the introduction of the *lijia* system was an expression of this assertion of imperial control over the country, and also that social conditions were ripe at that time for this change.[2]

Land registration had already begun in 1368. At that time, 164 officials were sent out to survey the land in Zhejiang and Jiangxi.[3] In the same year the equal-work-men (*jungongfu*) were organized in Nanzhili and three prefectures in Jiangxi for corvée services mostly on construction work in or around the capital Nanking. The *jungongfu* were conscripted on the basis of land. One *qing* of land was to provide one man. There were provisions for pooling together if one whole *qing* was not held by the same owner, and also for the hiring of substitutes if a household did not have enough persons to supply the labour according to its landholdings.[4] In 1369 or 1370 the compilation of the *jungongfu* registers were ordered,[5] but as population registers they were superseded in 1370:11 by the system of household certificates (*hutie*). The household certificates were based upon a system that had already been adopted in Ningguo Prefecture.[6] It was not an uncommon feature of Ming administration that procedures in existence in some areas were extended to the whole country. It should, however, be noted hat the adoption of procedures from one area did not mean that similar or different procedures for the same purpose could not have been in operation in other parts of the country.

The household certificates were issued to every household, and duplicates were kept in government offices as population registers. This registration was probably extended to all areas under effective government control. The certificates contained for each household information on their place of registration (*jiguan*), the number of adult males and persons (*rending*), the surnames and personal names of members of the household, and in addition there was probably a description of the household property. The order to issue the certificates does not mention property, but the surviving copies of certificates include this item.[7] With the property included, the certificates did not only serve as population registers but could also be used for tax assessment.

These household certificates were superseded in 1381 by the Yellow Registers for Taxes and Corvée (*fuyi-huangce*). These Yellow Registers were a development of the household certificates in several points. They were to be revised every ten years. The registers recorded details of the previous registration for persons and property, changes over the intervening ten years for every person and item of property, followed by the figures of the registration currently in progress. Finally the Yellow Registers were based upon the *lijia*; registers were compiled for each *lijia*, and the compilation was the responsibility of the persons on service in the *lijia*.[8]

All the inhabitants of a *lijia* were enrolled in the Yellow Registers irrespective of their professional registration or economic status. The Ming dynasty continued the division of the population into hereditary professional classes which had been a prominent feature of Yuan population policy.[9] This was however greatly simplified under the Ming, with only three major groups: civilians (*min*), soldiers (*jun*), and artisans (*jiang*). There were several subgroups but apart from the salt-producing households (*zao*), who are sometimes regarded as a separate group, their numbers were insignificant.[10] These hereditary groups were perpetuated in order to secure a supply of certain types of corvée labourers for the government.

It has previously been assumed that the soldiers and artisans were not enrolled in the Yellow Registers but only in the special professional Yellow Registers kept by the ministries or other government agencies under which they served.[11] However, it has now been established that, with the exception of soldiers on service in guards or batallions, they were all registered in the Yellow Registers and performed the regular *lijia* corvée besides their professional corvée.[12]

The Yellow Register for a *lijia* was divided into two parts. One part listed the 110 households participating in the regular corvée service. The other part was a supplementary list for registered households or persons who did not have to perform corvée, such as widows, widowers, orphans and childless. Later, children under the age of ten and absentee landlords (*jizhuang*), who had to perform their regular *lijia* corvée where they were registered, were added to this list. They were called 'odds and ends' (*jiling*).[13] With the introduction in 1391 of the principle that the *lijia* could not lie across the boundaries of the subdistricts, a further category 'supernumeraries' (*daiguan*) was created. These did not take part in the regular corvée and were probably included in the supplementary register. Even if some of the households in the supplementary register were then liable to taxes and corvée,[14] the division of the Yellow Register into these two parts underscores their fiscal emphasis.

2. Subbureaucratic government organizations before 1381

The *lijia* from 1381 were not the first attempts to organize the population into subbureaucratic government groups. *Li*-leaders are already mentioned in the areas under the administration of Zhu Yuanzhang before the establishment of the Ming.[15] A *lijia* organization is mentioned in 1369 in Shanxi and similar institutions probably existed in other parts as well.[16] In 1370 Small Yellow Registers (*xiaohuangcetu*) are reported in Huzhou Prefecture, Zhejiang, based upon an organization (*tu*) of 100 households and with both *li*-leaders and *jia*-heads (*jiashou*). The purpose of the *tu* was to press and collect taxes, and to meet military needs. It is not easy to determine the exact nature of this organization. Descriptions of the *tu* are very similar to the *lijia*. This may well be because the people writing these descriptions were influenced by the 1381 text, but the organizational difference makes it clear that the Small Yellow Registers and the *tu* did exist before 1381. Yamane thinks that they were not confined to Huzhou Prefecture, and that they may in some way have been connected with the household certificates.[17]

In early Ming, together with these units for household registration, there were also established units all over the empire more directed towards the community aspects of subbureaucratic government. In the beginning of the Hongwu period an order was issued for the establishment of *lishe* and *xiangli* altars all over the country. The *lishe* altars were for the worship of the 'five soil and five grain spirits' and the *xiangli* altars for the worship of unconsoled spirits.[18] These were the spirits of persons with no descendants to perform their sacrifices, often persons who had met an untimely death.[19] The altars were erected in each *li* of 100 households and they were simple earthen structures. They were established in most places c. 1375, and this can be regarded as the time when *li* were established all over the country on the initiative of the central government. The number of *lishe* and *xiangli* altars in a district often corresponded to the number of *lijia* created in 1381, so it seems to be a reasonable assumption that the *li* created for worship were the forerunners of the *lijia* in the 1381 system.[20]

In the pre-1381 *li* the responsibility for the worship was rotated mostly among old and respected persons. There were five ceremonies per year, and at the end of each ceremony there was communal wine drinking and reading of pledges of good conduct. The leaders of the *li* were also responsible for the maintenance of good order. To that end *Shenming* and *Jingshan* pavilions were erected. Records of bad conduct were posted at the *Shenming* pavilions and records of good conduct at the *Jingshan* pavilion.[21]

To what extent these early units for population control were related to the natural village is hard to say. The principle was to have 100 households in each *li*. However, when we recall the experience of earlier dynasties, particularly that of the Yuan, it seems reasonable to assume that some flexibility was practiced during early Ming, when the power of the dynasty was still in its infancy.

3. Internal organization of the *lijia*

The *lijia* introduced in 1381 was primarily intended for the collection of taxes and corvée. The taxpaying households in the *lijia* were organized at two levels, which is probably the reason why there were 110 households and not one hundred. The ten economically most powerful households in the *lijia* were selected to be *li*-leaders (*lizhang*). These were the households paying most taxes and having most adult men (*ding*). The other 100 households were divided into ten *jia* and were called *jia*-heads (*jiashou*). The service in the *lijia*, which is often called the regular corvée (*zhengyi*), was performed on a rotational basis over ten years. In each year there would be one incumbent *li*-leader and ten incumbent *jia*-heads, the so-called *xiannian*.[22]

The incumbent *li*-leaders were responsible for administering the affairs of the *lijia*. Their duties included certain functions in the assessment and collection of taxes and conscription of corvée, certain ceremonial, judicial, educational, and agricultural duties, compilation of the Yellow Registers, payment of expenses within the *lijia* and contributions to the government. These duties varied according to time and place; the most consistent duties were the fiscal.[23]

The incumbent *li*-leaders were assisted in these duties by ten incumbent *jia*-heads. It is not clear in the sources how these *jia*-heads were selected. There are two possibilities. Either that in each year one household was selected from each *jia* to assist the *li*-leader, or that one whole *jia* could in each year perform the duties. In the latter case the *li*-leader and the *jia* could be more or less permanently paired. Heinz Friese seems to assume that the duty of *jia*-head was rotated among the ten households within the *jia*, and that the ten incumbent *jia*-heads from the ten *jia* assisted the incumbent *li*-leader.[24] Ray Huang and several Japanese scholars accept the second possibility,[25] and it will be shown later on the basis of Shandong in the sixteenth century that this is probably correct.

Here we will only add an indication that the relationship between a *li*-leader and a *jia* appears to have been established on a reasonably stable basis from the early years of the *lijia* system. In the 1391 regulations for the Yellow Registers it was ordered that during the compilation of the registers each household should fill in their registration form and hand it over to the administrating *jia*-head. He in turn would hand over the registration form for his own household together with those from the ten other households in the *jia* to the *li*-leader.[26] This only makes sense if each *li*-leader was permanently regarded as a member of the *jia*, and acted as the administrating *jia*-head for the purpose of registration.[27]

4. The *lijia* in local society

The laws of 1381 and 1391 for the compilation of the Yellow Registers and the organization of the *lijia* have no provision for modifying the size of the *lijia* in order to accommodate the natural village. The natural village is best defined as a number of households living in relative proximity, having a certain degree of inter-relationship between the households and a feeling of community distinct from feelings towards households from other natural villages. The natural village could have developed out of historical or geographical circumstances or could be based upon kinship. The community life of the natural village could be of direct use in some subbureaucratic government functions such as security, education, ideological control, and agricultural supervision. Consequently, disregard for the natural village in creating sub-bureaucratic government organizations could reduce their efficiency unless the official policy was modified. Such modifications were in previous dynasties included in government regulations,[28] but to this day they have not been discovered in the *lijia* laws of the Ming dynasty.

The reason why the *lijia* was to be organized strictly according to the numbers of households can be found in the fact that the *lijia* was primarily a fiscal unit.[27] Taxes were levied on land. The official rate at the beginning of the dynasty was 0.0535 *dan* per *mou* from domain land (*guantian*) and

0.0335 *dan* from private land (*mintian*).[30] These figures are probably administrative guidelines for the levy of taxes rather than uniformly applied rates. The land was registered in the Fish-scale Registers (*yulintuce*) and also in the Yellow Registers.[31] If these two registrations were reliable and the tax payments were forthcoming, it would not matter whether there were considerable variations in the size of the *lijia* for the collection of taxes. Under such circumstances the *lijia* would only have provided clerical assistance for the bureaucracy. However, it appears that the compilation of the Fish-scale Registers was only carried out with care in Zhejiang and southern Jiangsu.[32] More important perhaps was the fact that the *lijia* was involved in the collection of the tax from the households in the *lijia*, and that it was the responsibility of the incumbent *li*-leader that all the tax of the *lijia* was paid. If one household could not pay its tax, the *li*-leader would have to pay it from his own resources and at the same time, or later, attempt to get contributions from the other members of the *lijia* to reduce his losses.[33] Under these circumstances it was important that the *lijia* were of roughly the same size, so that there would not be too great differences in these possible deficits. If only the payment of land taxes had to be considered, it would probably have been a more satisfactory solution to have based the subbureaucratic government units upon divisions of land. For the *lijia* system such a development started in the sixteenth century and continued into the Qing dynasty.[34]

In early Ming the conscription of labour for corvée was an important feature of population control. This must be seen in relation to the economy of the day, which after the disturbances in late Yuan virtually returned to a natural economy with only scanty circulation of reliable money currency.[35] This was one of the reasons for the *jungongfu* system, which had been extended to the whole of Jiangsu in 1375 and continued around Nanking after 1381.[36] At the national level it became an important function of the *lijia* to raise the manpower needed for corvée. The corvée was divided into the regular corvée – the *li*-leaders and *jia*-heads and other services connected with the *lijia* and tax collection, i.e. the *li*-elders (*lilaoren*) and tax captains (*liangzhang*). Besides these services there were numerous services for the government at all levels. These were called miscellaneous corvée (*zayi*).[37]

The procedures for the conscription of the miscellaneous corvée in early Ming are not well documented in the sources. Perhaps more elaborate regulations did not exist before the introduction of the equal corvée (*junyao*) in the second half of the fifteenth century.[38] The general idea in early Ming seems to have been that the officials in charge of the corvée would weigh each item of corvée against each other item and then distribute them evenly to each *lijia* in the district. In the *lijia* the miscellaneous corvée was then according to the Yellow Registers conscripted from the male adults (*ding*), in the first instance perhaps the *ding* of the incumbent *li*-leader and *jia*-head households,[39] in such a way that the heaviest corvée fell upon the *ding* from the households in the highest tax classes. These tax classes were introduced in 1384 and were assessed according to the number of *ding* and the general wealth of the household.[40]

Under such a system it was important that the strength of each *lijia* was more or less the same, and the strict adherence in the official policy to the organization of the *lijia* according to numbers should be seen in this light. If the *lijia* were of comparable strength for the collection of taxes and conscription of corvée, the officials dealing with the fiscal matters could to a certain extent limit the scope of their work to dealing with the *lijia* instead of with each household. Such considerations must have carried a certain weight in the early years of the dynasty when the administration was not yet fully developed. At the same time the *lijia* provided – under the restraints of a not fully developed bureaucracy – the means to distribute the burden upon the population with a certain degree of equality.

The equal distribution of burdens on the population seems to have been an important consideration at the time. The founding emperor of the Ming dynasty, Zhu Yuanzhang, is on record as having several times expressed concern that the people should not be exhausted by excessive demands for public duties.[41] This could be achieved by demanding relatively little from the population in the form of taxes and corvée. This policy was apparently adopted to such a degree that Ray Huang in his studies of the Ming fiscal system has concluded that there was undertaxation in the beginning of the dynasty in relation to the ability of the population to pay.[42] The policy of Zhu Yuanzhang could also be achieved by ensuring that nobody was subjected to unequal demands.

It is not important for our purpose to discuss whether this concern expressed by Zhu Yuanzhang for the livelihood of the people was genuine. This will be of interest for biographers who want to describe the personality of the emperor. The fact is – and we have little reason to doubt the value of the sources – that such concern was expressed, and to us as well as to contemporaries it makes perfect political sense, considering how extreme impoverishment of parts of the community had threatened the life of the previous dynasty. It is in the light of this wish to distribute the burden equally and the realization of the limited administrative capabilities – either as a temporary state of affairs or as a desirable state of affairs – that we must view the apparent insistence that

43

each *lijia* should be of the same size without regard for the natural village.

But was the law enforced? Japanese historians have over the last four decades discussed and studied the relationship between the natural village and the official subbureaucratic government organizations which some of them call administrative villages. The main work has been done by Shimizu Morimitsu. He makes it quite clear that this kind of study is extremely difficult, since the sources relating to this level of the administration rarely give an explicit description of how the laws were carried out. Shimizu's general conclusion is that the administrative villages were always organized with regard to the natural villages, so that the community functions of the latter could facilitate administration. This is also his conclusion for the *lijia* of the Ming.[43]

Oyama Masaaki holds the view that the *lijia* was an artificial organization based on the number of households, and that at least until the middle of the dynasty households were administratively divided to maintain the prescribed number in each *lijia*.[44] Other historians stress the territorial base of the *lijia* almost from the beginning. Tsurumi Naohiro supports this view with a table showing how the traditional territorial units from Song and Yuan were absorbed into the *lijia* system with only few alterations.[45] Kuribayashi has found examples from Shandong explicitly stating that there were a number of villages in the *lijia*. He concludes from this evidence that the *lijia* respected the natural villages. Unfortunately his sources are late Ming gazetteers, and he does not indicate whether he believes the information to be valid for early Ming.[46] Some caution is called for in applying the evidence from the later period to early Ming, since some developments could have taken place in the meantime. Manipulations of the *lijia* system could have obliterated possible inconvenient divisions of the natural villages, and there could have been a tendency to establish new villages within the boundaries of the *lijia*. These remarks do not mean that we have to reject the general conclusions of these scholars. They are only meant to emphasize the extreme caution needed before conclusions can be made on the evidence.

In Japan the discussion has continued on the problem of co-operative systems in Chinese society. This discussion has of course been fuelled by developments in village organization in Modern China. Some scholars have on the basis of comparative studies rejected the historical existence of co-operative systems in Chinese villages, because there was no commonly owned land. Others have maintained that, considering the special conditions in Chinese society, such co-operative systems did exist, and that in the Ming dynasty the *lijia* had a role in these systems. Their studies of the Ming period have been based on the areas of the lower Yangzi river and Fujian Province with extensive irrigation which needed constant attention. Their argument is that as the *lijia* were organized to maintain the level of tax collection, then the leaders of the *lijia* also had to promote co-operative measures in order to insure constant or rising production in the *lijia*, so that taxes could be collected. The *lijia* was an instrument for the leaders to raise the manpower and tools necessary for water control. At the same time they could also control the co-operative systems that might have existed in the villages, and other community functions at the level of the village, the *lijia* or the subdistrict (*du*).[47] The sources I have used for Shandong have not yielded evidence to support any of the different views on natural villages and co-operative systems. The discussion seems to me to be somewhat speculative and to be based on too scattered evidence to draw any conclusions yet. Great variations probably existed according to time and place. The discussion certainly stimulates the digging-up of evidence, and in the end the conclusion may well be that the administrative villages were generally created in relation to the natural villages, and that at least some Chinese peasants were intelligent enough to see the advantages of some co-operation. But the evidence may also prove to be too diversified to allow any conclusion.

Perhaps the most important point to emerge from the Japanese discussions is that when the leaders of the *lijia* were selected according to wealth then the government in fact endorsed and supported the social status of the richer landowners or landlords in their local communities. When the importance of the *lijia* in local administration faded away, this official recognition of the social status of landownership also came to an end. So the disappearance of the *lijia* may have contributed to enhancing the importance of degree-holding rather than landholding for social status.[48] Our sources have provided no material for discussing this stimulating hypothesis, but the whole study certainly corroborates the fading importance of the official subbureaucratic government system in Ming local administration.

5. The *lijia* and the subdistricts

The only deviation from the principle of the *lijia* organized strictly according to numbers is found in the 1391 regulations. They state that the *li*-leaders were not allowed – during the compilation of the Yellow Registers – to go outside the traditional territorial subdistrict (*du*).[49] The *du*, which was a remnant of the *baojia* system in the Song,[50] was not used for subdistricts in the north in Ming times. It is however reasonable to assume that this provision also covered the other traditional subdistricts, such as the *xiang*, which had persisted in the north since the Tang dynasty. This assumption is confirmed for Jinan Prefecture in the local gazetteers for which information is available for the Ming dynasty. In most cases we see the *lijia* divided between the *xiang*,[51] and in the one case where this is not recorded we are left with the impression that this was the situation.[52]

In Jinan districts had from four to nine subdistricts. The *xiang* that had existed before the Ming dynasty appear to have had deep roots, but in the reshuffling of the districts in early Ming some had to be divided between two districts. One example is the division of the *xiang* between Qidong, Qingcheng, Zouping Districts and Wuding Subprefecture. The main problem there was the creation of Qidong District, which demanded the transfer of several subdistricts from the surrounding districts. This resulted in two subdistricts divided between Qidong and Qingcheng and one divided between Qidong and Zouping. Between Qingcheng and Wuding there were one or perhaps two divided subdistricts. Each part of a divided subdistrict kept its original name and formed a subdistrict in its respective district. In the case of the Zhengde Subdistrict, which was divided between Qidong and Qingcheng, it is interesting to note that the tradition of the old *xiang* survived, as the numbered series of the *lijia* was on the basis of the old *xiang*. Nos. 1 and 2 *lijia* were in Qingcheng and nos. 3 to 7 were in Qidong. The *lijia* were kept within the boundaries of the subdistricts with one possible exception. In Qidong it was reported that some members of no. 2 *lijia* of Jiahui Subdistrict were living in Liangzou Subdistrict. It is not possible to establish whether this had been the case at the beginning of the dynasty or whether it was only the state of affairs at the time of writing in 1617. In Qidong the subdistricts were again reorganized in 1461 into four subdistricts, to the north, east, south, and west. The former subdistricts were absorbed wholly into the new, but they apparently kept their identity, since there were again nine subdistricts in 1685.[53]

The number of *lijia* in each subdistrict in Jinan varied from two to twenty-five. When the *lijia* were not allowed to lie across the borders of the subdistrict, then there would often be a surplus of potential *lijia* member households, because the number of households in a subdistrict rarely was a multiple of 110. These surplus households were the 'supernumeraries', who in contrast to the 'odds and ends' had to perform corvée under the direction of the *li*-leader. The supernumeraries did not have to serve in the rotation of the regular corvée, so they were probably the first to be called upon when conscription was made to the miscellaneous corvée.[54] One consequence of this policy was therefore

46

that the *li*-leaders might have had an interest in having as many supernumeraries as possible and were thus reluctant to increase the number of the *lijia* after a population increase within the subdistrict. As a certain amount of the miscellaneous corvée was performed for the benefit of the local yamen – either official duties or duties for the personal benefit of the officials – it seems likely that the officials shared this attitude. With the extra supernumeraries they could raise their demands without unduly exhausting the households performing the regular corvée. The officials probably also had an interest in keeping the number of *lijia* as low as possible, since their number influenced the allocation of corvée for the provincial or central government between the districts, and no official – even the most honest and conscientious – would want his district to be allocated too large a share of this corvée.

6. *Lijia* and the *she*

In the sources that have been examined in Jinan Prefecture no information on the relation between the *lijia* and the natural village has been found. However, in north China it may not be so important to examine this relationship, because the *she* inherited from the Yuan seems to have played an important part in the establishment of the *lijia* in early Ming. Gui E, who as a local official in Beizhili had been actively engaged in the problems of the *lijia*, wrote around 1530 that he subprefectures and districts in Jiangxi, Huguang, etc., divided the *lijia* according to villages, whereas in Beizhili, Henan, etc., the *lijia* were divided according to *she*.[56] Kuribayashi has found a few examples in Shandong outside Jinan Prefecture, where the *lijia* are called *she*.[57] In 1570 it is also seen in an administrative document from the provincial governor,[58] so there seems to have been a certain tradition for the use of the term *she* instead of *lijia*.

In Jinan Prefecture there is no direct evidence that the *she* continued in the *lijia*. In Pingyuan District there may, however, be indirect evidence that this had happened. The *she* in northern China were supplemented in the early years of the dynasty with other subbureaucratic government units called *tun*. The *she* were for the people already living in the area. The *tun* were established for migrants being moved by the government from other provinces, primarily Shanxi and Shaanxi, to be settled on land that could easily be brought under cultivation. The land of the local people was measured according to a large *mou*, and that of the migrants according to a small *mou*.[59] The use of the large *mou* was probably introduced as a tax concession to the thinly populated northern provinces in comparison to those of the south. The use of the small *mou* for the migrants indicates that with the influx of new population such tax concessions were no longer regarded as necessary.[60]

In the 1590 Pingyuan gazetteer it is stated that the district was divided into forty-six *lijia*. Of these, twenty-two *lijia* were large *lijia* (*dali*) for the local population (*tumin*), while twenty-four were small *lijia* (*xiaoli*) for the small people (*xiaomin*).[61] This indicates that there had originally been twenty-two *she* and twenty-four *tun*, and that the *she* had been used as a basis for the *lijia* in early Ming. It is not clear whether the difference between the *she* and the *tun* had disappeared altogether in the sixteenth century. Gui E writes that he initiated reforms in Chengan District, Beizhili, to remove the difference between large and small *mou*. He further claims that the reform spread to the whole of Guangping Prefecture, and that all the districts in Beizhili, Honan, and Shandong wished to introduce similar reforms. He laments however that the reform met with strong opposition from the powerful official families.[62] If the problem had existed in other districts than Pingyuan in Jinan Prefecture, then the absence of references in the gazetteers would indicate that it had been solved at some time, perhaps following Gui E's reform. The problem may not have existed in many of the other districts, since it should be noted that Pingyuan District is on the border to Dongchang Prefecture, which seems to be the prefecture in Shandong which had the greatest influx of migrants.[63]

7. Revisions of the *lijia*

With the emphasis on the equal size of each *lijia* for the purpose of equalizing the tax and corvée burden, it is to be expected that the number of *lijia* within the subdistricts would be revised during the decennial compilation of the Yellow Registers according to fluctuations in the number of households.[64] However, in the sources describing the procedures for the *lijia* and the Yellow Registers there is no specific order that such a redistribution should be made when the population figures warranted it. There are only directions for supplementing the *lijia* when there were vacancies both at the level of *li*-leaders and the level of *jia*-heads. A vacancy among the *li*-leaders was to be filled by the *jia*-head household within the *lijia* that was considered the strongest in terms of adult males and tax payment. The *jia*-heads were supplemented from the ranks of the 'odds and ends', presumably by a household whose circumstances had changed in the intervening ten years so that it was now liable to perform corvée. If there were no such households in the *lijia*, it was then permitted to transfer households from another *lijia* within the same subdistrict.[65]

From reading the instructions concerning the compilation of the Yellow Registers and the organization of the *lijia* it is easy to get the impression of an implicit understanding that the number of *lijia* should follow fluctuations in the number of households.[66] The reason this is not clearly stated can be that adjustments were not intended, but this seems unlikely, since corrections were carried out from time to time. A more likely explanation may be that the authors of the regulations in 1381 and 1391 did not feel any need for specific instructions regarding the increase or decrease in population, since the fluctuations had not yet been so manifest as to warrant a redistribution. The 1391 regulations give the impression that they were issued as additional regulations to the 1381 law to cater for abuses and problems which had become evident in the period between the first and second registration, and this may be the reason why this particular problem was not dealt with.

If the need for adjustments in the number of *lijia* was brought to the attention of the central government as a consequence of changes in the population, it would probably only have been after the completion of the second registration in 1391. Additional instructions would then have been issued in the years before the third scheduled registration when the instructions for this were being drafted in the Ministry of Revenue. This period coincided with the death of Zhu Yuanzhang and the civil war that followed.[67] These events had already caused the third registration to be postponed by two years,[68] so it is likely that sufficient attention was not given to working out the instructions for this registration, if any were issued at all.[69] It is furthermore conceivable that the local officials were not too anxious to draw attention to the problems arising from population fluctuations. Redistribution of the *lijia* would mean additional work in re-allocating the corvée, and, as long as the fluctuations were not too marked, the absence of adjustments to the *lijia* would not have had serious consequences.

There is thus an alternative explanation for the lack of direct orders to redistribute the *lijia* to the one preferred by others. Following a seventeenth-century author, Kawakatsu thinks that the number of *lijia* became static in 1391 because the emphasis in the organization of the *lijia* was moved from households to land following the new regulations with regard to subdistricts. This had become possible with the land survey of the Fish-scale Registers in 1387.[70] Ping-ti Ho also claims that Zhu Yuanzhang, after the introduction of the Yellow Registers and the Fish-scale Registers, became more interested in perpetuating the fiscal structure than in adjusting it to changes in population and wealth.[71] There

49

may be some validity in such arguments that the policy of Zhu Yuanzhang resulted in making the system inflexible. The inertia of the system and the limited administrative capability of the bureaucracy are other factors to be considered, but it appears that political events at the turn of the century over which Zhu Yuanzhang had no influence must be taken into consideration as well. Whatever the cause was, we must regard the failure to enforce revisions from the early years of the *lijia* system to have been a considerable weakness in the system, and this must have had considerable influence on its decline, starting in the late Hongwu period.

In Jinan Prefecture changes are found in the number of *lijia* in eleven districts, while no changes are found in eleven other districts. Details are not available for the remaining eight districts and subprefectures.[72] In the districts where changes happened there were usually only one or two during the whole dynasty. Dates for the redistribution are only given in a few districts, and it is not possible to draw any conclusions from these as to the general circumstances behind the changes.[73] Presumably they took place when an official felt the need to make corrections and he had the will and power to carry them through with the support of the provincial and central government. Certainly redistribution did not take place when the numbers warranted it. In the Licheng gazetteer from 1640 it is mentioned that some *lijia* could have over 1,000 households while others had only a handful of lineages.[74] This was at a time when the *lijia* had lost much of its significance, but we do get the impression that the author did not think that this difference was completely without relevance. This may be a special case, but discrepancies in the size of the *lijia* seem to have been a constant concern of the officials, so we are forced to think that any changes in the *lijia* system met with considerable opposition from the population. The households in the larger *lijia* would have had a vested interest in preserving the status quo, since this would give them an *a priori* advantage in the allocation of corvée even if the officials took corrective measures against the unequal strength of the *lijia*.

The only major redistribution for which details are available took place in 1512 in Zhanhua District. This coincided with a general policy of the central government to revise the *lijia* system,[75] but the direct cause given in Zhanhua was the bandit incursions into Shandong in 1511–1512, which were claimed to have led to a population decrease. The result was that the number of *lijia* was cut by one-half from forty-eight to twenty-four, still in four subdistricts each with six *lijia*. The redistribution was done on the order of the provincial government and involved an assistant administration commissioner and the assistant prefect of Jinan Prefecture.[76]

50

8. *Lijia* and population figures

Underlying the discussion in the preceding section is the assumption that during the Ming dynasty there were population fluctuations in the districts of Jinan Prefecture which warranted redistribution. It is generally acknowledged that the figures for the Ming period tend to show a static picture of the population and that this cannot be correct. It has been estimated that the population more than doubled from 1368 to 1600. Although there is reason to assume that the increase was more rapid in the south than in the north,[77] this would still indicate that there were considerable fluctuations in Shandong province. The reason for the failure of the sources to reveal the true figures is that the population records were often those used for fiscal purposes, and it is well known that such figures tend to become erroneous.

The picture of population development we get from the district gazetteers in Jinan Prefecture is extremely diversified. In some districts a constant rise in the number of households is recorded, in some a stagnation, and in others the number of households decreased. When it comes to the number of persons living in the prefecture, the situation is even more complicated. This is due to the counting of heads in some districts and the counting of male adults in others. As the male adults (*ding*) in the Ming dynasty tend to represent a fiscal unit rather than all the male adults living in the districts,[78] such figures are virtually worthless for estimating the population.

In Jinan there are figures available for two districts which have a ring of authenticity, since they show a fairly steady increase in the population and also a certain degree of consistency in the person/household ratio. This ratio was in the vicinity of ten to one, which seems to be a characteristic demographic feature of north China including Shandong.[79] Figures of Qidong District:[8]

Year	Households	Persons	P/H Ratio
1391	4,360	47,813	11.0
1452	5,280	51,330	9.7
1462	6,718	62,310	9,3
1472	6,930	69,074	10.0
1492	7,515	71,140	9.5
1512	7,689	74,919	9.7
1551	11,340	101,290	8.9

Figures for Shanghe District (only available from 1492):[81]

Year	Households	Persons	P/H Ratio
1492	8,111	79,890	9.8
1502	9,896	99,896	10.1
1512	9,634	110,090	11.4
1522	9,936	115,835	11.7
1587	11,314	123,986	11.0

There are figures for Qidong District after 1551, but their reliability is doubtful.[82] The 1586 Shanghe gazetteer admits that there was a degree of under-registration at least on the last year due to increases in taxes and corvée. This had caused 'idle and lazy' people to enter the Buddhist and Taoist orders or to 'sneak away' to live elsewhere. Even among those who remained in the district some were in hiding and not registered.

These developments in Qidong and Shanghe Districts can be contrasted with the development in, for example, Putai District:[83]

Year	Households	*Ding*	D/H Ratio
Hongwu	17,354	36,817	2.1
Yongle	17,921	37,153	2.1
Chenghua	12,914	35,368	2.7
Zhengde	10,878	27,642	2.5
Jiajing	9,196	11,073	1.2
1567	8,335	10,850	1.3
c. 1586	14,654	14,675	1.0

The sudden rise in the household figures during the Wanli period is a common feature in districts that had shown a decline or stagnation in these figures over the preceding two hundred years.[84] It is so drastic that it cannot represent a real increase in population but must be a result of changed registration procedures. It is unlikely that the district officials had been unaware of the increase in the population. The statistical diversity is probably best explained by assuming that the figures recorded in the gazetteers were drawn from different kinds of registers in the districts. Besides the Yellow Registers other registers were kept in the yamen. One of them would have been the equal corvée registers introduced together with the equal corvée (*junyao*). This began in Shandong between 1483 and 1486.[85] There is no record of the use of the unofficial population registers – White Registers (*baice*) – in Jinan Prefecture. These are reported in other parts of the country from c. 1500,[86] and it is of course possible that they existed in Jinan Prefecture as well. Furthermore, in the reforms carried out in the second half of the sixteenth century other registers than the Yellow Registers are mentioned.[87] The conclusion must be that there were in the yamen archives a selection of different population data available for the compilers of the gazetteers. Each set of data served a specific purpose and could be different from others serving different purposes. The data available to us depends upon the availability of the registers to the compilers of the gazetteers and the selection made by them.

Irrespective of actual population developments it is sufficient to note for the purpose of analysing the *lijia* system that changes in the number of *lijia* were not enforced when the recorded population figures warranted it. Even if we only take into account households registered for taxation, it does not appear that the adjustments were carried out. Putai District may be a case where the population figures are fiscal figures, but the number of *lijia* was only reduced from sixty-three in the Hongwu period to fifty-nine in the Jiajing period.

THE FUNCTION OF SUBBUREAUCRATIC GOVERNMENT AFTER THE ESTABLISHMENT OF THE *LIJIA*

1. Population registration and other fiscal duties

The *li*-leaders were responsible for the compilation of the Yellow Registers in their *lijia*. Each household filled in their registration form and handed it over to the administrating *jia*-head, who in turn handed it over to the *li*-leader. The heaviest work load was on the *li*-leader on service in the tenth year of the decennial rotation.[88] There was a certain amount of paperwork involved in the distribution of the registration forms, their collection and supervision, and the forwarding to the yamen. They were usually assisted in this work by people in the *lijia* who could write and calculate. These were the *li*-registrar (*shushou*) and the *li*-tax assessor (*suanshou*), who in the beginning of the dynasty only served in the years of registration. Their service was not regarded as a part of the regular corvée, and if no qualified persons were found within the *lijia*, then persons from outside could be hired to perform the duties. As the clerical work in the *lijia* increased with higher levies of taxes and particularly other duties, the *li*-registrars and *li*-tax assessors showed a tendency to become permanent and, with the increased responsibilities, more powerful positions.[89]

The *li*-leaders were also responsible for the population in the *lijia*. It was their duty to make sure that nobody escaped from the *lijia* in order to avoid corvée, and if they escaped, the *li*-leaders had to report it to the authorities, so that the fugitives could be apprehended. The *li*-leaders also ensured that no member household in the *lijia* concealed fugitives from other *lijia*. All these were criminal offences, and the Ming Code prescribes punishments of the *li*-leaders and the household heads if they falsified or obstructed registration.[90] A special kind of supervision exercised by the *li*-leader over the population was the control or 'purification' (*qingli*) of the military households and their registers in the *lijia*.

For tax collection in the *lijia*, the *li*-leader would assist the tax captains in areas where these were appointed. In areas with no tax captains the *li*-leaders would be in charge of pressing and collecting the taxes under direct instruction from the yamen personnel.[92] So far no evidence that tax captains were appointed in Shandong in the first half of the dynasty has been found.[93] We must therefore assume that the *li*-leaders in Jinan Prefecture in this period worked directly under the yamen. This seems plausible, since the number of *lijia* in the districts of Jinan averaged c. 50 and only in two districts exceeded 100.

The *li*-leaders were responsible for the supervision of the households in their *lijia*. If any of them cheated with their returns on *ding* and property, the *li*-leader was to suffer the same punishment as the culprit if he did not report it. He was also to report on natural disasters in his *lijia*, such as drought, flood and pests. If he reported that his *lijia* could not pay its taxes as a result of a bad year then the payments were deferred to the following year. However, if the deficiency in tax payments was due to cheating or absconding of households, i.e. to the neglect of the *li*-leader, then the remaining members of the *lijia* would have to make up the deficiency.[94]

The sources are not very informative with regard to the function of the *li*-leaders in raising the manpower for corvée. In assessing the households and distributing the corvée between them, the *li*-leaders were assisted by the *li*-registrars and *li*-tax assessors and perhaps the elders. After 1384 the assessment included a division of the households into the tax classes. This division provided a convenient guideline for the *li*-leaders and *li*-registrars in their allocation of the corvée duties, and more important perhaps it made it possible for others – both officials and the households concerned – to check that the distribution of corvée was fair. In at least one prefecture it was apparently part of the regular corvée of the *li*-leaders to dispatch the soldiers and artisans to their corvée duties.[95]

2. Tax captains

Above the level of the *lijia*, the subbureaucratic government system was supplemented by the tax captains (*liangzhang*), who were responsible for the collection and forwarding of taxes from the *lijia* within their tax areas (*qu*). The normal size of this *qu* was an area that yielded 10,000 *dan* in taxes, but in practice they seem to have been smaller. The status of tax captain was originally considered to be closer to the status of officials than was normal for other corvée duties. Meritorious tax captains could be appointed officials, and at the beginning of the dynasty they went each year to the capital (Nanking) to receive their instructions from the emperor in person. After the Hongwu period, and particularly after the capital moved to Peking in 1420, their status changed to that of corvée. It was impossible to ask all the tax captains to come to the capital each year, since the majority of them were from the middle and southern provinces. With the loss of the personal attention of the emperor, the tax captains became more easily the victims of excessive demands from officials. For some of them this led to their ruin, while other tax captains were able to use their position to enrich themselves from the inhabitants of their tax area. The result was that the social esteem of the tax captains fell drastically.[96]

In Shandong, as in the other northern provinces, there is no evidence that *liangzhang* were appointed at the beginning of the dynasty or later. However, as first pointed out by Liang Fangzhong and later by Japanese scholars, some kind of tax captains, the *dahu*, were appointed at least during the second half of the dynasty in the five northern provinces of Shandong, Henan, Beizhili, Shanxi and Shaanxi, and possibly in Sichuan. They are first mentioned in 1509 in connection with the *liangzhang* as extorting money from the people. This indicates that they had operated for some time before that date.[97]

3. The *lijia* contributions

During their year of incumbency the *li*-leaders and *jia*-heads had to pay minor expenses within the *lijia* for educational and ceremonial activities, relief for the poor, and support for prospective scholars.[98] Probably from the very early years of the *lijia* system, the incumbent *li*-leaders and *jia*-heads also had to pay for some expenses on behalf of the bureaucracy. These would include, on a modest scale, catering for official visitors to the district, often in such a way that the *li*-leaders in the city would arrange banquets, etc., while the *li*-leaders in the countryside had to meet the expenses of gifts and the dispatching of visitors on their further journey. The *li*-leaders would further be asked to provide paper, ink. etc., for use in the offices of the yamen.[99] Such contributions were not a part of the original duties of the *lijia*, but it was a convenient way for the officials to meet such expenses, for which there were no other budgetary allowances.[100] Later in the dynasty they came to be known as '*lijia* contributions' or simply '*lijia*'.

In the Hongwu period there were already demands from the central government for *lijia* contributions, the so-called *shanggong*. At first these contributions consisted of local produce considered a necessity either for the imperial household, for the central government or for the military forces. Some of these contributions were offset in the tax payments, but this was not universal and the reimbursements do not seem to have covered expenses.[101] Contributions to the local government agencies, normally known as *gongfei*, were not reimbursed and they became increasingly heavy. Besides the provision of stationery and entertainment these contributions could be such items as travel expenses for examination candidates, welfare expenses, ceremonial expenses, repair of buildings and provision of household utensils.[102] Other contributions could be the personal service of the *li*-leader in attendance at the yamen,[103] and a particularly heavy labour service was the postal service. Such service was provided in areas where there was no established regular postal service. Whenever there was a need for public transport, the *lijia* were required to provide the necessary manpower, horses or boats. As travel routes could change quicker than the regular postal services were re-routed, this imposition could be very heavy in some districts.[104]

It was the nature of the *lijia* contributions that they responded to *ad hoc* demands from the bureaucracy. If such demands were illegal and for the private benefit of the government personnel, they were difficult to control and the system led to considerable abuse.[105] Even when the *lijia* contributions tended to become institutionalized as fixed amounts, the arbitrariness of the levy continued, since it provided flexibility in the fiscal system. However, it also appears that the *lijia* contributions were one of the main obstacles to a fair economic administration in the later part of the dynasty.

The *lijia* contributions were paid both by the incumbent *li*-leaders and *jia*-heads. There is no indication of a country-wide policy for dividing the burden between the *li*-leader and the *jia*-head. The only example known so far is from a district in Sichuan where the *li*-leader paid 30% of the contribution, while the rest was divided among the *jia*-heads. As long as the demands for *lijia* contributions were not too heavy, it was not a major problem for the households to provide them once every ten years. However, when the levies increased, some of the incumbent households could no longer meet the expenses from their income during the year of service. They either had to make savings during the nine years of rest or they had to borrow money. Both solutions were a major problem for many poorer households and probably contributed to an intensification of the gap between poor and rich.[106]

4. The non-fiscal duties of the *lijia*

These have been described by Yamane Yukio and Sakai Tadao from various sources as follows: maintaining public order, instruction of the people, settlement of disputes, encouragement to agriculture, mutual assistance and other incidental work in the *lijia*. This included apprehension of fugitives, for which the non-incumbent *li*-leaders could be used. In the first years of the *lijia* system the *li*-leaders were in charge of these non-fiscal duties assisted by the *jia*-heads.[107] From various sources it also appears that the duties which had previously been performed under the *li* of the *lishe* and *xiangli* in connection with the *Shenming* and *Jingshan* pavilions were transferred to the auspices of the *lijia*.[108] In an order of 1383 it appears that the *li*-leader was now to chair the wine-drinking ceremonies which were conducted at the conclusion of the ceremonies at the *lishe* altar in the spring and autumn. During these ceremonies the participants were admonished to respect the old and virtuous, observe the rituals, and act in accordance with the criminal code. It is not clear whether these ceremonies were actually performed in the *lijia*, since the instructions mention 100 households and not 110, but it is clear that the *li*-leaders presided over them.[109] This is also clear in an order of 1384, which stated that it was the duty of the *li*-leaders to induce the inhabitants of the *lijia* to follow the appropriate social order, to encourage them to attend to their agricultural duties, and to warn them against bad conduct. At the end of the year the *li*-leaders would further investigate the conduct of the people, criticize the bad and commend the good.[110]

The *li*-leaders may not have been the only ones responsible for the non-fiscal duties in all the *lijia* of the whole country. Some sources mention that the tax captains shared the responsibilities of the *li*-leaders.[111] It also appears that families with examination graduates had a special function in the instruction of the people.[112] The role of the *lijia* in non-fiscal duties was probably not finally settled until the *li*-elders (*lilaoren*) in 1394 took over most of the educational and judicial duties of the *li*-leaders. This may have been done because the rotational service of the *li*-leaders, together with their other duties, made them unfit to fulfil these functions.

5. *Li*-elders

In the non-fiscal duties that had apparently been laid upon the *lijia*, the *li*-leaders were assisted or superseded by the *li*-elders (*lilaoren*). An examination of the system of elders in the Ming dynasty is greatly hampered by the term itself. There seems to be general agreement that the elders had special privileges and duties as leaders of the people and scrutinizers of the bureaucracy even if there was no official definition of their status.

Institutionalized elders are first mentioned in the Ming dynasty when the *qisu* were abolished in 1388:8. These *qisu* had judicial power in petty cases and had probably been established shortly after the *lijia* system in 1381. The subsequent formal establishment of elders was in 1394. However, there are records from between 1388 and 1394 showing that prefectures, subprefectures and districts selected elders to be sent to the capital for consultation with the central government. During this period the elders apparently also retained the privilege and duty imposed upon them in the Great Proclamation (*Da-Gao*) to report on the abuses of local officials.[113]

In 1394 the *lilaoren* were entrusted with judicial power in petty cases. In 1397 they were also given power over education, encouragement of agriculture and mutual assistance in the *lijia*. Their duties were finally laid down in great detail in the Precepts for Popular Instruction (*Jiaomin pangwen*) in 1398. There were two reasons for the appointment of the *li*-elders. First, they could relieve the *li*-leaders of some of their duties in the *lijia*, so that they could concentrate on the fiscal side of their responsibilities. Since there was no time-limit on the service as *li*-elders, they could probably perform many of the community functions better than the *li*-leaders. The only limitation on the service of the *li*-elders may have been that their performance was reviewed every three years. Second, they could relieve the judicial bureaucracy. The government complained that many local officials were unable to pass judgements in minor cases and referred them to higher authorities. The introduction of the *li*-elders was meant to remedy this shortcoming of the local bureaucracy, and at the same time it may have been a deliberate act to curtail its power.[114]

The first part of the Precepts for Popular Instruction is concerned with the judicial aspects of the *li*-elder institution, in many ways similar to the duties of the *she*-leaders of the Yuan dynasty. The *li*-elders were primarily to concern themselves with civil matters, but in some cases they could also pass judgement in criminal cases if the accused was a first-offender. However, in serious criminal cases such as burglary, fraud, and loss of life, the *li*-elders could only hear the case with the consent of all parties. The *li*-elders were to hear the cases in the *Shenming* pavilion, and they were allowed to punish by beating with the light and heavy bamboo, but not to arrest people and hold them in custody. The cases were normally decided by several elders selected from the *lijia* among those above the age of fifty, together with the *li*-leader and *jia*-heads. In all cases of a nature to be handled by the *li*-elders, the plaintiffs were strictly forbidden to bypass the *li*-elders and bring them directly to the officials. If this regulation was disregarded, then the plaintiff would be punished, and if a *li*-elder refused to settle a case, he would also be punished.

In the field of instruction of the people, the *li*-elder would arrange for a disabled person to walk around in the *lijia* led by a child. They would strike a wooden bell and proclaim the Six Sacred Maxims:

«Honour and obey parents»
«Reverence and respect superiors»
«Work for harmony in the community»
«Instruct and admonish the young»
«Let each be content with his work»
«Avoid evil conduct»

In a *lijia* that was scattered over a large area there would be a wodden bell for each *jia*. The *li*-elders arranged the sacrifices, especially the wine-drinking ceremonies in spring and autumn, and they carried out instruction in the school, *shexue*. During the wine-drinking ceremonies and in the *shexue* they would read the three parts of the Great Proclamation. When encouraging farming they would ensure that everyone in the *lijia* attended to his duties even to the extent that a drum was sounded at the fifth watch at night so they could supervise that everybody left early for the work in the fields. In the fields they were to supervise mulberry, cotton and irrigation work. As for bandits within the *lijia* area, the *li*-elder would assemble the men of the *lijia* to apprehend them, and after the culprits had been arrested they were sent to the officials.[115] However, in the sphere of public security it is worth noting that there was no mutual responsibility between the households in the *lijia*.[116]

The system of *li*-elders seems to have declined rapidly after its introduction at the end of the Hongwu period. This decline to some extent followed the general decline of the *lijia* system as an instrument of subbureaucratic government. There were however also weaknesses in the system of *li*-elders itself as described in 1428 by the magistrate in Xincheng District, Jinan. He complained that the *li*-elders used the law for their own benefit. With such opportunities there were people who bribed their way into the position of *li*-elder so that they could use it to slander officials to their superiors and to make extortions from the people. The result was that old and upright people were no longer selected for the position.[117]

The police duties of the subbureaucratic government could also be performed by the *zongjia* and *xiaojia*. In 1438 they are mentioned as assistants to the elders for the maintenance of public order in Songjiang Prefecture of Nanzhili. Their existence is mostly recorded in middle and southern China. There are no clear records to show their terms of service. In some cases they were selected on the basis of the subdistrict, in others according to the number of households. In one such case one *xiaojia* was conscripted for each ten households and one *zongjia* for fifty households.[118]

FACTORS IN THE CHANGE AND DECLINE OF THE *LIJIA* SYSTEM

The *lijia* system was created for a static society, and in this respect it must be regarded as a considerable achievement of the early Ming bureaucracy. Although there was no doubt a certain degree of under-registration of the population in the 1380s and 1390s, the figures appear to have an accuracy which most pre-modern societies could be proud of and which in China was not attained again before 1776.[119]

The Yellow Registers were compiled from the outset with the purpose of providing a reliable instrument for the levy of taxes and corvée. It is a common feature of such population registers to develop serious under-registration if the methods of checking the registers are inadequate. This was the case in the Ming dynasty. There is evidence that the Yellow Registers in some areas were not changed during the dynasty but only copied meticulously from the first registers.[120]

Ping-ti Ho claims that there was a change of emphasis in the Yellow Registers from 1381 to 1391 from being records of the whole population towards being records of the fiscal population. In my view the 1391 regulations were intended to clarify matters that had arisen out of the first registration. The order in 1391 that young males over the age of ten were to be enrolled in the regular register so that they were ready to perform corvée when they turned sixteen should be seen as a measure to ensure that they entered the corvée service at the right time rather than as a shift of emphasis towards fiscal population. It is possible that such amendments may subsequently have led to an emphasis on fiscal population, but there appears to be no change in official policy.[121]

The *lijia* system was based upon a mutual responsibility between the households in the *lijia* to supply the government with tax and services. For a reasonable functioning of such a system it was not only necessary that each *lijia* had more or less the same economic strength but also that all the households in the *lijia* had sufficient strength to meet the requirements. Such a situation apparently existed at the beginning of the dynasty when, after a considerable redistribution of land, most households were to some extent equal in economic strength. However, subsequent development was towards concentration of wealth in fewer households, and many households became too poor to meet the levies imposed upon them.[122] The result was a certain degree of illegal migration or non-registration. Since the households that remained still had to contribute the taxes and services of the whole *lijia*, their burden became heavier, thus forcing more households to abscond or to seek refuge with wealthy households or in monasteries. This development continued as a vicious circle until some *lijia* became more or less depopulated, at least in terms of registered population. Such developments are repeatedly described in the sources and are evidenced in practice by the reduction in the numbers of *lijia* in many districts, even if the evidence available to us today suggests population increase.[123]

To keep the *lijia* functioning in its original form would also have required honesty on the part of those who undertook the registration and allocation of the duties in the *lijia*, i.e. the *li*-leaders, the *li*-registrars and the *li*-tax assessors. In the absence of such honesty an effective method of checking their operation was required. The government was fully aware of malpractices and instituted elaborate procedures from the district level up to the national level, where the registers were checked in the Lake Posterior Archives in Nanking. Even if this control was backed up by heavy punishment for cheating, it did not succeed, and we must conclude that it was simply too ambitious considering the administrative capabilities of the bureaucracy. Furthermore, the punishments were so heavy that they would only have been applied with reluctance by most officials, and they were subsequently modified drastically in 1451.[124] It was inevitable under such circumstances that there was considerable tampering with the Yellow Registers, and there developed during the dynasty a whole vocabulary for the various manipulations of persons and property.[125] It should, however, be noted that records of malpractices are more likely to have been included in the sources than records of law-abiding and smooth operations of the *lijia*, so our picture of the system tends to become distorted. However, there can be no doubt that there were numerous problems in the *lijia* system relating to reliable and fair operation of taxes and corvée, but it should also be remembered that the *lijia* system continued to operate well into the sixteenth century.

NOTES TO CHAPTER II

1. According to the Ming Code it was illegal not to register a household or to be an accomplice to such acts. Commoners were also forbidden to have slaves. In 1588 the élite (*xiangshen*) were allowed to keep slaves. *Minglü jijie fuli* 4/1–2, 9; Nishimura Kazuyo, «Mindai no doboku», *Tōyōshi kenkyū* 38.1 (1979), 27.
2. Kuribayashi Nobuo, *Rikōsei no kenkyū*, (Tokyo, 1971), p. 11.
3. *Ibid.*, pp. 3–4; Heinz Friese, *Das Dienstleistungs-System der Ming Zeit (1368–1644)*, (Hamburg, 1959), p. 42.
4. Yamane Yukio, *Mindai yōeki seido no tenkai*, (Tokyo, 1966), pp. 8–10; Friese, p. 42; *Ming shi (MS)* 78/1904.
5. *DMHD* 206/1 dates the introduction to 1369. In the *Ming Shilu (SL)* a similar instruction is dated 1370:7:*xinmao*. Friese, p. 45; Yamane (1966), p. 9.
6. Kuribayashi (1971), p. 4.
7. Ho (1959), pp. 4–7; Yamane (1966), p. 19
8. Wei Qingyuan, *Mingdai huangce zhidu*, (Peking, 1961), p. 24; *DMHD* 20/1–2. Translated in Leif Littrup, «The Yellow Registers of the Ming Dynasty – Translation from the Wan-li Da-Ming Huidian», *Papers on Far Eastern History* 16 (1977), pp. 83–84.
9. Wei, p. 12.
10. The division of the population into professional groups is rarely recorded in the gazetteers. The only records available are from Deping District in 1512 and Zichuan District in 1543, 1553, and 1602. The official registration of numbers of households was in 1602 in Zichuan; *min* 6,868, *jun* 2,588, *zao* 39, *jiang* 280. Five minor groups in the same registration totalled only 31. *Deping xianzhi* 1796/3/2; *Zichuan xianzhi* 1602/12/1.
11. Wada (1939), p. 96; Ho (1959), p. 15.
12. Wei, p. 54; Kuribayashi (1971), p. 14.
13. *DMHD* 20/1–3.
14. Tsurumi Naohiro, «Mindai no kireiko ni tsuite», *Tōyō gakuhō* 47.3 (1964), 43 ff. For a further discussion of the *daiguan* see p. 46–47 below.
15. Kuribayashi (1971), p. 4.
16. *Ibid.* and Yamane (1966), pp. 14–15.
17. Kuribayashi (1971), p. 5; Yamane (1966), pp. 16–18.
18. *Huang Ming zhishu* 7/33, 36.
19. *Leling xianzhi* 1762/3/47; Taylor, p. 36.
20. Kuribayashi (1971), pp. 5–7.
21. *Ibid.*, pp. 7–10.
22. *SL* 1381/1; *DMHD* 20/1; Kuribayashi (1971), p. 11; Littrup (Yellow Registers), p. 82.
23. Yamane (1966), pp. 41–42; Kuribayashi (1971), pp. 54–56.
24. Friese, pp. 27, 76.
25. Ray Huang, *Taxation and Governmental Finance in Sixteenth-Century Ming China*, (Cambridge, 1974), p. 34; Tsurumi Naohiro «Mindai ni okeru gōson shihai», in

Higashi-Ajia sekai no tenkai, II (*Iwanami kōza sekai rekishi*, v. 12), (Tokyo, 1971), p. 73; Oyama Masaaki, «Fueki seido no henkaku», *ibid.*, p. 314.

26. *DMHD* 20/1–2.

27. The above discussion of the relationship of the *li*-leaders to the *jia* seems necessary to help to clarify the organization of the *lijia*. That it has not yet been generally accepted seems to be clear from the description given by Mi-chu Wiens: «In each *li*, the household with the largest number of male adults and the largest amount of property was chosen as the *li-chang* (village head). The remaining 100 households in each *li* were divided into ten *chia*, and *chia-shou* (section headmen) were selected to lead each *chia*. The *li-chia* service required the eleven financially better-off households within each *li* to serve as village head and section headmen each year.» See Mi-chu Wiens, «Changes in the Fiscal and Rural Control Systems in the Fourteenth and Fifteenth Centuries», *Ming Studies* 3 (1976), 58.

28. Shimizu Morimitsu, «Chūgoku no gōson tōchi to sonraku», in *Shakai kōseishi taikei*, v. 2, pt. 2 (Tokyo, 1949), pp. 8–41.

29. Oyama (1971), p. 320; Kawakatsu Mamoru, «Mindai rikō hensei no henshitsukatei – Oyama Masaaki-shi no 'sekiko no igi' ron no hihan», *Shien* 112 (1975), 523.

30. *DMHD* 17/3.

31. Wei, pp. 74–79, ill. 5.

32. Ho (1959), p. 108.

33. Kuribayashi Nobuo, «Mindai kōki no nōson to rikōsei», *Tōyō shigaku ronshu* 4 (1955), 375.

34. Obata Tatsuo, «Kōnan ni okeru rikō no hensei ni tsuite», *Shirin* 39.2 (1956), 92–101.

35. Kuribayashi (1971), p. 12; Wolfgang Franke, «Zur Grundsteuer in China während der Ming Dynastie», *Zeitschrift für vergleichende Rechtswissenschaft* 56 (1953), 93.

36. Yamane (1966), pp. 10–13.

37. *Ibid.*, p. 37.

38. Friese, p. 90.

39. Zuo Yunpeng, «Mingdai yaoyi zhidu sanlun», *Zhongguoshi yanjiu* 1980.2, 18–19; Mori Masao, «Nihon no Min Shin shidaishi kenkyū ni okeru gōshinron ni tsuite», *Rekishi hyorōn* 308 (1975), 48.

40. Wada (1939), p. 101; Yamane (1966), p. 189, *DMHD* 210/17.

41. Friese, pp. 44–45.

42. Huang, p. 183.

43. Shimizu, pp. 49–58.

44. Oyama (1971), p. 320; Kawakatsu (1975), pp. 522–526.

45. Tsurumi (1971), pp. 70–71.

46. Kuribayashi (1971), p. 30.

47. Tsurumi (1971), pp. 79–81; Tsurumi Naohiro, «Kyū Chūgoku ni okeru kyodotai no shomondai», *Shichō* (New series) 4(1978), 63–79.

48. Oyama (1971), pp. 341–343; Tsurumi (1971), p. 66.

49. *DMHD* 20/2.

50. Shimizu, p. 43.

51. *Binzhou zhi* 1583/1/35; *Leling xianzhi* 1762/1/65; *Linyi xianzhi* 1673/4/1; *Putai xianzhi* 1592/5/4; *Qidong xianzhi* 1617/6/2; *Qingcheng xianzhi* 1612/1/11; *Wuding zhouzhi* 1588/2/1; *Xincheng xianzhi* 1693/1/3; *Zhanhua xianzhi* 1619/1/9; *Zhangqiu xianzhi* 1596/1/4.

52. *Zichuan xianzhi* 1602/1/2, 3/1.

53. *Qidong xianzhi* 1617 /2/3, 6/2, 1685/1/13; *Qingcheng xianzhi* 1612/1/6, 11; *Wuding zhouzhi* 1588/2/1; *Zouping xianzhi* 1660/1/5. Some of the transfers of subdistricts are in the Qidong gazetteer dated to the Hongzhi period. From the other gazetteers it is clear that the date should be the Hongwu period.

54. Kuribayashi (1971), p. 19.
55. *DMB*, pp. 756–758.
56. *Babian jingshi leizuan* 35/13.
57. Kuribayashi (1971), pp. 29–30.
58. *SDHJL* 4/26.
59. *Babian jingshi leizuan* 35/13.
60. Wada Sei, *Minshi Shokkashi yakuchū* (Tokyo, 1957), pp. 56–58.
61. *Pingyuan xianzhi* 1590/1/20.
62. *Babian jingshi leizuan* 35/13–14.
63. Kataoka Shibako, «Kahoku no tochi shoyū to ichijo benbō», in *Shimizu hakase tsuito kinen Mindaishi ronso* (Tokyo, 1962), p. 141.
64. Wada (1939), p. 98.
65. *DMHD* 20/2.
66. In a discussion of the grading of prefectures according to tax quotas initiated in 1373 Ray Huang writes that it was apparently expected that the tax quotas of all territorial units would be revised from time to time to reflect the changes in population and land data. Such regular revisions seem never to have been carried out. Huang, pp. 21–22.
67. *DMB*, pp. 398–402.
68. Wei, p. 107.
69. No pre-registration instructions for 1403 are included in the *Houhuzhi* as there are for 1381 and 1391. Pre-registration instructions only begin again in 1452, which seems to indicate a general lack of interest in the first part of the fifteenth century to making adjustments to the registration and the *lijia* system. *Houhuzhi* 4/1–6.
70. Kawakatsu Mamoru, «Mindai no kishōko ni tsuite», *Tōyōshi Kenkyū* 33.3 (1974), 53–54.
71. Ho (1959), pp. 9–10. He overlooks the fact that a *lijia* had to be supplemented from the surrounding *lijia* if there were no substitutes available.
72. See appendix I.
73. Dates are given for Zichuan where two *lijia* were ceded to a district in Qingzhou Prefecture (1602/1/2). Lijin increased the number from 34 to 40 in 1462 (1673/4/1) and in 1512 there were reductions in Wuding (1588/2/1) and Zhanhua (1619/1/4).
74. *Licheng xianzhi* 1640/3/16.
75. *Houhuzhi* 8/2.
76. *Zhanhua xianzhi* 1619/1/4; Li Guangbi, *Mingchao shilüe*, (Hubei, 1957), pp. 88–90.
77. Ho (1959), p. 264; Perkins, p. 15.
78. Ho (1959), p. 26.
79. Michel Cartier et Pierre-Étienne Will, «Démographie et Institutions en Chine: 'Contribution à l'Analyse des Recensements de l'Époque Impériale (2 ap. J.–C. – 1750)'», *Annales de Démographie Historique* (1971), 230.
80. *Qidong xianzhi* 1617/15/4.
81. *Shanghe xianzhi* 1586/3/3.
82. For 1569, the 1617 gazetteer gives 16, 729 households and 141,220 persons (ratio 8.5). The 1685 edition gives the same households but only 102,020 persons (ratio 6.1). For 1617, the edition of that year gives 24,900 households, the number of persons being undecipherable. The 1687 edition has 24.000 households and 100.608 persons (ratio 4.2). The P/H ratio continued to be between 4.2 and 5.2 up to 1687. *Qidong xianzhi* 1617/15/4, 1687/3/2.
83. *Putai xianzhi* 1592/4/1.
84. E.g. *Deping xianzhi* 1576/3/1, 1796/3/2; *Leling xianzhi* 1762/2/42; *Lijin xianzhi* 1673/4/1. There were examples where this did not happen. *Zichuan xianzhi* 1602/12/1; *Laiwu xianzhi* 1673/4/1.

85. Taniguchi Kikuo, «Mindai Kahoku ni okeru ginsa seiritsu no ichi kenkyū – Santō no mongin seiritsu o chūshin ni shite», *Tōyōshi Kenkyū* 20.3 (1961),4.
86. Wei, p. 226.
87. *SDJHL* 4/3.
88. Yamane (1966), p. 42.
89. Kuribayashi (1971), p. 52.
90. *Minglü jijie fuli* 4/1–5, 31–33; Friese, pp. 24–26.
91. Yamane (1966), p. 42.
92. *Ibid.*, p. 40; Liang (1957), pp. 65–66, 85–90.
93. Taniguchi Kikuo, «Mindai Kahoku no daiko ni tsuite», *Tōyōshi Kenkyū* 27 (1969), 483; Liang (1957), p. 58.
94. Wada (1939), p. 100.
95. Kuribayashi (1971), p. 51.
96. *Ibid.*, p. 54; Liang (1957), *passim.*
97. Taniguchi (1969), pp. 474–483.
98. Yamane (1966), p. 41.
99. Yamane Yukio, «Mindai richō no shokuseki ni kansuru ichi kōsatsu», *Tōhōgaku* 3 (1952), 84.
100. Kuribayashi (1971), p. 98.
101. Huang, pp. 34–35.
102. Yamane (1952), p. 84.
103. Kuribayashi (1971), pp. 92–93.
104. Yamane (1952), p. 86; Kuribayashi (1971), p. 90.
105. Kuribayashi (1971), pp. 99, 103.
106. Yamane (1966), pp. 47, 52.
107. *Ibid.* pp. 41–42.
108. Kuribayashi (1971), p. 55.
109. *DMHD* 79/4.
110. *SL* 1384:4:*renwu.*
111. Liang (1957), pp. 43–49.
112. *DMHD* 20/22.
113. Kuribayashi (1971); Chang, pp. 53–55.
114. Wada (1939), pp. 111–113; Kuribayashi (1971), p. 56; Yamane (1966), p. 55; Chang, p. 57.
115. The Precepts are paraphrased in Wada (1939), pp. 113–117. They are translated in Elmquist, pp. 277–301, and in Chang, pp. 63–72.
116. Wada (1939), p. 117.
117. Wada (1939), p. 118.
118. Sakai Tadao, «Mindai zen shoki no hōkōsei ni tsuite» in *Shimizu hakase tsuitō kinen Mindaishi ronsō*, (Tokyo, 1962), p. 587; Yamane (1966), p. 63.
119. Ho (1959), p. 3, 22.
120. Wei, p. 224.
121. Ho (1959), p. 11.
122. Wada (1939), p. 104.
123. Wei, pp. 200 ff.
124. *DMHD* 20/2, 6.
125. A convenient but by no means exhaustive list is given in Wei, p. 108.

65

III. Subbureaucratic government and taxation c. 1550–1570

INTRODUCTION

The tax and corvée system of the early years of the dynasty was designed for a society with a stable population and very little circulation of reliable currency. Throughout the dynasty the government was very reluctant to make radical changes in the basic tax and corvée quotas, assessed in grain or other agricultural products and in adult males (*ding*). Zhu Yuanzhang appears to have deliberately created inequalities in the tax quotas in order to punish the supporters of his adversaries in the civil war. Further injustices developed as the economy took off at unequal pace in different parts of the empire. The answer to these problems was commutation of taxes and corvée to payments in silver, since the rates of commutation could be adjusted to alleviate inequalities. The first commutation of taxes to silver payment is reported in 1433 and became more widespread with the gold-floral silver of 1436 in southern provinces.[1]

In this chapter I attempt to describe the tax and corvée system of Shandong Province in the middle of the sixteenth century. The chronological limits have been determined by important events in the taxation system and by the availability of sources. The period c. 1550–1570 covers the official introduction and abolition of the first Single Whip by the provincial authorities.[2] Following the various measures in this Single Whip policy, it is possible to get some insight into the fiscal system of the province. Of equal importance is, however, the availability of sources. The entire period is covered by the *SDJHL*, whereas the coverage provided by the local gazetteers is less satisfactory. None of the available gazetteers for Jinan Prefecture were compiled during this period. Indeed there is only one – the 1553 Lingxian gazetteer – still known to be extant.[3]

For some topics it may be an advantage to use later editions of the gazetteers, since they sometimes contain information that had subsequently come to light or that had become less controversial, so it could be published. However, for the subbureaucratic government and taxation system it seems in general to be an advantage to use gazetteers compiled during the period under investigation. This is definitely the conclusion in my study. Some of the gazetteers compiled during the Qing period have detailed information on taxation reaching back to the Ming dynasty, but seldom before the Wanli period. At that latter time the Single Whip and remeasurement of land caused a major change in the tax system. The figures produced for acreage and tax during these reforms were in many later gazetteers used as the base figure (*yuane*) for the calculation of taxes. For the conditions before the Wanli period the gazetteers give little information, even those compiled during late Ming. The reason for this is perhaps that the records available for the compilers were too inadequate to make a detailed survey of the taxes in the previous period. Such an assumption conforms with the general picture of a tax system riddled with fraud and evasions that had been perpetuated since the early days of the dynasty. It is, however, difficult to believe that there did not exist some sort of coherent tax records which might have been included in the gazetteers if the compilers had so wished.

For the period 1550–1570 we have the *SDJHL*, which gives abundant information on the tax system. For our purpose it has the weakness that it almost exclusively deals with taxation at the district level and rarely illuminates the situation at lower levels. For the historian the *SDJHL* also presents the problem that it was written for officials of the time. It is of course an advantage to have a source that appears to be an administrative document, but it has the disadvantage that it only summarizes or makes amendments to regulations and customs which were probably well known in the bureaucracy but of which we have no other source of information. This disadvantage is common, particularly for the historian attempting to disentangle fiscal history. However, special problems do arise when we use a fiscal source to examine the role of the subbureaucratic government system in society as a whole and not only in the taxation system.

TAXES

1. Land assessment and ownership

The scarcity of information on taxation means that we can only get a rather confused picture of the development in the taxation system until the middle period of the sixteenth century. Tax was levied upon land, but there appear to have been no general regulations for levies applied over the whole province or even within Jinan Prefecture. The confusion is probably greatest for the historian, as perhaps it was for contemporary officials arriving in the districts and trying to understand the conditions of the tax system. For the people living in the districts, and for lesser functionaries and other clerical staff who kept the books in the yamen and had long experience of local conditions, the confusion was probably much less.

The tax to be paid from a given piece of land must have been fairly common knowledge even if it could not be deduced from official regulations. Tampering with the tax records could have resulted in inequalities in taxation, but such inequalities were probably embodied in the price of the land when it was sold or mortgaged. So if there was a high turnover in land the tax to be paid in most cases must have been established fairly clearly. Unfortunately we do not possess the sources necessary to investigate the frequency of land transactions, but it is unlikely that there was not a certain amount of these. The recorded changes in the population figures may not reflect the actual size of the total population, but they can indicate changes involving landowners. There is furthermore evidence of migrations in the province which would also have led to some transactions in land.[4]

As was mentioned in Chapter II, there was a difference in the northern provinces between land occupied by the people living in the provinces at the beginning of the dynasty and migrants arriving during the Hongwu period. This difference was in fertility, location and relation to towns, and in the size of the *mou*. For the migrants the *mou* would normally be 240 *bu*, while the large *mou* could be up to 1,200 *bu*.[5] However, there is not much evidence that this policy was widespread in Jinan Prefecture.

This does not mean that a uniform measurement existed in Jinan Prefecture. In one district the *mou* could be 600 *bu* in early Ming and later this was changed to 240 *bu* per *mou*.[6] In another district there could be 304 *bu* per *mou* before the later standardization.[7] In both these cases the later revision of the *mou* resulted in an increase of the acreage. A similar change in acreage is recorded in other districts.[8] However, there are districts where the acreage did not change substantially during the dynasty, not even during the remeasurements of the Wanli period. It is possible that the standard *mou* had been used in such districts from the beginning of the dynasty,[9] but the lack of change in acreage can also be due to factors not revealed in the sources.

In the beginning of the dynasty land had been divided into different fiscal categories. The main division was between domain land (*guandi*) and private land (*mindi*). The latter could be subdivided into good private land and saline private land. Other categories could be silk-floss land (*huarongdi*) and confiscated land (*moguandi*), etc. [10] The policy of the government had been to tax domain land heavier than private land,

68

regarding the difference in taxation as a rent paid to the landlord, i.e. the government.[11] In Jinan Prefecture there is evidence of this heavier taxation in Deping District, where in 1512 the tax measured in *dan* of grain per *mou* was c. 6.25 times greater on domain land than on private land if the horse fodder (*macao*), which was only levied on private land, is not included.[12] This heavy taxation on domain land was probably partly offset in the calculation process. In Binzhou it is reported that on good private land one *dan* equalled one *dan*. On domain land one *dan* was equal to two *dan*, and on saline land to three *dan*. In this way the tax on domain land was reduced by 50% and on saline land by 66.6%.[13] The difference between the different types of land was probably confused by manipulations of the kind described by Ray Huang for a district in southern China.[14] The distinction between domain land and private land disappeared in Deping District in 1542 and in other districts progressively until the land measurement reforms around 1581. The amount of domain land and other special categories was usually very small in Jinan, at the most a few per cent of private land.

Land could also be graded according to fertility. The Yangxin gazetteer from 1682 states that the upper, middle and lower land in 1391 totalled 2,520.96 *qing*, thus indicating that a three-level grading of the land was applied in early Ming. Similar gradings were introduced in the other districts in the Wanli period, so the Yangxin evidence is hardly proof of such grading in early Ming. The compiler of the gazetteer may simply have projected backwards the Wanli grading without possessing proof of its earlier existence.[15] The size of the *mou* could also be according to the fertility of the land. We do not know when this was first practised in Jinan Prefecture. In the middle of the sixteenth century some districts adopted the policy of remeasuring the land and calculating the size of the *mou* according to the fertility of the land. The most detailed description of this policy is found in the 1771 edition of the Licheng gazetteer translated by Ping-ti Ho. Unfortunately no date is given for the introduction of this policy, but it corresponds well with other evidence for the period 1550–1570. In Licheng the land was divided into gold, silver, copper, tin, and iron land with the respective conversion *mou* rates of 1, 1.166, 1.5, 2.5, and 3.[16] A similar system is described in 1562 by the governor Zhang Jian, when he rebuffed the argument that the Single Whip with a uniform levy on all kinds of land was unequal by saying that in some districts land was graded into gold, silver, copper, and iron land.[17] This system must have been introduced around 1550. The only reference we have to the actual introduction is probably for Shanghe District, where the magistrate Shen Guang in 1550 ordered a remeasurement of the land. The people were to make personal depositions and each *mou* was to be 240 *bu*. The measure to be used was the 'great foot' which was 1½ times the official foot. The number of feet were to be according to the fertility of the land.[18] Even if 'metallic' gradings are not mentioned in Shanghe, it appears to have been the same system.

Li Kaixian wrote around 1560 that the 'metallic' gradings according to the quality of the land had been introduced in the districts around Zhangqiu, and he advocated their introduction to that district as well.[19] This indicates that the process had not started substantially before 1550, since a large district such as Zhangqiu had not changed in 1560. From the remarks of Li Kaixian and Zhang Jian this policy seems to have enjoyed a certain popularity during this period, but to what extent it was applied in all the districts of Jinan is hard to say.

2. Inequality of taxes

The sources covering this period give a slightly clearer picture of the differences in taxation between the districts than for those within each district. The introduction to the *fulu* chapter in the *SDJHL* describes how in the beginning of the dynasty the tax had been very heavy on the eastern prefectures of the province. The reason was that people absconded from these prefectures leaving a heavy tax burden for those remaining. In contrast to this, there were more and more people settling in the western prefectures, particularly after the canal from the north to the south had been opened in the Xuande period. With more people in these prefectures more land was brought under cultivation. This land was not necessarily reported in the national tax accounts, so the burden of taxation in relation to population and cultivated land was lighter in the western prefectures. This inequality had been regulated when the tax payments were commuted to silver, so that the tax in an eastern district was commuted to 0.2 taels per *dan* of grain, while in a western district it was 0.7 taels per *dan*. This difference in commutation caused some discontent in the province, since some people thought that with these commutation rates taxation was much heavier in the western prefectures. It is interesting to note that the compilers of the *SDJHL* considered it necessary to explain this point in a work that was probably meant to be consulted by officials and other administrative personnel. The explanation given is that in the eastern prefectures there were considerable amounts of uncultivated land, so that one *mou* could pay tax for 2–3 *mou*, while in the western prefectures 3–4 *mou* could join together and pay the tax for one *mou* of land.[20]

The difference in commutation rates is clear for the 1550 figures.

However, they also indicate that the difference in taxation was not strictly according to prefectures. In that year the highest commutation rate for the summer taxes was in Puzhou, Dongchang Prefecture, with 0.7513 taels per *dan*, while the lowest was in Yizhou, Yanzhou Prefecture, with 0.2190 taels per *dan*. For the autumn taxes the highest commutation rate was in Caozhou, Yanzhou Prefecture, with 0.9925 taels per *dan*, while the lowest was in Rizhao, Qingzhou Prefecture, with 0.4223 taels per *dan*. For horse fodder calculated in *dan* of grain the commutation rates were highest in Fanxian, Dongchang Prefecture, with 0.1484 taels per *dan*, while the lowest was in Qihe, Jinan Prefecture, with 0.0546 taels per *dan*. There were minor fluctuations in the annual levy on Shandong Province in summer and autumn transferred-revenue taxes, and these fluctuations were used by the officials to adjust differences between districts. These adjustments, however, are very small. In 1550 they were also used to eliminate the smaller decimal digits in the tax figures, for example the commutation rate in Puzhou was reduced to 0.74 taels per *dan*. The officials recognized that the adjustments they made in 1550 were not adequate for all districts; some still had to be reduced and some increased. They preferred to postpone these adjustments, taking advantage of the fluctuations in the annual levy on the province rather than making an overall adjustment. Figures are not available to show the overall trend of such adjustments, but in Jinan Prefecture we have the commutation rates for the autumn transferred-revenue taxes for 1550 and 1571 in four districts. In Licheng the commutation rate was increased by 8.5%, in Qingcheng by 18%, in Pingyuan by 13% and in Qihe by 9%. These figures should be compared to the increase in the total transferred-revenue from the autumn taxes for the whole province of c. 4.5%.[21] We cannot draw any unconditional conclusions from these figures, since they may have been influenced by several factors such as the commutation rates for summer taxes and horse fodder, but they do show that the commutation rates were used as a convenient instrument to rectify inequalities without interfering with the basic tax levy calculated in *dan* of grain.

We do not know the actual degree of inequality between districts. The above description does, however, indicate that it was not too conspicuous – at least as seen by officials. The description also indicates that the officials regarded the available figures and registers for the different districts with regard to population, taxpayers and land as reasonably realistic.

Unfortunately we do not have concrete examples of adjustments between households or other fiscal units within a district. There is no doubt that inequalities existed beten taxpayers in the various districts.

The introduction to the section on taxes in the 1576 edition of the Dezhou gazetteer – after praising the system at the beginning of the dynasty – states:

> But after some time malpractices began. Although the officials planned and scrutinized [the tax records] very carefully, how could fraud be completely stamped out? Cases of reckless conspiracy by the powerful, clever tampering by the *li*-registrars and deceitful cheating by absentee landlords were numerous. There were fields with no taxes and taxes with no fields . . . [22]

Such cases where the rich were able to use their position for their own benefit are found in other gazetteers as well. The same thing is described in the documents in the *SDJHL*. In 1555 the provincial officials expressed fear that the tax system was being tampered with when land was sold by not keeping the tax and the land together. The land could be sold, but the tax still had to be paid by the former owner, who in this way got the immediate advantage of a higher price for the land but in the long run was disadvantaged by having to continue to pay the tax. The officials were aware of such practices but found it difficult to get sufficient information to prevent them.[23]

How the common people felt about the unequal taxation we do not know. Many of the inequalities that are reported as contravening existing statutes could probably be dated back several generations. The common people probably resented the advantages enjoyed by wealthy and powerful households. However, for the more wealthy in sixteenth-century Shandong tax inequalities between different plots of land were probably evened out by inverse capital valuations. In this way inequalities may not have had too great an impact upon the economic circumstances of the wealthy, and they might have felt no pressing need for major reforms which could upset the balance between land prices and tax payments.

3. Granary rates

By means of the granary rates (*cangkou*), taxes were levied at different rates according to the wealth of the taxpayers. These rates were levied not upon the land itself but on the tax payments. This meant that a tax payment with a high granary rate would pay more in silver per *dan* of tax calculated in grain than would be paid with a lower granary rate. The rate was determined according to the granary for which the particular tax payment was destined, and for deliveries to the capital or to the border defences the rate could be high. The allocation of granary rates was made within the districts and subprefectures on the basis of tax classes, so that the households with the highest tax class would pay the highest granary rate.[24]

The tax classes used for the allocation of granary rates were those also used for corvée. In Zhangqiu District the nine tax classes had been used for tax collection before 1541. In that year the system was simplified, so that only the three main divisions (*deng*) of the tax classes were used.[25] In 1570, when the granary rates were reintroduced after they had been at least partly non-operational under the early Single Whip, it is specifically mentioned that the equal corvée registers were used for the allocation of granary rates. During the time when the granary rates had been inoperational, sufficient attention had apparently not been paid to the division into tax classes in these equal corvée registers, and many households had managed to change their tax class from upper to lower. So when the granary rates were reintroduced, it was first necessary to upgrade some of the households.[25]

There are no records showing when the granary rates were introduced in Shandong. Ge Shouli claims that this system had originated in the early years of the dynasty, but his remarks are so general that they cannot be accepted as proof of such an early existence.[27] However, it is clear that the origin of the granary rates is to be found in the system of taxation before the taxes were commuted to payment in silver. When the taxes had to be paid in grain or other products, it was the obligation of the taxpayer to deliver the grain at the designated granary or to pay the costs of transportation.[28] Early Ming laws apparently stipulated that corvée related to tax collection (other than the regular *lijia* corvée) should be levied according to tax classes. Sources from the fifteenth and the early sixteenth century indicate that this had been applied in many parts of the empire until c. 1530.[29] When the tax payments were commuted to silver, the cost of transportation was no longer significant but was maintained in the granary rates, apparently as an extra source of income for the government. With the granary rate levied according to the tax classes it is reasonable to assume that originally transportation costs had been levied in the same way. The result would then have been the levy of higher taxes on the more wealthy households, which in Shandong probably served to counter – to some extent – the advantages the more wealthy households enjoyed from favourable land holdings.

The amount of the granary rates varied with the distance to the granary. It is not possible to give a complete picture of these variations on the basis of existing sources. It was claimed in 1570 that the granary rate could cause the payment for one *dan* of grain to vary from 0.3 taels to 1.3 tales.[30] Generally it is not easy to discover from the tax figures what the actual payments were because of the many ways of commutation. This is certainly true for the autumn taxes recorded for 1571 in Chapter I of the *SDJHL*. However, a comparison appears to be useful between some of the transferred-revenue summer taxes measured in wheat (*xiaomai*). The commutation rates per *dan* of wheat for all the districts of Jinan are given in appendix II.

With the granary rates allocated on the households according to the tax classes, the tax payments were not only a result of land holdings. In the north of China the land holdings played a much smaller part in the assessment of tax classes than was customary in the southern parts of the country. The number of *ding* and other assets in the household played a comparatively greater role. The reason was that the land was of relatively lower quality in the north, and climatic conditions made it difficult to improve productivity by using more labour, one factor being that there were extended periods of the year when labour could not be used in farming. From the point of view of conscription of corvée, the consequence of this was that personal services could be demanded from the adult males during the idle periods without interfering with farming.[31] Consequently the number of adult males was more important for determining the tax classes than in areas where the labour could be used throughout the year for farming.

The fact that the granary rates were not levied according to the land itself but according to tax classes could be more of a curse than a blessing for the less favoured people even if their purpose had originally been to help them. This is the impression we get from the sources in the sixteenth century, even from those admitting that it had originally been a good and fair system.[32] The trouble arose from the strong incentive of the households in the upper tax classes to get their assessment lowered when both corvée and granary rates were levied according to tax classes. The influential households could do this by various illegal means with the connivance of officials, lesser functionaries or other personnel in the yamen or at least of the *li*-registrars. They could tamper with the land registers and register their land under the name of other persons with or without their knowledge, or they could divide their households so that each part would get a lower tax class. The list of ways of cheating with the land registers seems almost inexhaustible. With the tax classes also depending upon *ding* and assets other than land, the possibilities for cheating were further enhanced, since such items were often easier to conceal than the land itself.

An interesting aspect of Ming taxation policy was that it was often profitable for the owner of a plot of land to transfer the nominal ownership to someone else, even if the original and actual owner continued to pay the taxes levied upon the land. By transferring the registered ownership he could obtain lighter corvée and granary rates than would have been the case if the property was still registered in his name. This was because the corvée and the granary rates served as a kind of progessive taxation on the people classed as wealthy in the registers. In this respect there are many similarities between corvée and granary rates, and it could be argued that the granary rates should rightly be discussed together with the corvée. I have, however, intentionally included them with taxes, as they were closely connected with the system of taxation. This point is further justified because the discussion of granary rates was included in the chapters on taxation in the *SDJHL*.

CORVÉE

1. Miscellaneous corvée

The miscellaneous corvée (*zayi* or *zafan-chaiyi*)[33] consisted of various services for the goverment – either local or central – on a regular basis. It was levied on the male adults (*ding*), from 1385 according to the tax class of the household. This meant that in comparison to a uniform levy on each adult male the basis of the assessment was more complicated but also more realistic if correct assessment could be maintained. A number of male adults were assigned to each corvée item and served in rotation. The frequency of the service depended on how many *ding* were listed in the Yellow Register as belonging to households in the appropriate tax class.[34] The services were graded according to the burden they were estimated to impose on the households. The heaviest services could be those performed at a considerable distance from home. Work in the Yizhou charcoal factory c. 150 km west of Peking was such a service for the people of Shandong.[35] They could also be services where the households had to use their own wealth to guarantee successful completion, such as weighers (*douji*) in the granaries.[36]

The general picture we get from the sources for the administration of the corvée system is that it was not a very systematic operation. However, we have to concede that the sources are probably deceptive, since in most cases we only have the initial orders for the system, which – considering how the Ming bureaucracy allowed for local variation – only provided the framework. This had to be elaborated by local officials, but the local sources leave us to a great extent in the dark. The operation of the system in a locality is usually only revealed by descriptions of shortcomings and corruption, rarely in a positive light. And no matter whether they are positive or negative the descriptions only faintly show the circumstances of individual households, if they are indicated at all. This of course is a problem for the historian, not for the household at that time. For the people who had to perform the work or pay the money there were no great uncertainties. With changing population patterns – and fortune or misfortune for the individual household – services or payments had to be transferred between households at the regular assessments of the corvée, and there must have existed guidelines as to how this was to be done. It would be inconsistent with the emerging picture of the workings of the bureaucracy to assume that such guidelines did not exist. This is further supported by the fact that wealthy and influential households made considerable efforts to manipulate their assets and *ding* in order to avoid services to which they were liable.

During the period under consideration the main complaints are these manipulations with the tax classes, so it appears that the rules for allocation of corvée to the households according to tax classes were still in force. One such case was that some households agreed to perform certain duties assigned to the tax class they would have been in had their property and *ding* been assessed properly. They acquiesced in performing the service as long as they could get the lower tax class.[37]

The view that there did exist at the local level administrative guidelines for the allocation of corvée is based upon the assumption that the administration worked on a rational basis, and that it was generally in the interest of the officials to have the corvée and other duties allocated to households that had the strength to perform them. We can also assume that local powerful households had the same interest, at least to a degree that would have prevented major reforms of the corvée system which could infringe upon the advantages they had been able to obtain. This is probably a valid assumption for the early years of the dynasty, when the miscellaneous corvée was still relatively light and only involved a few households each year from a *lijia*.[38] However, as the corvée became heavier, the advantages to be gained from cheating became more obvious, and some reform of the corvée system was needed.

2. The equal corvée

The solution to the problem of the corvée system was the equal corvée, which was initiated in Jiangxi Province before 1450. Later it spread to other parts of the country. In 1488 the emperor ordered the equal corvée to be introduced all over the empire.[39] It was probably introduced in Shandong between 1483 and 1486 by the governor, Sheng Yu. The sources state that Sheng Yu introduced the nine tax classes (jiuce), and Taniguchi is probably justified in taking this to mean the introduction of the equal corvée.[40] Of course this also means that the nine tax classes were introduced at this time at least in part of the province. In 1555 and 1561 some districts had four main divisions (deng) of tax classes and others five divisions.[41] We do not know whether these were remnants of tax classes from before 1483, or whether they were simply variants of the nine tax classes introduced by Sheng Yu.

The equal corvée introduced by Xia Shi in Jiangxi in the 1440s functioned on the basis of the lijia. The regular lijia services were performed by its members every ten years, and the equal corvée – as the miscellaneous corvée included in the new system came to be known – was performed five years later. This meant that in the year when jia no. 1 performed the regular services, the equal corvée services would be performed by jia no. 6. The equal corvée services to be performed by individual households among li-leaders and jia-heads were distributed according to their tax class and recorded in the equal corvée registers.[42] In the Jiangnan area, where the corvée was relatively light in relation to the capacity of the households conscripted to the equal corvée, it was possible and sufficient only to conscript the households once every ten years. The Daxue yanyibu from 1487 says that the equal corvée should not be introduced north of the Yangtze river. What is meant is probably that the equal corvée in a ten-year rotation could not be applied, because it would put too great a strain on the households on duty. Instead we see in the north the equal corvée performed at intervals of two to five years or even every year.[43] Writers in sixteenth-century Shandong complained that of all provinces annual service was only necessary there. Such statements cannot be taken as evidence for the situation in other provinces, but we have no reason to doubt that they accurately described the situation in Shandong, since they are made in official administrative documents and are followed by an elaborate proposal on how to give the households one year of rest out of ten.[44]

In Shandong the equal corvée and the equal corvée registers were, at least from 1529, assessed and compiled every second year, and this biennial compilation continued at least until the early 1570s.[45] A biennial compilation could imply that the equal corvée was only performed by the households every second year, but there is no evidence for this. Over the period under consideration here the services were apparently performed each year. The biennial compilation can be taken as a sign that the provincial administration suspected that the decennial compilations of the Yellow Registers were inadequate in view of the geographic, social and economic mobility of the population, and perhaps also as a sign that the administration had the capability to perform more frequent compilations.

It is even possible that the equal corvée registers were used as legal population records. In 1533, when a new magistrate Li Xing arrived in Zichuan, he discovered that a clan previously surnamed Gong-sun had changed this to Sun. He scolded the members of the clan for this inappropriate change of surname, and at the following assessment of the equal corvée their name was changed back to Gong-sun.[46] This does not rule out that the Yellow Registers were still regarded as legal records of family names. This incident took place one year after the previous compilation of the Yellow Registers. Hence the following compilation was nine years away, and Li would have left the district before then. But in the meantime the equal corvée registers served his purpose.

The corvée in north China in the sixteenth century had several special features. The most obvious is the absence of a special cateogry of militia corvée (*minzhuang*). Such services existed in the north, but they were levied as part of the equal corvée, whereas in other parts of the country they were often levied separately, e.g. by a certain number of men per *lijia*. The *lijia* services in the north were mostly connected with the postal transport system and supplemented such services. Many services that would normally have been regarded as *lijia* corvée were listed under the equal corvée after their commutation to silver payment.[48] This happened all over the country but was particularly prevalent in the north. The reason for this tendency to include the commuted *lijia* corvée (*lijiayin*) in the equal corvée is not explained in the sources. The commutation of the *lijia* services came later than the commutation of the equal corvée and this was most marked in the north. The commutation of the *lijia* corvée to *lijia* silver was introduced gradually, so Kuribayashi deduces from this that it was more convenient for the officials to include the collection of the commuted items in the collection of the equal corvée silver.[49] This explanation seems plausible, but the reason may also be that the officials preferred to have as many items as possible levied according to the biennial assessments of the equal corvée, and made the transfer when the *lijia* corvée was commuted to silver payment.

3. Commutation of corvée

The commutation of corvée to silver payments started generally in the second half of the fifteenth century, i.e. about half a century later than the commutation of taxes.[50] In Shandong the first instance of corvée commutation took place around 1470. In 1468 the central government ordered commutation of the corvée in the Yizhou charcoal factory, which provided fuel for the capital. This commutation must have applied to the workers coming from Shandong, and the reason this item was chosen for commutation was the inconvenience of long travel for the workers. This order from the central government is reflected in Shandong, where the governor in 1473 petitioned to commute to silver payment 20,884 wood choppers (*kanchaifu*) each paying three taels of silver.[51] Fuel-men-silver (*chaifuyin*) is mentioned for Zhucheng District in 1481 and a few years later for Zhanhua, so it seems that this commutation actually took place.[52]

Subsequent commutations appear to have been relatively gradual. Recorded instances are found in the 1510s and 1520s, but as commutation seems to have been well established by 1533, it was probably applied to several corvée items already during the Hongzhi and early Zhengde periods.[53] By 1571 all the equal corvée listed in the *SDJHL* are recorded in terms of silver, both the silver corvée (*yinchai*) and the labour corvée (*lichai*). This did not necessarily mean that silver was paid to the officials or tax collectors. The commutation figures served first of all as a convenient instrument for comparison between the different items of corvée when they had to be allocated on the households in the different tax classes. Silver corvée was collected in silver by the *dahu*, and the money was used by the officials to hire persons to perform the duties.[54] The commutation figures probably represented the cost of the labour at the time the corvée was commuted, and was apparently not changed following later fluctuations in the cost of labour.

Labour corvée was different. It appears that these services were still the responsibility of specific households during the period until 1571 and probably until the corvée was entirely commuted in the Single Whip of the Wanli period. They were conscripted from the households in the upper tax-classes, and these households had the choice of performing the services by one of their members or hiring a substitute.[55] The official commutation figures probably represented the price of the substitutes at the time the silver valuation was made. We do not know when this happened. It is possible that such a convenient instrument for allocating corvée between households was introduced together with the biennial compilation of the equal corvée registers in 1529. A review of the equal corvée in the whole province was apparently also conducted in 1549.[56] The purpose of this review was to determine the distribution of corvée between districts and subprefectures, and for such a purpose it was no doubt helpful to have all the corvée items valued in silver. So it is also possible that 1549 was the base year for the valuation of the labour corvée in silver.

The cost of providing substitutes for labour corvée rose during the period, and this increase had to be paid by the households conscripted to the corvée, i.e. the corvée heads (*touhu* or *zhengtou)*) and their assisting households (*tiehu*). This surcharge was called *datao*. In some cases it was officially recognized (*mingbian*) and was perhaps taken into consideration when the corvée was allocated. However, there were also cases where the *datao* was not officially recognized (*anbian*), and the surcharge thus became an extra fiscal duty of the households. As the burden of the labour corvée fell heaviest on the households in the upper tax classes, this was a further inducement for these households to attempt to get into a lower tax class. This problem was apparently solved in 1569, when Governor Jiang Tingyi ordered that the *datao* a household would have to pay for an item of labour corvée was to be registered in the household tax bill so that it could not be required to pay more for substitutes. This was for some reason not *mingbian*, but it seems to have served the same purpose,[57] and the *datao* figures for all the labour corvée are listed in the *SDJHL*. For most items of labour corvée the *datao* figures are two to three times higher than the original silver valuation.

The problem with the *datao* could of course have been solved by changing all labour corvée to silver corvée. The reason this did not happen immediately in 1569 was probably because the officials were not confident that the various levels in the administration were able to handle the collection of silver and the hiring of persons to perform the services. Certainly, such problems had existed when other labour corvée had previously been transferred to silver corvée.[58] It appears that transfers had proceeded gradually during our period; the last recorded was in 1570.[59] But later in 1570 the new governor Liang Menglong[60] issued a prohibition against further transfers from labour corvée to silver corvée as part of his policy against the Single Whip and for a return to the situation existing before 1550.[61] As with the Single Whip, this order was probably only effective for a short period, but it is worth describing in greater detail, since it gives some insight into the allocation of corvée in the sixteenth century.

Liang ordered a new valuation of the burden of the different kinds of labour corvée in the province. If the number of heavy corvée corresponded to the number of households in the upper three tax classes, each of these households would be conscripted as corvée heads. If the wealth and number of *ding* in any of these households were in excess of what was needed for the particular labour corvée, then the surplus wealth and *ding* would be assigned to light corvée duties. If any of the households did not have sufficient wealth and *ding* to match the heavy corvée, then assistant corvée heads (*tietou*) were conscripted from the households in the middle tax classes. If there were not sufficient households in the three upper tax classes for the heavy labour corvée, then two or three households in the middle tax classes would jointly be corvée heads. Each of these households would only perform this heavy corvée from one half of their wealth and *ding*, the other half being assigned to light corvée as an alleviation. The other households in the middle tax classes were conscripted as corvée heads of light labour corvée. Only households in the upper seven tax classes could be conscripted as corvée heads, and the eighth tax class could be conscripted as assistant households. Normally labour corvée was not levied on the ninth tax class, but if there was not enough wealth and *ding* in the upper eight tax classes, then it was permitted to levy 0.02 taels of silver per *ding* upon one-third of the households in the ninth tax class considered to be the most wealthy of the households in that tax class.[62]

4. *Men*-silver and *ding*-silver

The equal corvée in sixteenth-century Shandong was not only levied from *ding* according to tax class. In the 1533 edition of the Shandong provincial gazetteer the items listed in the *SDJHL* under equal corvée are divided into two groups. The first group is items levied on households as payments towards the expenses of the corvée (*yihu-chuzi-zhe*) and the second group items for which *ding* were levied or conscripted to perform the corvée (*yiding-chuyi-zhe*).[63]

It is possible that some of the miscellaneous corvée was levied on households instead of *ding* in Shandong and other northern provinces from the beginning of the dynasty. This is claimed by authors in the sixteenth century who wrote that the *zuyongdiao* system of the Tang had been applied by the dynastic founders, the *zu* being land taxes, the *diao* being levies on households, and the *yong* being levies on *ding*.[64] We have no evidence that this was actually the case, and such statements should be regarded with caution. It is possible that the levies on households were introduced some time in the fifteenth century before the commutation of corvée really began. In other parts of the country there was a tendency during that period to change levies of the miscellaneous and later equal corvée from *ding* to land.[65] This was probably a result of the increase in the corvée duties together with the concentration of land in the hands of fewer households. Under such circumstances it would have been increasingly difficult to levy all corvée on *ding*, and it became necessary to find alternatives. The special circumstances of agriculture in the north

6 – Subbureaucratic government . . .

compared to the rest of the country meant that it was probably less attractive in the north to make land the object of corvée levy, so the alternative was a levy on the households.

From the evidence available we can, however, only say with certainty that the levies on households were introduced in the first part of the sixteenth century, apparently together with the commutation of corvée. It appears that all the commuted items in 1533 were levied on the households, but this could not continue to be the case with additional commutations. The result of this would have been that the levies on the households were too heavy in relation to levies on *ding*, and this would have created all the problems of cheating and evasions arising from too heavy levies. The solution was to levy silver on the *ding* as well. This apparently happened around 1540 and resulted in the creation of the terms *ding*-silver (*dingyin*) and *men*-silver (*menyin*).[66]

Men (literally 'door') is used in the following years almost interchangeably with household (*hu*) when talking about tax classes for the levy of corvée.[67] The *men* were divided into nine classes, and this division was determined by the household wealth, which included land holdings, houses, animals, ready capital and promissory notes,[68] or in other words the accumulated assets of the household.[69] It is not stated that the *ding* of the households were included in the *men* grading. However, the *men* grading appears to have been identical with the normal grading of the households into the nine tax classes, which was definitely done on the basis of *ding* as well as other assets.[70]

As time went on the *men*-silver and *ding*-silver were clearly defined, so that around 1565 in Putai District they were as follows:

Tax Class	Men-Silver	Ding-Silver
		per *Ding*
1	4.0 taels	0.7 taels
2	3.0 taels	0.6 taels
3	2.0 tales	0.5 taels
4	1.0 taels	0.4 taels
5	0.9 taels	0.3 taels
6	0.7 taels	0.2 taels
7	0.4 taels	0.2 taels
8	0.1 taels	0.15 taels
9	0.0 taels	0.07 taels

The district corvée totalled at that time 3,758.46 taels.[71] In 1571 the district levy was 3,756,18 or if the surcharge on labour corvée is included, 5,029 taels.[72] Unfortunately we do not have details of how many households there were in each tax class, so we are unable to ascertain whether these figures were the sums actually collected or whether they had to be increased in order to cover the district corvée levy. Such policies were apparently necessary in some districts.[73]

During the reorganization of the corvée in 1571 Liang Menglong ordered the levies of *men*-silver to be 3.5 taels from the households in the first tax class, decreasing by 0.5 taels per tax class to 0.5 taels from the seventh class. The two lowest tax classes were not levied *men*-silver. The *ding*-silver was levied with 0.9 taels on the first tax class, also decreasing proportionately with the ninth tax class paying 0.1 taels per *ding*.[74] He further ordered that the *men*-silver should primarily be used for silver corvée, thus upholding the policy recorded in 1533 that the household levies were used for commuted corvée, while the labour corvée was conscripted from *ding*.[75]

The *ding* does not appear to have been completely unrelated to the number of male adults in the taxpaying households. This supports Ping-ti Ho's view that the north was different from the south in this respect.[76] Liang Menglong complained in 1570 that many wealthy households with many *ding* had bribed the *li*-registrars to remove the male adults (*chengding*) from the register. To remedy this situation he ordered a thorough survey of the population in order to have all the *chengding* registered for corvée. This shows that the presence of an adult male had up to that time made the household liable to pay *ding*-silver, but also that the registers had not been kept in sufficient order to strictly maintain this principle.[77]

OTHER SERVICES

In addition to the chapters on taxes and equal corvée the *SDJHL* also had chapters on the *lijia* corvée, postal services (*yichuan*), horse administration (*mazheng*), and salt administration (*yanfa*). The *lijia* corvée will be desribed in Chapter IV. The salt administration handled levies on the salt fields and does not appear to have had much connection with the subbureaucratic government organization or the taxes and corvée in general. The postal services and the horse administration show some of the problems generally encountered in the corvée system, and as they affected most of the population in the province they will be briefly described.

1. Postal services

The postal service was an important levy in Shandong, as the main road from Peking to the south passed through the western part of the province. The people had to provide most of the burden of the service such as horses, donkeys, wagons, boats, hostels, and goods necessary for the travellers, in addition to personal attendance. In 1565 the contribution to the service for the whole province – which of course included the postal services within the province – was 277,480.54 taels, which can be contrasted with the equal corvée at the same time of 556,754.24 taels.[78] The service had been organized in the Tianshun period on a ten-year rotation. The *ding* from households of the upper tax classes were conscripted as corvée heads, while poorer households were to assist them. The ten-year assessment of this corvée continued until 1565, when it was changed to every five years, because the governor and regional inspector regarded the ten-year rotation as too heavy for the people.[79]

The postal service corvée was different from the equal corvée in one important respect: the services levied in a district were determined according to the acreage of land in the district which was designated as station-land (*zhandi*). From the beginning of the dynasty the postal services had been levied on *ding* according to tax payments or landholdings. From around 1500 there was a general trend towards levying the postal services on land.[80] The 1533 Shandong gazetteer lists them under a category of 'levying person-corvée on land' (*yidi-chuyong-zhe*),[81] and in the *SDJHL* all the items conscripted are according to a certain acreage of station-land. It is not revealed how this station-land was chosen. In Pingyuan District, where the total acreage had originally been 5,021.68 *qing*, 2.375 *qing* was registered as station-land. It is clear from subsequent figures for acreage in the district that the station-land was not separate from other land, but only a special category from which the postal services were levied in addition to other taxes. Whether the station-land got concessions in normal tax payments or whether the postal services were used as an additional levy on this land is not clear.[82]

No explanation is given for how the corvée head and assistant households were conscripted from the land, but the most likely way was that when, for example, a horse was levied from eighty *qing* of station-land one household from the upper tax classes would then be selected as corvée head and be responsible for the service of the horse. However, the work or expenses provided by the corvée head was only to correspond to the amount of station-land owned by the household, while the balance up to eighty *qing* was to be provided by the assistant

84

households either in labour, money or other goods.

The postal service followed the general trend towards commutation to valuation and payment in silver. Each *qing* of land was in most districts calculated as 0.9 *qing* of station-land, and with the commutation each *qing* of station-land was levied one tael, or 0.9 tael per *qing* according to the normal measurement.[83] We do not know when the commutation started, but it must have been well advanced in 1558. In that year the government ordered reduction in services at the postal stations, and the savings were to be sent to the capital and used towards border defence expenses.[84] Complete commutation was achieved in 1570, when the money was simply collected from the station-land and the hiring of labourers and other services became the responsibility of the officials. This meant that the corvée heads and assistant households were abolished, and one can argue that the postal services ceased to be a corvée and changed into a tax. The levy on the station-land had been increased to 1.35 taels per *qing* of station-land and this continued after 1570. The reason given for the reform was that the corvée heads and assistant households had fallen too far into debt, so that they could no longer perform their duties.[85]

2. Horse administration.

Horses were bred by the people for the defence purposes of the central government. The government provided the horses, and those conscripted to this service were responsible for stabling and breeding so that new horses could be provided at given intervals. The areas designated for breeding were originally the metropolitan areas, but when the burden became heavier this spread to Shandong and Henan. Most sources date this introduction in Shandong to 1429, and some a few years later. Li Kaixian claims that breeding was originally introduced in all the prefectures of the province, and that the three eastern prefectures by crafty schemes later managed to unload the whole burden onto the three western prefectures. There is no evidence to support this claim; all other sources are unanimous that only the western prefectures were required to breed horses, since conditions in the eastern prefectures were considered unsuitable at the time when this stabling service was introduced, and they were also too far away from the capital.[86] The argument that the eastern prefectures were unsuitable for horse breeding was apparently not valid in the sixteenth century. A metropolitan censor complained in 1571 that much land was saline and there were no pastures in the western prefectures of Shandong, with the result that no horses were bred there. To maintain the delivery of horses, the households assigned to this service had to pool money together to buy a horse from the eastern prefectures for delivery to the government. He complained that it was not a good idea to requisition horses from prefectures that did not have the facilities to breed them, and that the eastern prefectures in this way made a profit by selling horses to the western prefectures.[87]

In the 1533 Shandong gazetteer it is said that the stabling service was levied from the *she* (*yishe-chuzi-zhe*). In this context the *she* could mean the *lijia*, but there is no further clarification. From the beginning the breeding was levied upon *ding*, one mare per five *ding* and one foal per three *ding*. In 1493, when the levy was changed in Beizhili from *ding* to land, the levy in Shandong remained on the *ding* but was changed to one mare per ten *ding* and one foal per five *ding*. The *ding* got no exemptions from taxes or other corvée.[88] Among the households assigned to stable service, one from the upper tax classes was selected as corvée head, while the other households were assistant households.[89]

Commutation of the stable service is reported in 1542 after a bad year in some districts that had heavy levies of horses. In 1555 the government ordered that commutation could only continue if there were severe economic hardships, and the provincial authorities were consequently forced to revert to delivery of horses from all districts. In the following year there were several attempts to commute and reduce the number of horses to be delivered. The provincial authorities realized that the delivery of horses was a heavy burden upon the population. It was no longer fair, because the wealthy households had managed to get exempted from the service. The government was aware of the problem, but it was still concerned about sufficient supplies of horses. In 1567 the commutation was allowed for 50% of the horses, and this was raised in 1570 to 70%.[90]

The assessment of the households for stabling service had originally been carried out every ten years. From the 1540s there was a movement to change this to assessment every five years. However, when the equal corvée was assessed every two years, confusion could arise if households had their tax class substantially changed during the biennial assessment. The solution to this problem was that changes would only be made in the stabling service assessment during the five-year period if any household in the biennial assessment was downgraded to one of the three lower tax classes. In such cases their service would be changed from corvée head to assistant household.[91] In Binzhou Subprefecture the provision of horses was in the late 1560s organized every five years and was based upon groups of ten households. Horses were delivered in spring and autumn.

The ten households worked in rotation, so that during the five years each of them would once be responsible for the provision of the horse, while the other nine households in each delivery were assistant households. After five years there would be a new assessment of the corvée. It was claimed by the magistrate who introduced the reform, Wan Pengcheng, that this system was fair and that no household would suffer excessive exhaustion.[92] The delivery of horses from Binzhou was sixty-three both in spring and autumn. Nineteen of these had to be delivered in kind while the rest were commuted at twenty-four taels per horse.[93] This meant that there would be sixty-three groups, and as there were seventy-eight *lijia*, the households selected were probably all in the upper tax classes.

From the 1540s there was also a movement to change the levy from *ding* to other items. In 1544 it was changed to *men* in Zhangqiu District, and this apparently spread to other districts.[94] In 1561 the governor ordered Linyi District to change the levy from *ding* to land, so that the households with most land were selected to be corvée heads while those with smaller land holdings were assistant households. The reform was introduced only in this district, and the magistrate reported in 1567 that it had been carried out. In 1567 Governor Jiang Tingyi ordered that the stabling services were to be levied by 40% from *ding*, 40% from *men*, and 20% from land. Households with privileged exemptions were only allowed them for their own *ding*, and the households with much land and in the highest tax class were still to be corvée heads. In this way the burden of the stabling service was claimed to be a little more equal.[95]

THE *DAHU*

1. The function of the *dahu*

The *dahu* are not given a special section in the *SDJHL* as is the case with the items of corvée discussed above. They are, however, mentioned frequently, so there is no doubt that they existed and that in the minds of the officials they were a corvée conscripted from the people. The reason they are not dealt with separately in the *SDJHL* is probably that they were conscripted in each district according to local need, and were not entered in the consolidated provincial accounts for corvée services and payments which were used to distribute the corvée between the districts. In this way they resemble the regular *lijia* corvée as *li*-leader and *jia*-head.

According to Ge Shouli, writing in 1567, the *dahu* were assigned to collect tax designated for a certain granary from the taxpayers and to forward it.[96] At this time such taxes had a granary rate but, to the extent that the *dahu* had been in existence before commutation to silver payments, their duty would have been to receive the grain and forward it to the designated granary. The amount of tax they handled was small compared to that handled by the *liangzhang* in the southern provinces. Li Kaixian writes that the *dahu* originally had to collect and forward 100 taels in silver or 100 *dan* in grain.[97] This figure is corroborated by a story from Zhangqiu District. During the Jiajing period a man in the district found 100 taels which had been lost or left behind by a *dahu* from Yizhou Subprefecture in the eastern part of Yanzhou Prefecture. The man, Hou Zhisheng, picked up the silver, handed it over to the officials and later refused to accept a reward. The district official was delighted, and Hou Zhisheng was given a tablet to display on his house saying: 'The House of a Righteous Man'.[98] The figure of 100 taels in this affair is so striking that it strongly supports the claim by Li Kaixian that this was the sum a *dahu* was expected to collect and forward. This is further supported by the fact that in the Single Whip system proposal of 1555 two petty *dahu* were to be selected to forward 200 taels.[99]

Li Kaixian continues his description of the *dahu* by saying that they were in his time collecting and forwarding 200–300 taels. The 1583 Binzhou gazetteer says that in that subprefecture there were ninety *dahu* and each collected about 500 taels of silver. This is the highest figure available for the districts and subprefectures but admittedly information is very scarce.[100] These two statements indicate strongly that there was a considerable increase in the amount the *dahu* had to collect. The reason could be that the administration did not wish to increase the number of *dahu* along with increase in the collections assigned to them, either because this was not thought necessary or because there were not sufficient households available to perform the duties.

The *dahu* was responsible for delivering the money or grain at the designated granary. There are indications that they were allowed to charge the taxpayers for the transport of the grain. In the 1560s it is said in a discussion of grain destined for the frontiers that the regulated transport surcharge of 0.035 taels per *dan* of grain per 100 *li* was not sufficient when the *dahu* had to use three or four men to perform the service. As a result a calculation was made of the transport cost between Licheng District and the granaries in Dezhou, with the result that the *dahu* were then allowed transport expenses of 0.06 taels per *dan* per 100 *li*.[101] It is likely that the *dahu* were allowed to pass on the cost of transport to the taxpayers, but the system does not seem to have worked, as one of the major reforms of the *dahu* during the period was that they no longer had to forward the tax to the designated granaries but only to the prefectural administration, so that they could avoid ruining themselves.[102] Another way of solving the financial difficulty of the *dahu* was to levy money on other households to assist them. This happened in Binzhou Subprefecture in the late 1560s. When the *dahu* were conscripted, assistant households were organized to pay a fixed amount of ten taels to each *dahu*. Moreover the amount each *dahu* had to forward was fixed at 150 taels and 150 *dan* of grain, and in this way the ruin of their families was avoided.[103]

With the introduction of the silver corvée the *dahu* were also required to collect the silver used to hire persons for this work. There are several references to this collection, and we must assume that it was general for all silver corvée.[104] The money was normally handed over to the officials after the collection had finished, but in the case of some of the corvée of a military nature the *dahu* could be involved in a way that resembles the corvée heads of the labour corvée. If the collection had not been finished, so that the wages for the soldiers sent on training could not be paid, then in the case of labour corvée the corvée head would have to pay the money, while in the case of silver corvée the *dahu* would have to pay.[105] Other instances where the *dahu* had to perform functions similar to the corvée head was in the procurement of certain goods for the central government. A number of live deer requisitioned for sacrifices had been commuted to silver payment at some date, but in 1555 the Ministry of Works suggested that this was not convenient, presumably because it was difficult for the government to buy live deer. The solution was that the *dahu* were to continue to collect the silver and then buy the animals and forward them. As this inolved considerable effort on the part of the *dahu*, the silver to be collected was doubled from eight to sixteen taels so that the *dahu* were not ruined. Another instance was in the procurement of military clothing. After the levy had been commuted to silver, the *dahu* were ordered, when they had collected the money in the fourth month, to buy cloth and have it dyed, and when the cotton was harvested in the seventh month they would have the clothing made with padding. The finished clothing was forwarded to the prefecture before the tenth month.[106]

In some cases the *dahu* actually performed duties that were normally regarded as equal corvée or *lijia* contributions. In 1567 it is mentioned in the middle of a list of small *lijia* contributions for branch offices of the central government in the province that the *dahu* should pay four taels as wages to the clerks (*shushou*) in a branch office of the Ministry of Revenue.[107] In 1569 the weighers in the granaries of the Confucian schools in Jinan Prefecture were abolished, and *dahu* were ordered to manage the collection and reimbursement of the silver in these granaries.[108] Both duties were probably on a very small scale but are mentioned here to indicate the flexible attitude the administration apparently had towards the duties of the *dahu*.

2. The *dahu* and the *lijia*

The origin of the *dahu* has so far been impossible to establish, since no sources relating to this have been found. However, Kuribayashi Nobuo has attempted to explain their origin during his researches on the *lijia* system. He begins with a description of the introduction of the Single Whip during the early years of the Wanli period in Caoxian District, Yanzhou Prefecture. The account, which was written by the magistrate Wang Qi,[109] says that according to the old system there were over 200 *dahu* who collected the taxes and corvée silver. As these duties were traditionally those of the *li*-leaders, Kuribayashi thinks that the *dahu* was simply another word for *li*-leaders. However, from the writings of Yu Shenxing he realizes that the *li*-leader and the *dahu* were not necessarily the same person. He deduces that the *dahu* were originally created by dividing the duties of the *li*-leaders when they became too heavy, so that the *dahu* collected taxes while the *li*-leaders continued to perform the other duties.[110]

Taniguchi Kikuo, who has so far done most of the work on the *dahu*, disputes Kuribayashi's point of view. He does it most strongly in a review of Kuribayashi's work,[111] but the argument is more fully presented in an earlier article. He bases his argument on the description given by Ge Shouli stating that the *dahu* were assigned to granaries, in which case it would be difficult to maintain Kuribayashi's argument. Furthermore, he cites cases from some northern provinces other than Shandong where the *dahu* are clearly mentioned as part of the equal or miscellaneous corvée, and he also points out that in several districts the number of *dahu* did not correspond to the number of *lijia*. This was certainly the case in Caoxian, which had seventy-four *lijia*,[112] and in Jinan Prefecture this is supported in Binzhou mentioned above and in Zhangqiu, where the *dahu* before 1586 numbered 116.[113] Taniguchi further points out that the number of *dahu* increased when they had to collect the commuted corvée payments, and possibly with increases in other burdens following the commutation of the land taxes.[114]

In the face of such criticism Kuribayashi's conclusion that the *dahu* originated directly from a division of the duties of the *li*-leaders can hardly be accepted. There is, however, evidence that the *dahu* were conscripted on the basis of the *lijia*. In connection with the order of 1571 to revert to the old system, Liang Menglong states that a practice that could not be completely eradicated was to conscript the *dahu* according to the *lijia* in a ten-year rotation. From the incumbent *jia* (*benjia*) two households from the upper tax classes were drafted as *dahu*, one who could write and one who could calculate. The allocation of the corvée duties to these *dahu* was according to the size of the *lijia*. The *dahu* collected the tax in small tax chests, which after weighing were emptied into a chest for the whole district. The officials then divided the silver into portions for each item of tax, and the *dahu* were ordered to melt it into ingots and forward it to the prefecture or provincial administration. Liang Menglong called on the officials to suggest how this method of 'combined collection and combined forwarding' could best be changed to comply with the order to revert to 'separate collection and separate forwarding'. It is not clear whether he had any objections to the way the *dahu* were conscripted.[115] This method of conscription is further confirmed in the 1602 Zichuan gazetteer, where it says that the *dahu* were still to originate from the *lijia*.[116]

THE SINGLE WHIP

1. Granary rates

As has been seen, there were manipulations with the tax and corvée system, so that people who were in a favourable position *vis-à-vis* the keepers of the tax records had their payments or services to the government reduced. Such manipulations were mostly for the benefit of wealthy households or the families of government officials. The latter also enjoyed privileged exemptions from some taxes and corvée. These exemptions were regulated for the whole empire in 1545 to stop abuses, such as claiming exemptions above the amount to which a given official was entitled or extending exemptions beyond the households.[117] However, this regulation does not appear to have immediately stopped the abuses.

The main problem for the provincial authorities in the 1550s was the manipulation of the granary rate and the *dahu*. In 1555 Governor Liu Cai held consultations with the officials in the province, and the conclusion they reached was that the Single Whip (*yitiaobianfa*) should be introduced where conditions allowed it. The prefect in Jinan Prefecture reported that the Single Whip had been in operation in Licheng and Changqing Districts for some time, probably from 1551.

The Single Whip in Licheng was applied to tax collection and eliminated the granary rate. The total tax from Licheng was 13,673.21 *dan*, of which 9,800 *dan* was transferred revenue. Each *dan* of transferred revenue was originally commuted to 0.43 tael of silver, giving a total of 4,214 taels. Under the Single Whip, tax was paid at a uniform rate, regardless of the tax class of the owner and whether or not he was an absentee landlord. The retained and transferred revenue was levied on each *dan* of tax according to their percentage in the total district tax. In this way the transferred revenue from each *dan* was 0.71673 *dan*, or when commuted to silver at the rate of 0.43 taels per *dan* it was 0.308194 taels per *dan*. The retained revenue per *dan* was then 0.28327 *dan* which was not commuted. To this was added a melting charge of 8%, giving a total of 0.3059316 *dan*. The melting charge was probably imposed to make payment in kind equal to payment in silver, since in the latter case the taxpayers had to make up the losses when the silver was melted. In addition a small charge was made of 0.00435 tael in mat-cover silver (*xicaoyin*) per *dan* of retained revenue. The only unclear point here is that the original (*yuan*) commutation rate is given at 0.43 taels, which suggests that there had not previously been any difference in the payment of silver per *dan*. However, during the deliberations, statements that the tax classes should be disregarded and that it was no longer necessary to specifically determine the granary rates for each *dan* of collected tax show clearly that the object was to eliminate the granary rate. The commutation figure of 0.43 taels per *dan* must then be regarded as the average figure for previous commutations.

In 1555 the governor ordered that a similar system should be introduced in the other districts, but it is doubtful whether the provincial authorities expected that this could be applied immediately in every district. At any rate, during the deliberations it was maintained that suitable conditions for the Single Whip existed in districts where there were not too great differences in the quality of the land and in the wealth of the people. In districts where this was not so, it would be better to continue with the collection of tax according to tax classes, i.e. granary rates.[118]

The provincial authorities also took the opportunity to continue a policy of reducing the number of decimal digits in the calculation of taxes. This had been going on at least since 1550, when it was enforced with only two decimal digits in district tax figures.[119] Recommendations were made in 1555 that this should continue for the districts, and that in addition the *dahu* should not be allowed to calculate payments from the individual taxpayers to more than two decimal digits.[120] The reason for this – according to an order from the governor in 1561 – was that trifling amounts could be used to imperceptibly increase the levies on some households to the benefit of others.[121] The sources give many figures to more than two decimal digits, so we must have some doubts about the implementation of this policy. It is however interesting to see that the officials were prepared to sacrifice complete equality in the levy of taxes, by abandoning the application of minute decimal digits – in order to simplify the administration and supervision of the tax system, which in the end would benefit ordinary taxpayers.

There can be doubt that the order to introduce the Single Whip in 1555 was followed, at least in some districts. In a letter to Liu Cai probably in 1557, Ge Shouli wrote that it had been necessary to change the uniform levy and instead create three grades, since it was difficult to use the Single Whip when poor and rich were assessed at the same rate. What Ge meant by that remark is not clear as he did not elaborate, but it is evidence that the Single Whip had been applied sufficiently to show that there had been problems in its application which had to be adjusted.[122]

Discussions of the Single Whip took place again in 1561 and 1562. Officials were ordered to hold meetings with the people to inquire about those who had been impoverished by the tax system and how the allotment of the taxes could be improved. The conclusion of the deliberations was in favour of continuing the Single Whip. The reason for this was clearly stated to be that the Single Whip had removed a considerable part of the fraud in the tax system, and that it was more suited to a situation where many officials did not have the necessary competence or moral standards that were required if the previous system was to be successfully continued. It was further argued that inequalities which could have arisen when land of different quality was levied at the same rate were to a certain degree offset through the new 'metallic' gradings of the land. There could still be cases where the 'metallic' gradings had not been introduced, or where they did not provide complete equality. In these circumstances the local officials were granted a certain discretion of action. It was, however, forbidden to give special consideration to single households. If special consideration was granted, it was to be to a whole *lijia*, to prevent individual households from obtaining unfair tax advantages over other households in the *lijia*. At the same time instructions for the management of the Single Whip were given to some subprefectures and districts in Dongchang Prefecture. This may indicate that the Single Whip was only introduced in these districts at this time. This gradual introduction is further shown by a clear statement in the discussions that a uniform policy could not be enforced in all districts of the province. Local discretion was allowed, but the general trend was to be towards the introduction of the Single Whip.[123]

2. The *dahu*

With the elimination of the granary rates it became easier to reform the *dahu* services. The concern of the provincial authorities was that the system of the *dahu* was no longer effective for the collection and delivery of taxes, because some of the *dahu* were apparently not efficient. 'Combined collection and separate forwarding' (*zongshou-fenjie*) was now to be substituted for the old system where each *dahu* had been responsible for both collection and forwarding, or 'separate collection and separate forwarding' (*fenshou-fenjie*). Each district was to be divided into a number of tax areas (*qu*), eight in large districts and six or four in smaller districts. In each tax area a tax chest (*gui*) was to be set up to be managed by wealthy and honest *dahu*. It is mentioned during the deliberations, but not in the governor's dicision, that there were to be two *dahu* for the taxes paid in silver and two for taxes paid in kind, the latter being mostly for retained revenue. Registers (*chili*) were compiled for each tax chest, and the *dahu* were to supervise the reception of the taxes at the chest. In this they were to be assisted by the *li*-leaders, who would direct the *shipai* to lead the households to the chest, where they would personally deposit their taxes. The obvious purpose of this was to prevent the taxpayers from being exploited by intermediaries. For forwarding of taxes, the officials were to match the content of each chest with the deliveries to the different granaries, so that payments to a granary did not have to be drawn from more than one chest. For the delivery itself two petty *dahu* (*xiaodahu*) were conscripted for each 200 taels of silver. [124]

It is not possible to ascertain whether this system of collection and forwarding was actually established in 1555. Li Kaixian, writing around 1560, mentions tax chests in Zhangqiu District. [125] Dongchang Prefecture reported that the order to introduce the 'combined collection and separate forwarding' was received in 1562, [126] and in 1570 the Left administration commissioner wrote that after the introduction of the Single Whip the tax was still divided into summer and autumn tax; and granary rates and *dahu* conscription were still operative. This had later been changed to the Single Bellstring method (*yichuanlingfa*) with 'combined collection and separate forwarding' and summer and autumn taxes paid together. [127] However, this had apparently not been the case in Dongchang Prefecture in 1569. [128] The conclusion must be that the reform of the *dahu* was introduced gradually, beginning in the late 1550s, but as with the granary rates there was considerable allowance for variations according to local conditions.

3. Corvée and Ge Shouli's opposition to the Single Whip

The Single Whip considered in the provincial administration in 1555 was only concerned with land taxes and their collection and forwarding. This is an indication that the term Single Whip was used for almost any reform that was carried out at that time with the intention of increasing simplicity and uniformity in the tax and corvée system. It is generally assumed that the Single Whip policy had as its primary purpose the regulation of the corvée system, which had become more and more unmanageable as more items were included and the illegal manipulations created greater inequalities. It should, however, be noted that authors writing about the Single Whip tend to perceive it as an instrument to regulate the particular part of the tax and corvée system in which they had or have an interest. This is illustrated in modern times by Kuribayashi's statement that the Single Whip was mainly aimed at regulating the *lijia* contributions,[129] while Tani writes that it was mainly aimed at regulating the stabling service.[130]

As stated above, the granary rates can be regarded as corvée, because they were levied according to the tax classes, but by contemporary officials they were conceived as part of the tax system. There were, however, movements in Shandong in the 1550s, at least in the later part of the decennium, to apply the Single Whip to corvée. Single Whip in connection with corvée usually meant that the corvée was levied according to land holdings, either by incorporating the payments for corvée into the land tax or by converting land holdings to *ding*. The main opponent of the Single Whip in Shandong at this time, Ge Shouli, concentrated his opposition on the point of levying corvée on land. He also expressed concern over the uniform tax rates and the 'combined collection and separate forwarding', but the levy of corvée on land seems to have been his greatest fear whenever he heard the phrase Single Whip, ever since he had first seen the consequences of such changes when governor of Henan in 1549–1550.

The problem with the levy of corvée on land was that the households that made a comfortable living – not to speak of great profit – from trade or other non-primary professions did not have to contribute to the corvée. This had been the case when corvée was levied according to *men* where assets besides land holdings were included in the assessment. When corvée was transferred to the land, it was levied from the people who also paid the taxes. In the view of Ge Shouli – while minister for revenue in 1567 – this could endanger the payment of taxes which were more important for the central government and the military forces on the northern border.[131] He apparently refused – at least in his writings – to admit that the previous system had become unequal following concentration of land holdings and various malpractices. Apparently, in the method for the levy of corvée according to tax classes, land was weighted so that the total corvée contribution according to *ding* and *men* of those with large land holdings was low in relation to those with smaller land holdings. This at least seems to be the major argument for the introduction of the Single Whip for corvée.

Provincial consideration of the levy of corvée on land is first recorded in 1563, when it was approved for some areas, but it had already developed in some unspecified districts in earlier years. The approval in 1563 came too late for it to be applied to all corvée during the equal corvée assessment in progress, so to give some immediate relief it was decided to transfer some items completely from the equal corvée to be levied on the land. These items were material money (*liaoyin*), charcoal money (*chaitanyin*), and fuel money (*muchaiyin*), which had increased in recent years, so that even if they only amounted to c. 50,000 taels compared to a total of 600,000 taels for all equal corvée, the change was probably significant for the taxpayers.[132] This was further enchanced by the fact that material money had increased comparatively more in the districts that were not directly adjacent to the Grand Canal. The districts on the canal had complained that money or labour to be provided for corvée work on the canal from distant districts had not arrived, so their burden had become excessive. The solution was to levy the canal corvée on the adjacent districts and then transfer to the more distant districts the material, charcoal and fuel money previously levied on the adjacent districts for delivery to the capital. For the distant districts this meant a real increase in their corvée burden, since they had previously, by illegal means, been able to avoid some of the canal corvée.[133]

When Ge Shouli became minister for revenue in 1567, he got the chance to enforce his own ideas about the Single Whip in Shandong and for that matter in other parts of China as well. In 1567:5 he obtained imperial approval for a memorial stressing that the officials should have the welfare of agriculture constantly in mind, because that was the basis of the state, and that, in particular, the levy of corvée on land should be prohibited and the 'combined collection and separate forwarding' should be abolished. His opposition to this method of collection was based upon the experience that officials took first from the tax chests the silver needed for the most urgent tax payments, so that there was no money at all for the less urgent payments if all taxes were not collected. At the same time the *dahu* supervising the tax chests withheld for themselves any surplus that may have accumulated in the chest, which under the old system could be used for making up losses during the forwarding. Now the petty *dahu* had to make up the deficits themselves. Finally it seems that the book-keeping procedures were not adequate to cope with the changes, so it was difficult to keep control of the tax from payment to delivery when it had to pass through several hands. This created a special problem when remittances were to be made to districts after bad harvests, particularly when no distinction was made between summer and autumn taxes, and things became almost impossible when calculations had to be made for the general remittance of tax arrears from before 1564.[134]

Ge Shouli's memorial gained approval for a general return to the old system of taxation, so he seems to have won a complete victory. Had this policy been carried out it would probably have meant a complete dismantling of the Single Whip. However, he had to relinquish office the following month,[135] and even if there is no evidence that the imperial sanction to his memorial was later withdrawn, it certainly was a setback for its implementation. It would have demanded a very vigorous policy from the central government to reverse the trend towards the Single Whip. After all, there is no evidence that the reforms carried out in Shandong since 1555 had obtained approval from the emperor or the central government.

4. The Single Whip after 1567

Jiang Tingyi, who as governor had to act upon Ge's memorial, did return the material money, etc., from levy on land to the equal corvée, but at the same time he introduced a Single Whip for the whole equal corvée. Investigations had revealed that even if the corvée was paid according to regulations and there were no manipulations, the stronger *lijia* still had advantages, since they could use their position to get assigned the less urgent corvée, while the weaker *lijia* had to perform the more urgent corvée, which was more difficult to fulfil. This seems to indicate that the corvée was still to a large extent levied with the *lijia* as a unit. The solution was to calculate all the silver to be paid for corvée in a district and then distribute it over all the objects on which corvée was levied.[136] So the arrangements of Jiang Tingyi complied with the very specific government order that the material money, etc., was to be returned to the equal corvée, but his 'Single Whipping' of all equal corvée can hardly have met with the approval of Ge Shouli. It also seems that Jiang did not enforce the return to the equal corvéee of other corvé, which in the previous years had tended towards levy on land in the districts. Anyway, Ge Shouli wrote in an otherwise laudatory letter when Jiang

97

left his position as governor that Jiang had allowed the levy of corvée on land.[137]

Jiang Tingyi also reviewed the 'combined collection and separate forwarding'. As mentioned previously, it was then revealed that this method had not been used in Dongchang Prefecture. Most districts in Jinan Prefecture preferred to return to the 'separate collection and separate forwarding'. As a result greater flexibility was allowed than had apparently been officially endorsed before, but 'combined collection and separate forwarding' was generally preferred.[138]

In 1570 the new governor Liang Menglong ordered an almost complete return to the tax and corvée system of before 1555. Corvée could not be conscripted according to land, only according to *men* and *ding*. There were to be granary rates and *dahu* to collect and forward taxes by 'separate collection and separate forwarding'. The tax classes were to be reassessed, households that had been discontinued were to be removed from the registers and newcomers included. *Men*-silver at specific rates was to be assigned to silver-corvée, and *ding*-silver also assigned at specific rates to labour corvée. One of the few concessions allowed by Liang was towards the problem of corvée levied on *ding*, which was very heavy on the less wealthy peasants. He ordered that in all households assets other than land were to be converted to *ding*, so that the wealthy could get a number of *ding*, and the households with privileged exemptions could get some *ding* in excess of the exempted. It was finally decided that the land belonging to absentee landlords was to be levied at 0.03 taels per *mou* towards the cost of the corvée. Liang also gave concessions to the *dahu*, who now had to manage both the collection and forwarding of the taxes. They would deliver the tax payments to provincial or prefectual offices, and officials would be in charge of further transportation to granaries.[139]

To what extent the Single Whip was actually introduced in the province is impossible to establish. There were obviously allowances for local variations. However, the officials appear to have worked from the assumption that developments were under way which were worth pursuing and encouraging, or, in the case of opponents, were worth a considerable effort to resist, including a memorial to the emperor. It has been impossible to get any picture of the development from the district gazetteers. The only references in the local gazetteers are in Putai District, where material, charcoal and fuel money in 1565 are listed under land taxes.[140] In Binzhou Subprefecture the Single Whip is mentioned in the late 1560s. The gazetteer says that the summer and autumn taxes were levied after the Single Whip and divided according to granary rate for reception and forwarding. The exhausted *lijia* were first to be selected and amalgamated in the tax registers. After that the *dahu* were to draw lots in the yamen for the granaries, so that the *li*-registrars could not tamper with the burden of each granary.[141] In other words the granary rate was abolished and land tax collected at a flat rate without regard for tax classes. The *dahu* were assigned to deliver taxes to specific granaries; the tax for each granary was still calculated on the basis of granary rates. Delivery to a distant granary could be unattractive, since transport expenses only covered part of the costs. As there is no reference to tax chests, the *dahu*, perhaps with the *shipai* as intermediaries, collected taxes from a number of households (or *jia*) whose accumulated tax payments, collected at the standard rate, corresponded to the amount of tax he had to forward. This system appears to have been Single Whip with 'separate collection and separate forwarding'.

NOTES TO CHAPTER III

1. Huang, pp. 46–52; Oyama (1971), p. 322.
2. Littrup (Single Whip), *passim*
3. Franke (1968), pp. 268–273.
4. *SDJHL* 4/1–2.
5. Kataoka, p. 142. The *bu* can more correctly be called 'square *bu*'. In the Ming dynasty it was a square of five feet (*chi*). The size of the *bu* and *chi* varied according to location. The standard *chi* in Ming was 0.311 m. This gives c. 580 m^2 for the standard *mou* of 240 *bu*. Wu Chengluo, *Zhongguo duliangheng shi* (1937: Shanghai, 1957), pp. 54, 114–117.
6. *Laiwu xianzhi* 1673/4/49.
7. *Qingcheng xianzhi* 1612/1/14.
8. *Leling xianzhi* 1762/3/46; *Jiyang xianzhi* 1765/3/4.
9. *Putai xianzhi* 1592/3/7.
10. *Zichuan xianzhi* 1602/10/1; citing the previous (probably 1548) edition.
11. *DMHD* 17/13.
12. *Deping xianzhi* 1796/9/13. We have no indication of the value of horse fodder in relation to grain in 1512. A very tentative calculation using the overall provincial rates for commutation to silver of transferred summer and autumn taxes and horse fodder in 1542 indicates that the horse fooder would increase the levy on private land by c. 12%. This would still leave the levies on domain land as c. 5.6 times greater than on private land. *SDJHL* 3/4.
13. *Binzhou zhi* 1701/4/14. Written by Zhao Dagang (*jinshi* 1541).
14. Huang, p. 84.
15. *Yangxin xianzhi* 1682/3/8.
16. Ho (1959), p. 105.
17. *SDJHL* 4/9.
18. *Shanghe xianzhi* 1586/3/1.
19. *Li Kaixian ji*, p. 707.

20. *SDJHL* 4/1.
21. *Ibid*. 3/6 ff, 1/1–46.
22. *Dezhou zhi* 1576/4/1.
23. *SDJHL* 4/2.
24. Memorial from Ge Shouli as minister of revenue 1567. *Ge Duansugong wenji* (GDSGWJ) 3/12. Also in *SDJHL* 4/14.
25. *Li Kaixian ji*, p. 707.
26. *SDJHL* 4/20.
27. *GDSGWJ* 3/12.
28. Huang, p. 40.
29. Oyama Masaaki, «Mindai ni okeru zeiryō no kachō to kosoku to no kankei», *Bunka kagaku kiyō* 7 (1965), 43 ff.
30. *SDJHL* 4/21.
31. Taniguchi (1961), pp. 7–9; Yamane (1966), pp. 188–191.
32. *SDJHL* 4/10.
33. The term *zafan-chaiyi* or simply *zafan* was often used in early Ming for the miscellaneous corvée. It was inherited from the corvée system of the Yuan dynasty. Yamane (1966), p. 37.
34. *DMHD* 210/17.
35. Huang, p. 57.
36. Yamane (1966), p. 72.
37. *SDJHL* 9/71.
38. Yamane Yukio, «Jūgo jūroku seiki Chūgoku ni okeru fueki rōdōsei no kaikaku», *Shigaku zasshi* 60.11 (1951), 47.
39. Friese, pp. 94 ff.
40. Taniguchi (1961), pp. 4–5; *Jinan fuzhi* 1839/35/3.
41. *SDJHL* 4/2, 7.
42. Yamane (1951), pp. 49–51.
43. *Daxue yanyibu* (1487. Taipei 1976 reprint), 31/15.
44. *SDJHL* 9/56–57.
45. *Ibid*. 9/57, 64.
46. *Zichuan xianzhi* 1602/23/3.
47. Yamane (1966), p. 160.
48. *Ibid*., p. 144.
49. Kuribayashi (1971), pp. 129–130.
50. Yamane (1966), p. 117.
51. Taniguchi (1961), pp. 15–16.
52. *SDJHL* 9/35.
53. Taniguchi (1961), p. 17.
54. E.g. *SDJHL* 7/26.
55. Iwami Hiroshi, «Kasei nenkan no rikisa ni tsuite», in *Tamura hakase shōju tōyōshi ronsō* (Kyoto, 1968), p. 47.
56. *SDJHL* 8/12 ff.
57. *Ibid*. 9/49–51.
58. *Ibid*. 9/7.
59. *Ibid*. 9/11.
60. *DMB*, pp. 898–902.
61. *SDJHL* 8/85.
62. *Ibid*. 9/53.
63. *Shandong tongzhi* 1533/8/21–24. This passage is repeated in *SDJHL* 7/1.
64. Yamane (1966), pp. 205–208.

65. Yamane (1951), p. 51
66. Taniguchi (1961), pp. 17–19.
67. F.ex. Ge Shouli, *SDJHL* 4/13.
68. Taniguchi (1961), p. 7.
69. *SDJHL* 9/75.
70. *Ibid*. 7/72.
71. *Putai xianzhi* 1592/4/2.
72. *SDJHL* 5/24.
73. *Ibid*. 9/75.
74. *Ibid*. 9/72–73.
75. *Ibid*. 9/74.
76. Ho (1959), p. 31.
77. *SDJHL* 9/71–72.
78. *Ibid*. 6/1, 11/39.
79. *Ibid*. 11/31–32.
80. Yamane (1966), p. 166.
81. *Shandong tongzhi* 1533/8/21–22.
82. *Pingyuan xianzhi* 1592/1/19, 1749/3/5. Ray Huang has shown that in some places the postal services became a surtax on all land of a district. Huang, p. 113.
83. In Jinan Prefecture the conversion rate to station-land was 0.8 in two districts and 0.7 in five districts. *SDJHL* 11/1–8.
84. *Ibid*. 11/32; *DMHD* 148/4.
85. *SDJHL* 11/39.
86. Li Kaixian ji, p. 707; Tani Mitsutaka, *Mindai basei no kenkyū* (Kyoto, 1972), pp. 292–295.
87. *SDJHL* 12/44–45.
88. Ibid. 12/26. The date for the revision is given as Chenghua 6 (1470), but this appears to be a mistake for Hongzhi 6. *DMHD* 150/9.
89. *SDJHL* 12/38.
90. *Ibid*. 12/27 ff.
91. *Ibid*. 12/45–47.
92. *Binzhou zhi* 1583/4/23.
93. *SDJHL* 12/4.
94. *Ibid*. 12/45.
95. *Ibid*. 12/38.
96. *GDSGWJ* 3/12.
97. *Li kaixian ji*, p. 708.
98. *Zhangqiu xianzhi* 1596/27/47.
99. *SDJHL* 4/3.
100. *Binzhou zhi* 1583/2/50.
101. *SDJHL* 4/28.
102. *Ibid*. 9/1.
103. *Binzhou zhi* 1583/4/22.
104. *SDJHL* 7/26, 8/78, 9/5.
105. *Ibid*. 9/6.
106. *Ibid*. 9/2–3.
107. *Ibid*. 8/62.
108. *Ibid*. 8/78.
109. The compiler of the *Xu wenxian tongkao*. Franke (1968), p. 194.
110. Kuribayashi (1971), pp. 172–173.
111. Taniguchi Kikuo, «Kuribayashi Nobuo, Rikōsei no kenkyū», *Tōyōshi Kenkyū* 31.2 (1972), 118.

101

112. *Houhuzhi* 2/52.
113. *Zhangqiu xianzhi* 1596/12/86.
114. Taniguchi (1969), pp. 114–124.
115. *SDJHL* 4/26–27.
116. *Zichuan xianzhi* 1602/13/1.
117. *DMHD* 20/19–20. Translated from the *SL* in Friese, pp. 33–35.
118. *SDJHL* 4/2–6.
119. *Ibid.* 3/7.
120. *Ibid.* 4/3.
121. *Ibid.* 4/7.
122. *GDSGWJ* 13/25.
123. *SDJHL* 4/7–10.
124. *Ibid.* 4/3, 7.
125. *Li Kaixian ji*, p. 708.
126. *SDJHL* 4/17.
127. *Ibid.* 4/19.
128. *Ibid.* 4/18.
129. Kuribayashi (1971), pp. 152 ff.
130. Tani, p. 248.
131. *GDSGWJ* 3/9–15, 13/25; Littrup (Single Whip), pp. 81–83.
132. *SDJHL* 8/37–38, 9/59–62.
133. *Ibid.* 9/29.
134. *GDSGWJ* 3/10–15; *SDJHL* 4/11 ff.
135. *MS* 112/3470.
136. *SDJHL* 9/54–55.
137. *GDSGWJ* 14/18.
138. *SDJHL* 4/18–19.
139. *SDJHL* 4/23–25, 9/70–76.
140. *Putai xianzhi* 1592/3/9.
141. *Binzhou zhi* 1583/4/22.

IV. The *lijia* before the second Single Whip

INTRODUCTION

The subject of this chapter is the *lijia* organization, the *lijia* corvée, and the involvement of the *lijia* with other kinds of corvée from c. 1550 to the early years of the Wanli period. This upper time-limit has been chosen because the Single Whip policy introduced during the Wanli period had profound influence on the subbureaucratic government system. The introduction of this second Single Whip took place at different times in the various districts, so no definite time-limit can be established. For the formal structure of the *lijia* organization we have to rely on information supplied in the Wanli or later gazetteers. We cannot be sure that this information is unconditionally reliable for the situation that existed thirty to forty years before the compilation of the gazetteers. However, the impression I get from the gazetteers is that the organization described in them was probably much the same as it had been for at least the last few decades. In some cases the gazetteers purport to describe the situation that had existed throughout the dynasty, while in Pingyuan and Laiwu it is specifically stated that the description given in the district gazetteer was of the organization that had been abolished with the introduction of the Single Whip.[1] With regard to the function of the *lijia* in the wider context of the tax and corvée system, the *SDJHL* remains the main source. In the latter part of this chapter the upper time-limit can consequently be set at 1571.

THE *LIJIA* ORGANIZATION

1. *Li*-leaders, *shipai* and *jia*-heads

In the reform of tax collection discussed and perhaps partially introduced in 1555 with the creation of tax chests, the *li*-leaders were to assist the *dahu* and instruct the *shipai* to escort the taxpayers (*huahu*) to the chest. This shows clearly that the officials regarded the *li*-leaders and the *shipai* as the persons in the *lijia* who normally assisted the bureaucracy and the *dahu* in fiscal administration. The *jia*-heads are not mentioned in this or any other source, indicating that they had administrative or supervisory duties over other households in their *lijia*. They are only mentioned as members of the *lijia* conscripted to certain corvée duties. In 1548 it is mentioned that messengers (*jiedi-zaoli*) were to be selected among the people working on transport corvée in the districts along the canal, while in all other districts they were to be selected among the incumbent *jia*-heads whenever there was a need for such services. Moreover *jia*-head runners (*jiashou-zaoli*) were conscripted until they were abolished in 1569.[2]

The *shipai* were the non-incumbent *li*-leaders (*painian-lizhang*)[3] and were apparently permanently assigned to their *jia*. This is shown in Laiwu District, where, before the introduction of the second Single Whip, the situation is desribed as follows:

> Ten households formed one *jia* and ten *jia* formed one *lijia*. Each *jia* had one man as *shipai* to press taxes. *One jia* performed the corvée each year in a ten-year rotation.[4]

According to this text, the *shipai* in Laiwu District could have been one of the ten *jia*-head households in the *jia*. However, the position of the *shipai* is further made clear in Pingyuan:

> Each *lijia* had nine *shipai*. Together with the incumbent *li*-leader there were ten persons. They served in a rotation over ten years.[5]

In Zhanqiu District there were also ten *shipai* per *lijia*,[6] but in Binzhou Subprefecture the situation is not evident from the sources. The 1583 edition of the district gazetteer mentions one *li*-leader and ten *shipai* per *lijia*, and this is repeated in the 1701 edition.[7] We cannot establish whether this is an error, which was then continued in the latter gazetteer, or whether it describes the actual situation in the subprefecture. If the latter is true, this indicates that the office of incumbent *li*-leaders was no longer rotated among the *shipai* but was of a more permanent nature. The *shipai* were then not potential *li*-leaders waiting for their turn in the rotation but were the leaders of each of the ten *jia* serving more or less permanently under the direction of the *li*-leader. Such an arrangement would not have been consistent with the original structure of the *lijia*, and also conflicts with the policy – to be described below – that the *lijia* corvée were still to be performed in a ten-year rotation.

Another example of the relationship between the *li*-leaders and the *jia* comes from Zichuan, where from the beginning of the dynasty:

One leader (*zhang*) administered ten households, which made up one *jia*. Ten *jia* made up one *lijia*.

The compilers of the gazetteers must have described the situation as known to them, which probably means that this description is accurate for the sixteenth century. We cannot be absolutely sure that they described the situation as it had existed from the beginning of the dynasty, but at least we can see that in the opinion of the compilers there had been no major changes during the intervening two hundred years, that is until changes were made about thirty years before the compilation of the gazetteer.[8]

If the compilers were correct, we can then answer some of the questions raised in Chapter II about the relationship between the *li*-leaders and the *jia*-heads. For pressing and collecting taxes the *li*-leaders were each year assisted by the non-incumbent *li*-leaders (*shipai*), who exacted the annual taxes and corvée from the *jia* of which they were permanent heads during the decennial rotation. For the *lijia* services provided on a rotational basis, the incumbent *li*-leader was the only one responsible among the ten *li*-leaders, and he was assisted in the performance of services or payment of money by the *jia* to which he was assigned. The *jia*-heads had no administrative functions, their only duty being to assist the incumbent *li*-leader with the *lijia* corvée and possibly other expenses within the *lijia*.

In other words the power over other households in the *lijia* rested in the hands of the ten households which, according to the registration in the Yellow Registers and/or perhaps other tax registers, were considered to be the most powerful in wealth and *ding*. It is open to doubt whether these ten households were actually the most wealthy in the *lijia*. Tampering with the tax classes, as seen above in the discussion of the granary rates, must also have influenced the selection of *li*-leaders. The simple fact that these were selected from the upper tax classes, as is stated in one source,[9] would further induce the powerful households to change their tax class when granary rates, equal corvée and *lijia* duties all fell most heavily upon the upper tax classes.

The position of *li*-leader could be hazardous if the members of the *lijia* were not able to pay their taxes and other contributions, leaving the *li*-leader to make up the deficiencies. They could however get some advantages from the position, as in Binzhou Subprefecture, where it had been necessary to have the taxpayers pay direct to the *dahu* because the demands of the *shipai* were excessive.[10] When the *shipai* could act in this way they must have been among the more powerful households. Perhaps the officials also wanted the *li*-leaders and *shipai* to be persons with a certain standing in the community, otherwise they could hardly be expected to function effectively. This is suggested further by the experience of Taian Subprefecture, where during the Jiajing and Longqing periods the corvée was so heavy that even the 'élite' (*jinshen*) could not avoid service as *li*-leaders.[11]

2. The *li*-registrars

Besides the incumbent *li*-leader and the *shipai* the *li*-registrar was an important person in the fiscal work of the *lijia*. In the sixteenth-century sources they are usually called *lishu*, but they were probably identical to the *shushou* of the early years of the dynasty and appear to have combined this function with that of the *li*-tax assessors (*suanshou*). In the gazetteers of the Wanli period they are only mentioned as having existed in Zangqiu District until 1586 under the title of tax-assessing *shushou* (*pailiang-shushou*).[12] Even in that gazetteer they are not listed together with the *lijia* officeholders and this, together with their absence from similar listings in other gazetteers, indicates that their position was without the legal basis enjoyed by other officers in the *lijia*.

The *li*-registrars are, however, mentioned frequently in the *SDJHL* documents, so their positions were recognized by the officials and appear to have been firmly established in the sixteenth century. During the 1555 reforms the seal-holding officials in each subprefecture and district were ordered to personally supervise the *li*-registrars in compiling a register of the land and tax of each household, and they were also ordered no longer to distribute trifling amounts of tax between the households.[13]

The importance of the *li*-registrars is perhaps best illustrated by an incident described in the «Tablet for Good Government» written by Li Kaixian for the magistrate of Binzhou Subprefecture in 1546, Ji Depu. Li Kaixian first describes how the corvée in Shandong was very heavy and how the people involved in the assessment cheated for their own benefit. One of the problems as Li saw it was that as soon as a district official had managed to understand and improve the corvée assessment he would be transferred, so officials never really got a chance to master the situation in their districts. During the biennial assessment of the equal corvée in 1546 the provincial treasury considered the corvée in Binzhou districts to be particularly heavy. From Li's observations and the subsequent action this probably meant that the corvée was particularly heavy on the less wealthy households. The provincial administration issued an order for a particularly careful assessment of the equal corvée in Putai District, which was under the jurisdiction of Binzhou Subprefecture. Ji Depu went personally to Putai to assist with the assessment, but as he was not familiar with the district he found it difficult to get quick and reliable information. Under the pretext of doing other business he then travelled around the district and summoned the *li*-registrars to the pavilions. Without revealing his real intentions he then got the *li*-registrars to report on property and persons within their *lijia*. The *li*-registrars 'did not conceal their feelings' - that is, they were not suspicious – and freely reported the facts. Their reports were subsequently recorded in the registers, and when the official assessment was later undertaken this information was used and malpractices eradicated.[14]

A story like this, reported in a laudatory essay for a meritorious official, probably gives too much credit to his achievements. We must of course doubt whether the *li*-registrars unsuspiciously revealed all facts and that the information obtained by Ji was accurate. However the figures for property and persons given to him were probably sufficiently at variance with those in the previous equal corvée registers to warrant the claim that he had achieved a fairer assessment. For our purpose here, it is more significant to see that Ji Depu knew which kind of persons he had to contact in order to get the information he wanted. His action furthermore proves that the position of the *li*-registrars was of a permanent nature, as 1546 was almost half way between two compilations of the Yellow Registers in 1542 and 1552.

The sources give no information about the recruiting of the *li*-registrars, and the only indication that they received any remuneration for their work is that the tax-assessing *shushou* in Zhangqiu were assessed at ten taels per year, and we cannot be sure that this applied during the period. If they did not receive a formal salary, they were definitely able to compensate themselves for their efforts by informal or illegal means. They received bribes from people who wanted favours in the assessment of taxes and corvée, and worked in collusion with rich families to contrive tax frauds.[15] The *li*-registrars in turn bribed dishonest officials and other government personnel, and one of the reasons for the introduction of the Single Whip after 1555 was to stop such malpractices.[16] With the elimination of the granary rates the opportunities for the *li*-registrars to make manipulations were dimished. However, no attempts to abolish the service of the *li*-registrars were apparently made during the period, and they are still reported in 1571, when they were involved in the assessment of stabling services together with the *shipai*.[17]

3. The *zhishi* and *zongcui*

In Zhangqiu District the officeholders in the *lijia* are listed in the 1596 gazetteer as *li*-leader and *laoren* serving in each *lijia* (*tu*), while in each *jia* there were also one *zongcui* and one *zhishi*. The *zongcui* was responsible for the distribution of tax bills and for pressing taxes. As this function appears to be identical with the one assigned to the *shipai*, the *zongcui* may be another word for the non-incumbent *li*-leaders, but this is not certain.

The *zhishi* in each *jia* were responsible for the 'purification' of the soldiers in the hereditary military households. This work would have included supervising the military households and registers, sending soldiers off to their service, and perhaps also reporting on deserters passing through or temporarily living in the *jia*. The district gazetteer states that the number of military households was very high in Zhangqiu in relation to the number of civilian households. In previous registers the military households had numbered over 10,000 and in the gazetteer compiled c. 1530 the total number of all households had been 13,170.[18] These figures provided in a very casual way are the only ones available for Zhangqiu, so it is impossible to say anything definite with regard to the size of the military population of the district. The relatively high proportion of military households in that part of the province is however evidenced in Zichuan District to the east of Zhangqiu, where, as has been seen in Chapter II, c. 25% of the households were registered as military in the sixteenth century.

Despite the fact that there were such large numbers of military households in some districts their administration is virtually not mentioned in the gazetteers. This is perhaps because the military households had to some extent lost their earlier significance as the mainstay of the military forces. They were, however, still sufficiently important to be mentioned in a memorandum concerning military administration, and particularly the problems involved in raising troops, written by the magistrate of Lingxian District between 1550 and 1553. He stated that it was important to be careful with the examination of the *lijia* registers in order to keep track of the military *ding* for the service. He implied that this had not been done, and that consequently it was difficult to raise the necessary troops. This memorandum was probably written in connection with the compilation of the Yellow Registers in 1552, which shows that in this magistrate's view these registers still had some useful function as an instrument for population control.[19]

No indication is given in Zhangqiu as to when the *zhishi* were introduced in that district. They appear to have been functioning at the time the gazetteer was compiled or at least not long before, since their description is followed by complaints that some troops had to serve each year and that the common people were unhappy about this. The cost of sending off a soldier could be as much as thirty to forty taels. The gazetteer implies that the households actually had to provide manpower for the army, but the cost figures given could mean that military households were only levied expenses and that the duty of the *zhishi* were mainly fiscal.

4. Elders, *zongjia, xiaojia* and *huofu*

For the non-fiscal duties in the *lijia*, the *li*-elders continued to serve to some degree in the districts of Shandong during the sixteenth century. In 1521 the *li*-elders were ordered to report on bandits in Deping District[20] and they are mentioned along with the *li*-leaders, *zongcui* and *zhishi* in the 1596 Zhangqiu gazetteer. Each *lijia* had one elder who was responsible for security at least in the sense of vouching (*baojie*) for the inhabitants of the *lijia*.[21]

One of the main functions of the elders had originally been to settle local disputes, thus relieving the bureaucracy of this burden. In this respect the elders appear to have lost their usefulness. In 1569 the magistrate of Binzhou, Wan Pengcheng, laid down regulations to be followed in litigation between the inhabitants of the subprefecture. He complained that small matters at issue between the common people dragged on excessively. The families involved suffered from this prolonged litigation, both losers and winners. But even worse, the innocent witnesses were under heavy economic strain when some cases could drag on for years. Wan now introduced a procedure whereby the families involved could avoid prolonged litigation by using Instruments of Conciliation (*yihedan*). If the contending families were prepared to draw up such a document and take it to the officials with a petition that the case be settled, then they could avoid having to present evidence. If they demonstrated sincerity the officials would then grant permission to close the case. Elders are not mentioned, and the need for such procedures shows that they were no longer active in a judicial role.[22] These procedures show that Wan did not consider any use of subbureaucratic government in settling legal disputes when he gave the initiative to the families involved. This, however, does not preclude assistance by community leaders in arranging such conciliation.

In the maintenance of public order the elders were assisted or superseded by the *zongjia, xiaojia* and night fire-watchers (*shangsu-*

huofu). Li Kaixian lists these latter services as one of his minor grievances against the existing corvée system. To grasp the details of his grievances is not easy from his description. However, it is clear that the *zongjia*, *xiaojia* and *huofu* were responsible for security against thieves and other miscreants. The services were, in Li's opinion, disliked by the people, so they attempted to evade them by guile. The *zongjia* conscripted from wealthy households had been used since the time of Zhao Zuoshan. Assuming that this man was magistrate of Zhangqiu District, he is probably to be identified with Zhao Ying who held this office from 1531 to 1534 and was the first in the Ming dynasty with this surname according to the 1596 gazetteer. About ten years later the magistrate was Zhao Jiefu, but according to the gazetteer Zhao Ying appears to have been the more active of the two.[23] Li Kaixian moreover writes that the system of *zongjia* was excellent when first introduced, which indicates that some time had elapsed between its introduction and his criticism. So the *zongjia* were probably introduced in the early 1530s, if not before by an unknown Zhao. The *zongjia* in Zhangqiu had to serve terms of three months, and the households designated to serve for a term used all the influence they could muster in order to evade it. The *huofu*, who may be identical with the *xiaojia*, had to serve once every few days.

Li Kaixian continued by describing the policies introduced by Wang Guosheng (H. Yeshan) when the latter was magistrate in Tangxian District of Beizhili around 1550.[24] Wang was a native of Zhangqiu and a *juren* in 1528, the same year as Li Kaixian,[25] who probably heard about these policies directly from Wang. Wang had abolished the *zongjia* and *huofu* in Tangxian, so it was no longer necessary to impose upon the wealthy households and burden the poor. These services had now been allocated among the townspeople and also among those performing corvée as *minzhuang* and *kuaishou*, which in Shandong were parts of the equal corvée.[26] From the description of Li Kaixian it appears that the services as *zongjia*, *xiaojia* and *huofu* were levied outside the normal and regulated equal corvée, and that the resentment of the people was more directed towards this irregularity than towards the services *per se*, or in other words the resentment was towards using the *lijia* to conscript additional services.

Elders are only referred to in a few instances in the gazetteers. In the *SDJHL* they are, however, mentioned several times in fiscal functions, so they must have been fairly widespread. The elders participated in the fiscal process as advisers to the officials in 1562 during the Single Whip reforms. *Li*-elders are specifically mentioned in this context but only together with more general groups such as the 'rural population' (*xiangmin*) or the 'people of the *lijia* and subdistricts', so whether or not

110

they enjoyed special status while advising the officials is open to doubt.[27] In 1563 it is stated that the division of the *men* into tax classes depended upon verbal reports from the *li*-elders. This must have been the case for a long time previously, as it was now recommended that registered land should be included in the assessment, which would then rely on written registers rather than oral reports. However, after the assessment was determined and checked according to the Yellow Registers, the *li*-elders were still invited to give their opinion.[28] In Binzhou Subprefecture the elders were even involved in the pressing of taxes and there is no reason to believe that this was exceptional.[29]

The fiscal work of the elders even went as far in some cases as using them for services normally provided through the equal corvée. In 1563 the doormen (*menzi*) were abolished at certains altars and pavilions in the provincial administration and also in the districts. These services had been performed by elders and local people, and it is possible that these particular services were regarded as carrying some honour so the use of elders was appropriate.[30] However the doormen at the office of the regional inspector were aboslihed in 1559, and the premises were then attended by elders.[31] The same happened in the Yizhou Military Defence Circuit in 1561, where they shared the duty with the *zongjia*.[32] Such developments can only mean that the social prestige of the elders was no longer the same as in the early years of the dynasty; at least the administration, by using them directly in fiscal work, did not act in a way that added support to the non-fiscal duties of the elders. In the case of their use as doormen it is possible that the elders themselves wanted such positions because they were able to benefit from them, but then the mere acceptance by the officials of such a thing indicates the administration's attitude towards the elders.

THE *LIJIA* IN THE FISCAL SYSTEM

1. The *lijia* and fiscal administration

From the previous description of the *li*-registrars it can be seen that the *lijia* was still during this period regarded as an important organization for assessment of taxes and corvée. The recurrent claim that the *li*-registrars exploited their position for their own benefit further suggests that the regulations allowed them a certain degree of discretion in determining taxes and corvée within their *lijia*. At the same time they were supervised by officials, as evidenced by the fact that the *li*-registrars bribed them to turn a blind eye to tampering with the registers.[33]

No description of the procedures for the daily supervision of the *li*-

registrars has been found. In 1544 the horse administration was changed in Zhangqiu District from levy on *ding* to levy on *men*. When this reform was extended to other districts in the province, the officials in the twenty-five districts concerned subpoenaed the *li*-registrars and *shipai* together with registers for the equal corvée and for the households who had previously been responsible for the delivery of horses to the district offices in order to make a fair assessment.[34] This was a special occasion, as was Ji Depu's action in Binzhou Subprefecture. Together these examples indicate that the administration had the capacity to undertake major re-assessments and also thought that useful results could be obtained. At the same time they indicate that daily supervision was less thorough, which of course does not preclude the possibility that the *li*-registrars were individually in regular contact with the officials.

The *lijia* continued to play an important role in the registration of the taxpayers. During the deliberations for the introduction of the Single Whip in 1555, the prefectural officials proposed that the seal-holding officials in subprefectures and districts should be ordered to establish registers for each *lijia*. They were to order one wealthy household (*fuhu*) with a good knowledge of local conditions to go to each household and check it carefully. Each *lijia* was to compile a register (*shouce*) in which the summer and autumn taxes and the number of *ding* would be clearly stated for each person and each plot of land. The registers, which were to be compiled every ten years, would then be sent to the subprefecture or district to be stamped with the official seals, and copies were to be made for granaries and treasuries. The registers were then to be sent to the prefecture.[35]

In the governor's order of 1555 this procedure was changed. He ordered the officials in subprefectures and districts personally to supervise that the *li*-registrars prepared the registers with figures for land and tax for each taxpaying household. In the yamen the officials were then to enter this information in two registers, one for retained and one for transferred revenue. These registers were then to be issued to the *dahu* as tax-collecting registers (*chili*). A tax bill was to be issued to each household, which would at the appropriate time take this bill together with the tax to the *dahu*, who in turn would match it against his *chili*. The subprefectures and districts were also to compile registers of all the taxpayers and send them to the prefecture. From these registers the prefecture was to extract information on taxation and print this on a proclamation which would be posted in each village, so that the taxpayers could know their tax commutation rates. The intention was to diminish the reliance of the taxpayers on the *li*-registrars and to make cheating by the latter more difficult.[36]

112

The difference between what was proposed and what was finally ordered may have some importance. The governor's order seems to require the involvement of local officials even at the primary level of compilation of the registers in the *lijia*. The original proposal does not mention the *li*-registrars, which could indicate that the prefectural officials did not want them to be the main agents in the compilation, or at least that they wanted them to be scrutinized carefully by wealthy households. According to the regulations, we would normally expect a wealthy household in a *lijia* to be either *li*-leader or *shipai*. The fact that these households were not part of the formal *lijia* structure may indicate that the officials putting forward this original proposal held the opinion that the households with wealth and power in most *lijia* were not identical to those registered in the upper tax classes from which the *shipai* were selected. In other words these wealthy households had themselves cheated considerably with their registration, and the officials knew this. However the officials may have preferred to use the wealthy households in this informal way, as they probably had very little chance of preventing them from cheating no matter what was done. The wealthy households were perhaps in a better position to give a reasonable assessment of all households in the *lijia* than were the *li*-leaders and *li*-registrars, and at the same time they could safeguard their own position. To the local officials this may have been an acceptable compromise. On the other hand, the governor appears to have preferred to rely on the *li*-registrars but at the same time also set up procedures to prevent some of the cheating. We should of course bear in mind that the Single Whip was among other things designed to diminish the cheating of the *li*-registrars.

The original proposal and the governor's order also differ in that the latter does not mention the use of the *lijia* in guiding the taxpayers to the tax chest, but this may be because the governor's order does not elaborate on the procedures to be followed at the chests. The proposal that the *dahu* should order the *li*-leaders to ensure that the *shipai* guided their households to the chest was repeated in the order by Governor Jiang Tingyi of 1569. He ordered that *dahu* were to be selected together with households from the upper tax classes which were to be heads of the tax chests. The seal-holding officials supervising the tax administration would prescribe the time-limits for the different procedures in collection and forwarding. The *shipai* would be supervised, presumably by the heads of the chests, and they would in turn ensure that the taxpayers delivered their tax in person at the granary. The order does not specify which granary, but it must have been one of the local granaries within the district. These granaries then operated as tax chests. Tax was to be paid three times during the year. One time was presumably the summer tax to be paid from the fifth to the seventh month, the other the autumn tax to be paid from the tenth to the twelfth month, and the third may have been the collection of the horse-fodder tax, but no clarification is given. When all three taxes had been received, the *dahu* would draw lots for the granaries to which the tax had to be delivered, and they would then forward it separately.[37] As in Binzhou, the reason for drawing lots was probably to prevent the *li*-registrars from profiting from the allotment of granaries to the *dahu*.[38]

Dongchang Prefecture reported in the same year that 'separate collection and separate forwarding' was still operating in that prefecture. The provincial administration allowed Dongchang to continue this procedure, since the land was level and taxes were easy to collect without excessive fraud. The administration also allowed a certain flexibility in other parts of the province but expressed concern that with 'separate collection and separate forwarding' the *lijia* was too heavily involved in tax collection. In some cases all tax was collected within the *lijia* and only on the last day handed over to the *dahu* for forwarding. Under these circumstances the *shipai* could keep some of the collected tax for themselves, to the disadvantage both of the taxpayers and the *dahu*, so the administration preferred 'combined collection and separate forwarding' where the *shipai* did not touch the tax payments before they were handed over to the *dahu*.[39]

The Yellow Registers were still compiled in the province and are mentioned in 1571 as the basis for the organization of the *lijia*.[40] There is, however, good reason to doubt whether they contained accurate descriptions of the conditions in the province, because the governor in 1555 ordered other registers to be compiled in the *lijia* every ten years. Probably the Yellow Registers did not play a significant role in the allocation of taxes and corvée, but they are mentioned in 1563 in connection with the Single Whip. In that year it was decided that in parts of Yanzhou and Dongchang Prefectures the corvée could be levied according to *ding* and land, as the land was predominantly spacious and level, so satisfactory results could be expected. In neighbouring districts in both Nanzhili and Beizhili a land remeasurement had equalized taxes and corvée levied on *ding* and land. This had been made easier by the appointment of capable officials. The same policy could be adopted in parts of Yanzhou and Dongchang, while in other parts of the province where the conditions were different it was considered better not to levy corvée on land but to continue levy on the basis of tax classes. The districts in Yanzhou and Dongchang did not want to levy corvée entirely on land, or for that matter entirely on *ding* or other assets, as each method could create inequalities, so they were allowed to organize the

114

tax classes according to land, *ding*, and other assets. When the assessments had been made, they were to be compared with the Yellow Registers and the opinion of the *li*-elders was to be heard.[41] The reference to the Yellow Registers may be because they had been compiled the previous year so they were fresh in the memory. The officials may also have felt that the Yellow Registers had some usefulness shortly after they had been compiled. However, they were only to be consulted after the assessment had been made, presumably according to the equal corvée and other available registers.

2. The *lijia* and the equal corvée

The general impression we get of the levy of equal corvée in the sixteenth century is that the allocation of the services was done on the basis of the wealth of individual households, and not by dividing all the services in a district with the number of *lijia* and then levying the same amount on each *lijia*. However, the number of *lijia* in a district could be used to determine the level of certain services levied upon it. In 1563 it is reported that the material money supplied to ministries in the capital had originally been levied on the equal corvée of the districts according to their number of *lijia*. This was no longer appropriate, because the number of *lijia* no longer corresponded to the actual situation in the districts after many households had absconded. The solution was to transfer the levy of material money from equal corvée to land.[42] Another instance of levy according to the number of *lijia* is mentioned in 1553. In determining the number of wall-defending militiamen (*shoucheng-minzhuang*), the frequency of official travel and the number of the *lijia* in the district had to be taken into consideration.[43] This may be a special case, since in other parts of the country the *minzhuang* services were often conscripted from the *lijia*. In 1569 the military circuit intendant in Caopu Defence Circuit proposed that the *minzhuang* and *kuaishou* were to be fully supported by their respective *lijia*, i.e. all the households that through equal corvée levies supported a given man were to live in the same *lijia*, so that they knew each other. In this way all the money levied for the service of each given man would be easier to collect.[44]

As stated in the previous chapter, items of corvée which were normally regarded as part of the *lijia* contributions were in Shandong included in the equal corvée. During the period under review there are instances of this change but the opposite also happened. Moreover the *lijia* was used to levy services included in equal corvée when the levies were increased between the biennial assessments. This happened for the material money in 1552, 1555 and 1557.[45]

Services as treasury men (*kuzi*) at the subprefectural and district treasuries were in 1570 changed from labour to silver corvée to be levied on the ninth tax class. The people hired for this service were only to guard the treasuries, while reception and disbursement were to be in the hands of a person performing corvée in the yamen or a rich and honest peasant. Dezhou petitioned to be allowed for the *kuzi* watchmen first to conscript from the No. 1 *jia* in each *lijia* twelve men from households with comparable strength in *ding*, so that one man served one month in rotation. This presumably meant that the following year twelve men from No. 2 *jia* would serve in rotation, and so on in a way that would resemble the corvée to be levied on the *lijia*. The proposal was not accepted by the provincial administration.[46]

In 1569 a discussion took place whether or not 'public-use silver' (*gongyongyin*) should be levied on the *lijia* instead of on equal corvée. This silver was used to cover expenses in the offices of the various yamens and expenses in connection with travelling officials, such as banquets etc. A decision had been made to transfer the *gongyong* silver for use in subprefectures and districts to be levied on the *lijia* and together with *gongyong* silver already levied on the *lijia* rename it 'contribution silver' (*gongyingyin*). *Gongyong* silver for prefectures was abolished as a separate account, and the silver for provincial offices was still to be levied on equal corvée. Governor Jiang Tingyi did not like the decision. He argued that the transfer would of course be beneficial to the equal corvée as the levy was reduced. However, in the equal corvée the burden was each year divided upon the ten *pai*, that is the ten *jia* of the *lijia*, while a levy on the *lijia* would mean that the gongyong silver was only levied on one *pai* (*jia*). He suggested that the *gongyong* silver should still be collected through the equal corvée, but the decision was not reversed.[47] In 1570 the *gongying* silver was still levied on the *lijia* and the *gongyong* silver on the equal corvée.[48]

Yanzhou and Dongchang Prefectures reported in 1567 that in many districts the salaries for clerks in the circuit yamens (*shushou*) and the *kuaishou* (yamen police) were levied on the *lijia*. This was done because there was apparently no other authorized way of providing the money. The provincial administration then decided that the salaries for the clerks were to be paid from local treasuries and from fines received by provincial and circuit administrations. The *kuaishou* were to be incorporated in the equal corvée and their number determined according to local conditions. At the same time there had been some complaints that the *lijia* had to provide the prefectural officials in charge of punishments with their necessary equipment. This was now to be paid

116

from fines received by subprefectures and districts.[49]

As a direct consequence of the above irregularities the provincial administration ordered that one register had to be printed with the regulations for equal corvée and one with the regulations for *lijia* corvée. The equal corvée was to be performed annually, those of the *lijia* in rotation. No levy was permitted of corvée not included in these registers. If such levies took place they were to be regarded as extortion and were to be punished without mercy.[50]

THE *LIJIA* CORVÉE

1. The corvée performed by the *lijia*

In the sources for Shandong for the period 1550–1570 no mention has been found of the terms *shanggong* or *gongfei*, which I have previously translated as 'lijia contributions'. The services performed by the *lijia* were not different in nature from other corvée, as had probably been the case earlier in the dynasty. The only difference now was the method of levy where the *lijia* were collected decennially and the equal corvée annually. This at least was the difference seen by Jiang Tingyi in 1569. As an indication that the nature of the services was no longer significant, I have chosen in this chapter to rename the *lijia* contributions 'lijia corvée'.

The *lijia* corvée listed in the *SDJHL* was heavily directed towards services in the public transport system. The heaviest services were the *qingfu* (blue-men) and *baifu* (white-men) who assisted in the postal or transport system. Their exact duties and the difference between them are not described during this period, but a reform in Binzhou in c. 1582 may give an indication. The *qingfu* were after this reform to transmit public documents and escort prisoners, while the *baifu* attended to the transport duties when official travellers arrived and left the subprefecture.[51] These titles were unique for Shandong Province, but similar services existed in other provinces under other designations.[52] Other *lijia* corvée that were levied in 1571 were lamp-men (*dengfu*), prisoner escorts and messengers (*jieren-jisonggongwen-fu*), prison warders (*shangsu-kanjianfu*), transport horses and mules, and horse-men (*zoudi-maluo* and *mafu*), 'bedding (*puchen*) and public-contribution silver (*gongyingyin*). Some other corvée items which were still demanded from the *lijia* but no longer levied separately are listed together with the above items. These were the sedan-chair men (*jiaofu*), key-holders (*tisuofu*), treasury watchmen (*kanku*), *jia*-head runners (*jiashou-zaoli*) and drummers (*zhonggufu*).

For *lijia* corvée the districts in Shandong were divided into five grades according to their geographical position in relation to official travel routes. The grades were I (*shangchong*), II (*cichong*), III (*xiachong*), Zero A (*shangdeng-buchong*) and Zero B (*cideng-buchong*). In Jinan Prefecture Grade I districts were Licheng, the provincial capital, and Dezhou, the northernmost subprefecture in the province on the trunk road from Peking to the south. Grade II districts were Pingyuan, Yucheng, Qihe, Changqing, and Feicheng on the trunk road, and Taian Subprefecture in the south of the province. Grade III districts were Zhangqiu, Zouping, and Changshan on the road east from the provincial capital, and Linyi and Jiyang on the road from Pingyuan to Zhangqiu, which provided a shortcut from the eastern prefectures in the province to Peking bypassing Licheng. Wuding Subprefecture, which must have been a centre for the northeastern districts, was also Grade III. Grade Zero A districts were scattered mostly around the northern and eastern part of the prefecture. They were all levied exactly the same amount of *lijia* corvée in 1571. Grade Zero B districts were Laiwu and Xintai in the southern mountainous area, and Lingxian southeast of Dezhou. These three districts had previously together with Linyi been regarded as a special category of Grade III districts.[53] Linyi District had now been upgraded to regular Grade III while the other three were downgraded. If they had been included in the Zero A grade their *lijia* corvée would have been reduced by several hundred taels and that was apparently not acceptable, so a special category was created in Grade Zero.[54]

2. Administration of *lijia* corvée

The list of *lijia* corvée in the *SDJHL* gives the impression that these services were well arranged on an orderly basis and incorporated in the overall fiscal system. The regulations had on the provincial level only started in 1566, but the problems of the *lijia* corvée had attracted official attention before then. In the years 1536 to 1547 the governors held deliberations together with the regional inspectors and provincial and circuit officials in order to find ways to regulate the *lijia* corvée. Some officials stated that the frauds of the *shipai* were excessive, and they considered remedying this by collecting silver. This was not however possible, because many households in the three lower tax-classes preferred to continue to perform the corvée in the form of labour instead of paying silver. Others proposed the *lijia* corvée to be distributed equally upon the *lijia* according to an evaluation of their respective strength. This proposal met with sympathy and may have been applied in

118

some districts, but in the end it was recommended that no fixed regulations should be adopted, since circumstances differed from district to district.[55]

Some of these differences are described in the introductory remarks to the *yinge* section of the *SDJHL*. The *lijia* were organized in *jia* according to the Yellow Registers. Each *jia* served one year in rotation. One method of levying the corvée was that all the *ding* in a subprefecture or district were calculated according to their tax class and silver collected from them. Other methods were the levy of *lijia* corvée according to the ten-part-tapestry (*shiduanjin*) method, levy according to tax classes, and finally levy on the incumbent *jia* serving in rotation.[56]

The ten-part-tapestry method is usually connected with the levy of equal corvée in parts of the empire where this corvée was levied in a ten-year rotation. In these areas landholding weighed relatively heavy in the assessment of the equal corvée. Illegal use of privileged exemption and other property manipulations caused inequalities in equal corvée assessment between the *jia* within a *lijia* or between the *lijia* themselves to be so pronounced that corrective measures had to be taken. One measure was the ten-part method (*shiduanfa*) in which all land in a district was divided into ten parts of equal size, in some cases with the *ding* converted to *mou* as well, and the equal corvée was then levied each year upon one of these parts. Another measure was the ten-part-tapestry method. The land (and perhaps converted *ding*) of each *jia* in a *lijia* was calculated. If the *jia* were then of different size, then this method allowed the deferment of corvée levy on some of the land in the stronger *jia*, so that the levy could be made on this land in the years when the weaker *jia* had to provide the equal corvée.[57]

The main feature of the ten-part and ten-part-tapestry methods was the strong emphasis upon the levy of corvée on land. It is unlikely that this was generallly adopted in Shandong for the *lijia* corvée, but some development in that direction cannot of course be completely excluded. The other aspect of the ten-part-tapestry method is the flexibility between the *jia* within the *lijia*. The use of the ten-part-tapestry method for the *lijia* corvée in Shandong Province would then imply that the weaker *jia* were aided by the stronger *jia* while the latter could not claim to have performed all their *lijia* corvée during their year of incumbency.

The use of a ten-part-tapestry method must mean that the *lijia* corvée was levied in a ten-year rotation. The same thing happened where the corvée was levied from the incumbent *jia*. The levies on *ding* graded according to *men* and on tax classes could indicate that the *lijia* corvée in districts where such policies were adopted was levied each year. If this was the case, it cannot have been widespread, since we have seen that the officials assumed that *lijia* corvée was levied in ten-year rotations. The allocation of the *lijia* corvée according to *ding* or tax classes can mean that such criteria were used for the allocation of the corvée between the *lijia* within each district, as had been approved, but not enforced, during the deliberations from 1536 to 1547. If this interpretation is correct, then the *jia* still served in rotation, but their burden was adjusted to their strength. This could further mean that such adjustments had not been made in the districts where the old system of the *jia* serving in rotation was still reported.

3. Problems with the *lijia* corvée

The *lijia* corvée imposed a heavy burden upon the population because even if some regulations already existed in the districts before the provincial regulations began in 1566, they were not enforced. The energy of the people was 'wasted', to a constantly increasing extent.[58] The problem of the *lijia* corvée is described most vividly by Li Kaixian. According to him, the statutory amount for the *gongyong* silver was in Zhangqiu District 200 taels in 1560. However, many miscellaneous expenses were levid upon the *lijia*, so the total amount exceeded 10,000 taels.[59] These expenses could be supplementary salaries to officials and lesser functionaries (*guanli-zhefeng*), winter clothes for orphans and old people, utensils for officials arriving to take up their posts, travelling expenses for officials from the Ministry of War who were assessing the levy of horses, expenses for offices and ceremonies, repair of buildings, etc. In one year a *lijia* could pay as much as 200–300 taels, and in the year before he was writing private persons had paid 700 taels. The people were ruined under such circumstances, and there was an urgent need to regulate the situation.[60]

Zhangqiu was on the main road from the provincial capital to the eastern prefectures, and this created special problems in the district. According to Li, it happened all too often that an official announced that he planned to arrive in Zhangqiu at a certain time and then when the time came did not arrive with his entourage. At the time for his scheduled arrival the bells in the district town began to ring, officials and other people in the district dressed up especially for his benefit and provisions for his travel were prepared. When he did not arrive the bells could go on ringing for days and nights, and all the preparations had to be made over again. The burden of this fell upon the *lijia*. To avoid such situations one person was stationed in the provincial capital and one at the Longshan postal station between that city and Zhangqiu. These men reported back when officials started their journey from Licheng, so that the officials in

Zhangqiu knew exactly when they had to be prepared. This was considered cheaper, but the expenses to keep the two persons stationed on the road still had to be paid by the *lijia*. Once the official arrived, lavish banquets were provided and precious gifts were presented to please him, even if he was not very important, and the *lijia* had to pay for this as well as catering for his entourage. To charge such expenses to the *lijia* was illegal,[61] and according to Li such prodigality had only started within the previous ten years.[62]

The *lijia* in Zhangqiu were further disadvantaged, since no reorganization had been undertaken according to changes in population such as the ones in districts like Xintai, Jiyang and Zhucheng. In some *lijia* in Zhangqiu there were only two to five *shipai*. Li therefore proposed to amalgamate the *lijia*, so that their number would be reduced by about one-half. It is interesting to note that Li mentioned only the *shipai* as an indication of the size of the *lijia*. He had said immediately before this statement that the statutory number of households in the *lijia* was 110. This may suggest that in the *lijia* only the *shipai* were of real importance, and that there could be any number of households at the level of *jia*-head even if only 100 of these had to be enrolled in the Yellow Registers.[63]

For details of the *lijia* corvée such as those given above Li Kaixian is our only source during this period. However, his statements should not be accepted uncritically. Many of his grievances are undoubtedly well-founded, such as the different items charged upon the *lijia* and at least some of his observations concerning the number of households in the *lijia*. This situation was widespread and would have been fairly common knowledge and easy to authenticate. But with regard to the figures for the levies of the different services he may not be so reliable. He was complaining about the plight of the people, i.e. the taxpayers. However throughout his writings on the conditions in Zhangqiu he made references to other districts, so he was really complaining about the plight of the taxpayers in Zhangqiu, and he appears to advocate that at least some of the excessive burdens should be shifted to other districts. With this aim in mind he may have greatly exaggerated his figures.

To alleviate the plight of the *lijia*, Li Kaixian suggested that some of the money could be obtained from transactions at the markets. Unregistered people who indulged in drinking and gambling were in charge of weighing at the markets (*douchenghu*), and in large markets they could receive as much as 3,000–5,000 *wen* and in smaller markets several hundreds. He suggested that one wealthy and honest elder should be selected together with one man from each *lijia*. The latter were to supervise the transactions at the market, collect the money and bring it to the elder, who was to be stationed in a pavilion. The elder was to keep records of the receipts for every item day by day and at the end of the month the seal-holding official was to audit these records. If the collection was not adequate to cover the cost of the *lijia* corvée, then the balance was to be collected from the *lijia*.[64]

We have no evidence to show that Li's proposal was adopted, but the idea of a commercial tax to pay for the *lijia* corvée was kept alive. In 1568 the magistrate in Putai District petitioned that the amount in excess of twenty taels of the tax on shop-signs should be used together with a salt tax to pay the *gongyong* silver of the *lijia* corvée. This petition may have been approved, since it is included in the 1592 gazetteer under the tax section. However, probably only small amounts were involved, as the tax was 0.001 tael per shop-sign and 0.002 tael per *yin* of salt.[65]

4. Regulation and commutation of *lijia* corvée

Regulation of the *lijia* corvée began in 1566, when this was proposed by the general administration circuit intendant in Jinan, Zhou Shiyuan, together with other officials. As was seen in Zhangqiu, some of the *lijia* corvée had already been commuted to silver payments or at least calculated in silver. This development towards commutation continued after 1566. The provincial administration promoted this policy in order to reduce the burdens on the people. However, commutation and regulation apparently met with some resistance. The source states that 'the feelings of the people are governed by ancient principles', which can mean that in the eyes of the officials the people resented any changes. In this specific case, however, changes in the levies would have disturbed the balance between households, and until such a balance had been restored under the new regulations a certain uneasiness would probably have been common among the taxpayers. The attitude of the people was apparently unable to prevent a unanimous feeling among the officials in the province that reforms were necessary.[66]

The corvée services continued to be levied upon the *lijia*, and their number in each subprefecture and district was determined in 1566 together with their degree of commutation. The *qingfu* and *baifu* in Licheng District had to perform corvée entirely in the form of labour. In the other Grade I subprefecture, Dezhou, the services were levied in equal corvée, probably because their number was very high there. In Grades II and III in Jinan the *qingfu* and *baifu* performed corvée two-thirds in the form of labour and one-third in silver, while in Grade Zero they were all to perform it as labour. Sedan-chair men for the officials were no longer to be conscripted separately but were selected among the *baifu*. Lamp-men were completely commuted, the rate being 0.45 tael per month. The lamp-men levy in Licheng District was particularly high but also in Dezhou where the officials often worked at night. Key-holders were to be levied at one tael per month on wealthy *li*-leaders, while the *jia*-head watchmen (*kanjian-jiashou*) were commuted at 0.6 tael per month. Treasury watchmen were to be taken from the wall-defending *minzhuang* and the key-holders, while the *jia*-head runners were selected from the key-holders and the *qingfu*. Drummers were levied at 0.8 tael per month, and the 'public-use silver' was of course also commuted as were the *lijia* horses in Grade Zero districts, while in Grades I–III two-thirds were provided in kind and one-third was commuted. 'Bedding' to be provided for travellers was not levied in districts with postal stations, but in the other districts this was all to be provided in kind, its quantity depending upon the grade of the district.[67]

In 1569 Governor Jiang Tingyi introduced further regulations for the *lijia* corvée. All items were now listed in silver except perhaps the 'bedding', where only the wages to be paid to attendants were commuted, while the provision of materials was apparently still made in kind. At the same time the governor reduced some of the levies in the districts. The commutation rates for *qingfu* were set at 0.7 tael per month in Grades I, II and III districts, and at 0.6 tael in Grade Zero. The *baifu* were commuted at 1.05 taels per month in Grades I, II and III, and at one tael in Grade Zero (and also in Licheng District). Both *qingfu* and *baifu* were to perform half of the service as labour and half in silver. Jiang Tingyi stated that this was the same as had previously been the case, so there may have been a change in this respect since 1566.

The sedan-chair men were still to be taken from the *baifu*. The lamp-men were conscripted with a certain number for each official, and in addition there was to be a reserve on stand-by to attend superior officials travelling through the district. The payment was 0.4 tael in Grades I, II and III districts, and 0.3 tael in Grade Zero. Prison escort and messengers, treasury watch-men and *jia*-head watch-men, who had hitherto been levied among the *jia*-heads, were to be abolished, as were the key-holders, the *jia*-head runners and the drummers. The *lijia* horses were commuted at 24 taels in Grade I districts and 22 taels in all other districts. The money was paid annually to the officials, who would then have to buy and maintain the horse. The commutation for the *lijia* mules was at 22 and 20 taels; similar rules applied to donkeys, but they were not levied in Jinan Prefecture.

Apart from minor adjustments in the levied amounts, no changes were made to the public-use silver. For the 'bedding, there appear to have been considerable reductions, as only one-half of the money for wages was to be collected and apparently there was also a reduction in the number of beds to be provided. 'Bedding' was to be administered by the lesser functionaries in the Military and Treasury Bureau in the local yamen, which could indicate that they were situated in the vicinity of the yamen in or around the district towns. If there were changes in the *lijia*, the seal-holding official would personally arrange them; the two lesser functionaries would certify the changes and all would be entered in the appropriate registers.[68]

Most of the 1569 regulations were still in force in 1571, but minor adjustments had to be made. The *qingfu* and *baifu* in Grades I, II and III districts were to be levied in a way that resembles labour corvée. Silver was no longer to be collected for the district treasury to hire people. Instead a list was drawn up with the order in which the people (or perhaps the *lijia*) had to serve. The commutation rates were the same as in 1569, but they must now have been only for the valuation of the corvée, which was now called 'actual corvée' (*shiyi*). In Grade Zero districts where these services were only required at irregular intervals, the districts were not allowed to collect silver each month. The names of the people to serve were also registered and they were then summoned when their service was required, and at least for the *qingfu* they could then each be required to report for duty with two helpers.[69]

Some kind of labour corvée was also introduced for the prisoner escorts and messengers and the key-holders. They had been abolished by Jiang Tingyi because they had a bad reputation. Their duty was to escort prisoners, but when there was no such work they were used for minor administrative work, in which they often did harm to the people by tampering with property. After their abolition the escort service had been performed by the *qingfu* in rotation, but then there were not enough of these for transport work. In 1571 the solution was to designate ten *lijia* runners in each district as prisoner escorts and messengers to perform these duties in the form of labour, and they were listed in a separate account in the *SDJHL*.[70]

At some unspecified time before 1571 the *qingfu* and *baifu* in Licheng district had been transferred from the *lijia* to equal corvée, as was the case in Dezhou. The reason was that the number of these services levied in Licheng was relatively high, and it had not been possible to collect all the silver. When the change was made to equal corvée, these services had been levied upon *ding* at 0.9 tael per year in the first tax-class, declining to 0.1 tael in the ninth tax-class. The total collection had then been 4,670 taels per annum, but the expenses for the *qingfu* and *baifu* had only been 3,600 taels. Even if not all the silver was collected after the

124

transfer to the equal corvée, as some households had absconded, there was still a surplus and this had been pocketed by the people who collected it. To avoid this the levy of *qingfu* and *baifu* in Licheng was in 1571 re-transferred to the *lijia*. The people would then only have to serve once every ten years and would have plenty of time to recover from the service.[71]

The prisoner escorts and messengers, and the *jia*-head watch-men acting as gaolers, who had all been abolished in 1569, were reintroduced in 1571 and were levied upon the *jia*-heads. If some districts did not need all the messengers, they were allowed to reduce the number at their own discretion. For the lamp-men, each official was allowed a certain number, and the money for those not serving constantly with one of the officials was to be collected each month. When the local officials went out on inspection and needed additional lamp-men, this money was to be used to hire additional people. The same happened when superior officials arrived, and if the funds in this account were insufficient, then the local officials were to lend one of their own lamp-men to serve temporarily, since it was not allowed to make additional levies upon the *lijia* on such occasions.[72]

The silver for the *lijia* corvée in 1571 was to be levied at 70% on *ding* and 30% on land. This had already been in operation for some unspecified time but presumably only for a few years following the general trend to levy corvée on land since the 1550s. A certain amount of silver was to be collected from each *mou* of land and each *ding*. Tax bills (*youtie*) were issued to the households, and the people who did so and collected the silver had to explain the levies in simple terms, so that the common people were able to understand them. The payments were to be divided into four seasons, from each tael 0.25 tael would be collected in each season to make it easier for the less wealthy to pay. The *li*-leaders belonging to the upper tax-classes would collect the silver, but they were to have no part in its disbursement. Two wealthy elders with a good reputation for honesty were to be selected together with a lesser functionary with a clear handwriting. They were to draw up two registers and between them to arrange the disbursement of the *lijia* silver. The district officials were to verify these registers, stamp the seal and sign them. The elders only had to serve for one-half year. At the end of the summer two other elders were to be selected to serve in autumn and winter, but the elders could only be replaced after a full year. The reason for this was probably that the accounts for the whole year in which these elders had served had to be settled and possible irregularities during their term of office investigated before they could be completely relieved of their responsibility. On the other hand, a rotation between at least two pairs of elders was probably designed to prevent them from using their positions to embezzle money continuously over long periods. The *li*-leaders were only allowed to spend two mornings each month handling money and taxes (*qianliang*), and they were to devote the rest of their time to farming so they would not be exhausted economically.[73]

Linyi District reported in 1571 that it had received the regulations for the assessment of the *lijia* corvée, and that it would collect the silver for the *lijia* horses from the incumbent *jia* at 70% on *ding* and 30% on land.[74] The silver collected by the *li*-leaders was probably delivered to the district treasury and from there disbursed according to the registers mentioned above. The elders appear to have had only a supervisory role in disbursement, since it is stated a few times that the granary servants (*cangzu*) in the local treasuries used the treasury money to hire labour or horses to perform the *lijia* duties.[75]

A certain flexibility was allowed in the disbursement of the silver from the district treasury. Linyi District reported in 1571 that the *lijia* corvée of the *qingfu* and *baifu* was performed by fifteen men in rotation. If this number was not sufficient to carry out the transport duties, then silver had been taken from the account of the commuted *lijia* horse silver to hire additional labour. The problem in Linyi District was that in the years before 1571 traffic through the district had increased considerably, since travellers from the eastern prefectures who were entitled to use the public transport system took the short-cut through the district on their way to Peking and thus avoided the provinvial capital. The result of this report from Linyi District was that the combined number of *qingfu* and *baifu* was increased by four men and the number of horses and mules by two each, so that hiring of additional labour was no longer needed.[76] This of course indicates that such flexibility was not regarded by the provincial administration as a normal state of affairs. This is also seen in the previously mentioned case of the lamp-men, when the local officials had to lend their own lamp-men to serve superior officials instead of making extra levies on the *lijia* or, as would have been the alternative, instead of taking the silver from other accounts.

Commutation to silver payments of the *lijia* corvée was apparently generally accepted in 1571, although some services were still best performed in the form of labour. The objections made by the lower tax classes mentioned in the deliberations between 1536 and 1547 are not repeated. Problems were, however, reported in Pingyin District, Yanzhou Prefecture, just south of Changqing District. The *baifu* in the district had previously been levied on the *ding* in the incumbent *jia*. Four or five persons had jointly provided one man who had performed the service for one month. When his term of service was over, he returned to farming, and both the people and the officials had reported that this system was convenient. However, a few years before 1571 commutation of the *baifu* had been implemented, so that the silver needed for wages, 14.4 taels per year, was deposited in the district treasury to hire labour when the need arose. The district was Grade III, so there was not much traffic, and apparently urbanization was not very advanced, since the sources claim that most people lived in the countryside. When the granary servants offered silver to hire labour for the *baifu* service, they received no response. The collection of silver was moreover difficult, threats of flogging had to be applied, and both the people and officials claimed that this was harsh. The decision was then made to revert to the former system, so the people acted as *baifu* in a decennial rotation, 'without resentment'.[77]

From the point of view of economic development it is interesting to note that the people of Pingyin District could not be enticed to work for money at that time. This stands in sharp contrast to the situation in Shanghe District, which a little later reported that commutation of corvée was beneficial, since it gave jobs to vagrants, who competed to be the first to be hired.[78] The explanation for this difficulty in Pingyin District may be that the officials did not want to hire certain kinds of people to perform *baifu* services. They may have preferred people with a certain standing in the community, i.e. taxpayers who were registered and who could be punished if they did not perform the services properly. They may not have wanted to hire vagrants or other people over whom they had little control and whose integrity they may have had reason to doubt.

NOTES TO CHAPTER IV

1. *Pingyuan xianzhi* 1590/1/20; *Laiwu xianzhi* 1673/4/4.
2. *SDJHL* 7/12, 10/44.
3. *Painian lizhang* usually means the non-incumbent *li*-leaders but is also used for all the ten *li*-leaders serving in rotation. *Shipai* is obviously derived from the latter meaning and means the 'ten *painian*'. Littrup (Yellow Registers), p. 84.
4. *Laiwu xianzhi* 1673/4/4.
5. *Pingyuan xianzhi* 1590/1/20.
6. *Li Kaixian ji*, p. 711.
7. *Binzhou zhi* 1583/2/42, 1701/4/31.
8. *Zichuan xianzhi* 1602/13/1.
9. *SDJHL* 10/30.
10. *Binzhou zhi* 1583/2/50–51.
11. *Taian zhouzhi* 1671/2/8. Probably a verbatim quote from the 1603 edition.
12. *Zhangqiu xianzhi* 1596/12/69.
13. *SDJHL* 4/3, 6.

14. *Li Kaixian ji*, pp. 644–645.
15. *SDJHL* 4/8, 26.
16. *Ibid.* 4/7, 20.
17. *Ibid.* 12/45.
18. *Zhangqiu xianzhi* 1596/14/96 and the preface to the former gazetteer included in the 1596 edition.
19. *Lingxian zhi* 1845/16/23.
20. *Deping xianzhi* 1796/5/7.
21. *Zhangqiu xianzhi* 1596/14/96.
22. *Binzhou zhi* 1583/4/23.
23. *Zhangqiu xianzhi* 1596/14/24–25, 21/73.
24. *Baoding fuzhi* 1607/8/32. Eighteen magistrates followed him before 1607.
25. *Zhangqiu xianzhi* 1596/11/44–45.
26. *Li Kaixian ji*, p. 711.
27. *SDJHL* 4/9–11.
28. *Ibid.* 9/58–61.
29. *Binzhou zhi* 1583/2/41.
30. *SDJHL* 8/41.
31. *Ibid.* 8/15.
32. *Ibid.* 8/30.
33. *Ibid.* 4/7, 7/15.
34. *Ibid.* 12/45.
35. *Ibid.* 4/3–4.
36. *Ibid.* 4/6.
37. *Ibid.* 4/17.
38. *Binzhou zhi* 1583/4/22.
39. *SDJHL* 4/17–18.
40. *Ibid.* 10/33.
41. *Ibid.* 9/60–61.
42. *Ibid.* 8/37.
43. *Ibid.* 7/61.
44. *Ibid.* 9/6.
45. *Ibid.* 7/47, 7/80, 8/1.
46. *Ibid.* 9/12–13.
47. *Ibid.* 9/16–18.
48. *Ibid.* 5/1 ff., 10/1 ff.
49. *Ibid.* 8/59–63.
50. *Ibid.* 8/64–65.
51. *Binzhou zhi* 1583/2/50.
52. Yamane (1966), pp. 51–52.
53. *SDJHL* 10/34.
54. *Ibid.* 10/1 ff.
55. *Ibid.* 10/33–34.
56. *Ibid.* 10/33.
57. Yamane (1966), pp. 119–127; Friese, pp. 106–110; Huang, p. 117; *DMHD* 20/14.
58. *SDJHL* 10/34, 47.
59. He said that the amount 'is not limited to 10,000' which may mean a lot but not necessarily 10,000.
60. *Li Kaixian ji*, pp. 705–706.
61. *DMHD* 20/12.
62. *Li Kaixian ji*, p. 712.

63. *Ibid.*, p. 706.
64. *Ibid*, p. 706.
65. *Putai xianzhi* 1592/3/10.
66. *SDJHL* 10/47–48.
67. *Ibid.* 10/34–35.
68. *Ibid.* 10/42–47.
69. *Ibid.* 10/28–29.
70. *Ibid.* 10/52.
71. *Ibid.* 10/51.
72. *Ibid.* 10/28–30.
73. *Ibid.* 10/30.
74. *Ibid.* 10/49.
75. *Ibid.* 10/50.
76. *Ibid.* 10/49.
77. *Ibid.* 10/50.
78. *Shanghe xianzhi* 1586/3/6.

V. The later Single Whip and subbureaucratic government

INTRODUCTION

The Single Whip method of taxation was officially abolished in Shandong in 1570 after it had been applied in various degrees and probably with several variations between districts for about twenty years. The order was given by Governor Liang Menglong with the approval of the Ministry of Revenue.[1] In his order to return to the former taxation system Liang emphasized that the cultivated as well as the uncultivated land in each district was to be calculated. The acreage in each *she* was to be established and granary rates allotted for all households in the nine tax classes of each *she*. Tax collection registers for the *dahu* (*chili*) and tax bills for the households (*youtie*) were to be issued and, as seen in chapter III, the *lijia* were in some way to be the basis for the conscription of the *dahu*. The *she* and *lijia* were probably identical; the difference in terminology may have been to emphasize that taxes were to be collected on land and corvée only according to *ding* and households.[2]

There can be no doubt that the abolition of the early Single Whip was the policy of Liang Menglong and his provincial administration. To understand the reasons for the later reintroduction of the Single Whip in relation to the social and economic conditions of Shandong, it is however necessary to understand why Liang ordered the Single Whip to be abolished.

Liang Menglong was from Beizhili,[3] and as a northerner he may have had the same reservations towards the Single Whip as some people in Shandong, notably Ge Shouli. These reservations are illustrated by Ge in his preface to an appraisal of Liang when the latter was transferred from Shandong to the governorship of Henan. Ge quoted Liang as having said:

> The levy of corvée on land suits the needs of the south. To cure the illness of the north with the policies of the south may be compared to the similar situation with food and drink. It would be like asking the people to eat shrimps and clams each day. There would be few who would not fall sick.[4]

130

Although most of what is said by Ge Shouli about the Single Whip must be treated with caution because of his bias, there can be little doubt that Liang did at some time express such views. We must assume that what Ge wrote was for public consumption and must have been seen by Liang, so he could hardly have attributed false or misleading statements to Liang.

Liang apparently also sought the advice of Ge Shouli when he became governor of Shandong, as we have Ge's reply with which he enclosed copies of his 1567 memorial and a letter to Jiang Tingyi.[5] Liang cannot have been unaware of Ge's thoughts, so his own ideas at that time must have embraced an acceptance of the abolition or at least substantial modification of the Single Whip in the province. We must, however, also consider the political consequences of his association with Ge.

Ge Shouli had retired as Minister of Revenue only about one month after his Single Whip memorial had obtained imperial approval in 1567. The reason for his retirement was that he supported Gao Gong, one of the grand secretaries, in the latter's struggle with another grand secretary, Xu Jie. Gao Gong lost at that time and Ge Shouli was retired. Gao Gong was re-appointed grand secretary and also Minister for Personnel in 1569:12 and showed his gratitude to Ge Shouli by having him appointed Minister for Justice in 1570:2.[6] So Liang's approach to Ge Shouli and his subsequent adoption of his ideas must also be viewed as a way to establish good relations with the men in power in the capital.

Liang Menglong was also a close associate of Zhang Juzheng, who at this time was increasing his power in the Grand Secretariat. Zhang's general policy was to create stability in the central government and assert its predominance over local administrations,[7] and Liang's actions in Shandong bear the distinct imprint of being part of this policy. He also said that he did not expect the policy he had introduced to last for a long time. When abuses became marked, corrections would have to be made.[8] This view contrasts sharply with that of the opponents of the Single Whip like Ge Shouli, who advocated a return to the old system, which had functioned so well since time immemorial and which in their view could continue to do so in the future.

I therefore conclude that the main reason for the abolition of the Single Whip in 1570 may not have been that it was unfit for the conditions in the province. Administrators including Liang Menglong may have questioned the suitability of the Single Whip, and as will be seen later such reservations were valid for some parts of the province. The introduction of the Single Whip had no doubt created local problems, for which adjustments had to be made, and Liang's policy seems to have been aimed at creating the administrative climate for devising a taxation policy which would be most suitable for the province. However, as far as timing was concerned the general political situation may have been more decisive in its abolition than the general opposition to the Single Whip.[9]

Contemporaries probably realized that the abolition of the Single Whip in Shandong did not mean that a return to the former method of levying taxes and corvée could be permanent even if the careful assessments which Liang ordered were carried out. The Single Whip was in the ascendant. It obtained imperial approval in Jiangxi Province in 1570 and evidently reforms along these lines were inevitable.[10] A number of officials in the province were probably also well acquainted with the Single Whip policy and favoured its introduction as a solution to the taxation problems. The Left administration commissioner under Liang Menglong was Wang Zongmu, who is credited with being the first to use the term Single Whip in a publication and to have given it a precise definition, after he had participated in experiments with such reforms in Jiangxi around 1560. He may incidentally also have been the compiler of the *SDJHL*.[11] A couple of years after 1570 Ge Shouli complained in a letter to the Grand Coordinator for the River (*hezong*) Wan Liangxi (probably Wan Gong serving c. 1572)[12] and a little later to the Governor Li Shida[13] about their wanting to use the Single Whip and levy corvée on land.

The Single Whip was introduced into various districts of Shandong during the Wanli period, when it became the policy of the central government to introduce it in all provinces.[14] This chapter attempts to follow the introduction and the effects it had upon the subbureaucratic government system, and also what other fiscal roles this system had to perform in the last quarter of the sixteenth century. The sources for this are the local gazetteers, supplemented by the private writings of the officials. The uneven coverage provided by the local gazetteers makes an assessment at a provincial or prefectural level difficult, since details are not available even for all districts of Jinan.

THE SINGLE WHIP OF THE WANLI PERIOD

1. Developments in the south around 1570

The first Single Whip in Shandong had primarily been concerned with the collection of taxes and their granary rates but also with the levy of corvée on land. This latter tendency had been emphasized in the south during the 1560s, when the Single Whip had been promoted by such men as Pang Shangpeng. In Zhejiang the general opinion was that the reforms of the corvée system introduced by Pang Shangpeng in the last years of the

132

Jiajing period marked the beginning of the Single Whip in that province. As regional inspector he introduced a reform in two districts, perhaps modelled after Wang Zongmu's attempted reforms in Jiangxi,[15] and this later spread to other districts in Zhejiang. The reform was called 'equal level' (*junping*) and was mainly concerned with the *lijia* corvée, but also with some of the heavier items in the equal corvé which were still levied in a ten-year rotation. The corvée of a whole *lijia* was consolidated and levied upon the land tax with an annual levy on all households in the *lijia*, so that the decennial rotation ceased. If households had both *ding* and land, then the *ding* were commuted to a certain number of *mou* of land and these households would pay according to the total figure. Households without land were to pay according to their *ding*.[16]

The Single Whip was also introduced in two districts of Jiangxi in 1568:3 after the reforms in which Wang Zongmu had taken part had been obstructed by local opposition.[17] All the corvée was to be commuted to payment in silver and all items assessed, including the surcharges. The amount of silver needed each year was to be levied on *ding* and land, and the households were divided into three classes. Those with only *ding* were in the lowest class and paid *ding*-silver. Those with both some *ding* and some land were in the middle class, and those with much land and few *ding* or much land and many *ding* were in the upper class. Tax bills were to be issued to the households with time limits for collection, and the services as corvée heads (*touhu*) and assistant households were abolished. According to the compilers of the *DMHD* this was the beginning of the Single Whip.[18]

2. The Single Whip in Shandong according to Yu Shenxing

The new wave of Single Whip which flowed over Shandong in the Wanli period was much more concerned with corvée than the first Single Whip. One of its main aims was to abolish the *lijia* corvée, which in many districts also resulted in the abolition of the *lijia* positions.

Among senior officials and statesmen who were concerned with the Single Whip in Shandong in this period Yu Shenxing stands out, not least because some of his writings on the subject have survived. On 1591:9:16 he retired from the position of Minister of Rites.[19] He seems to have been well aquainted with conditions in his native Donga District as well as the neighbouring Pingyin, which bordered on Jinan Prefecture. His writings about the Single Whip are contained in a letter to the governor of Shandong, Song Yingchang, who was promoted from the governorship on 1592:8:18 to become vice-minister of War and supreme administrator of the defences against the Japanese in Shandong, Ji, Liaodong and Baoding.[21] This letter was therefore probably written at the end of 1591 or in the first half of 1592. About ten years later Yu composed a tablet about the corvée system introduced by the magistrate Yao Zongdao in Pingyin District in the middle of the Wanli period.

The Single Whip was introduced into Donga District in 1573 or shortly thereafter. Yu writes in his letter to Song that it started in early Wanli, about twenty years before writing. Yu's letter to Song is obviously part of a discussion of the Single Whip.[22] It is not polemic but rather intended to inform the governor about the situation in Donga District with some reflections on why it was suitable in that district while it was said to be unsuitable in other districts. We do not know the other parts of this discussion. It may have been a general discussion in the province at that time as a continuation of the previous discussions in which Ge Shouli and Guang Mao had opposed the Single Whip, in the case of Guang Mao with a specific protest in 1577 against its introduction in Donga.[23] However, the controversy may have flared up in 1591, when the official who had originally introduced the Single Whip in Donga, Bai Dong, had a short spell as circuit intendant in the general surveillance circuit for Yanzhou and Dongchang Prefectures.[24]

Yu Shenxing made it quite clear in his writings that as far as he was concerned the issue at stake in the introduction of the Single Whip was not whether or not corvée was levied on land. That was only secondary to more important issues of regulating some of the problems in the corvée system and removing some of the malpractices. He was aware that the Single Whip was not a specific term to be used for one type of reform. The term could be used when the granary rates were abolished and the tax handled by 'combined collection and separate forwarding'. It was also used when the household tax-classes were abolished and the corvée was only levied according to *ding* or when tax and corvée were amalgamated and levied entirely on land. The Single Whip for *ding* was used when the *ding* were not graded according to tax classes but all paid the same amount in silver, and the Single Whip for land was when the land was not graded.[25]

In Donga District the Single Whip included abolition of granary rates, and 'combined collection and combined forwarding' (*zongshou-qijie*) of taxes. Corvée was levied according to *ding* and land. The tax classes were abolished and the land was not graded, so poor and rich paid the same amount for their *ding* and the land was levied a uniform amount without regard to its fertility. The money was paid into a tax chest and was then used to hire people to perform the corvée services. The silver for the *lijia* corvée was included in the levy.

134

Yu realized that such a system had advantages and disadvantages. The advantages were: 1. Corvée heads (*yitou*) were no longer conscripted. 2. *Dahu* were no longer conscripted. 3. The *lijia* corvée was abolished. 4. The equal corvée was no longer assessed.

Previously households from the upper eight tax-classes had been conscripted as corvée heads while those in the ninth tax-class had been assisting households. In addition to these the official corvée system in the district had also included 'agents' (*daidang*), who apparently were people who had the time (*xianmin*) to actually perform or arrange the corvée work. They received money from the corvée heads, who in turn collected from the assistant households. The agents were issued a certificate showing the amount of silver they could collect from the corvée heads, including the surcharges (*datao*). The collection of money by these households had presented problems. The amount collected from each assistant household could be a little as a tenth or a hundredth of a tael, and if they lived scattered over a considerable area, the corvée heads could find it difficult or inconvenient to collect all the silver, so they had to pay some of it out of their own pockets. They also tried to shift some of the deficit upon the agents, with the result that both suffered losses and they were generally on bad terms with each other. From the introduction of the Single Whip the households paid the corvée silver into the tax chest according to their *ding* and land. The silver was then paid to the agents, who thus avoided the burden of insufficient pay.

In the collection and forwarding of taxes the previous system had created hardship for the *dahu*, so that they had to sell their property in order to perform their duties. Yu did not specify which system had previously existed in Donga, but in Pingyin District this had been 'combined collection and separate forwarding', which had either not been abolished in 1570, as ordered by Liang Menglong, or had been introduced thereafter. In this respect Yu's ideas seem to correspond to the views of Ge Shouli on 'combined collection and separate forwarding'. After the Single Whip reform in Donga only one chest head was conscripted to supervise the reception of taxes. He only ensured that the correct amount was entered but had no further part in the administration of the taxes. The subsequent handling and forwarding of the taxes was probably managed by the officials without assistance from *dahu*, as was the case in the Single Whip of Pingyin District.[26]

The advantages of abolishing the *lijia* corvée and incorporating them into the general levy was that the households would no longer have to face excessive expenses involved during their year of incumbency once every ten years. Even the nine years of rest were not sufficient to build up the necessary economic strength. Yu did not elaborate on this point, but we must assume that one of the difficulties was the lack of facilities to save money during the rest period.

When the equal corvée was abolished, the need for biennial assessment of the household vanished. Consequently there would be no more manipulations on the part of the *li*-registrars, the favourably placed households (*shifu*), the *li*-elders or the officials involved in the process of reporting and registering household assets.

In the opinion of Yu Shenxing this system was working well in Donga and had the approval of the people in the district. He did not specify which people approved but did mention that he was aware of possible disadvantages to some people in the district. With the abolition of the equal corvée the *men*-silver disappeared and with it the assessment and levy of corvée on assets other than land. He said that this was to the advantage of merchants with no land but the landowners suffered. The abolition of the equal corvée also placed relatively larger burdens upon the ninth tax-class. The *men*-silver had only been levied on the upper eight tax-classes. Now corvée was only levied on the *ding* and the ninth tax-class paid the same per *ding* as the others, and in addition they were also levied corvée on their landholdings. Even so, he claimed that the Single Whip was justified in Donga because of the four advantages listed above.

He was aware of problems with the Single Whip in other districts where the conditions for the landowners were not as favourable as in Donga. He was referring in particular to the districts in north-eastern Jinan Prefecture, where the productivity of the land was low because of high salinity, and to districts in the southeast of Yanzhou Prefecture which had considerable tracts of uncultivated land liable to taxation. In such places a levy of corvée on land would be ill-advised when there were already difficulties in collecting the land taxes, so that the *li*-leaders (incumbent and non-incumbent, *lipai*) had to make up deficiencies. He saw, however, no reason why difficulties in such districts should prevent the use of the Single Whip with levy of corvée on land elsewhere.

Even in the districts with less favourable conditions some kind of Single Whip could, in Yu's opinion, be introduced. This would involve some degree of levy of corvée on land. If this was not done, the assessment of the households for the usual corvée had to be continued in order to levy *men*-silver. However, the levy of corvée on land was possible if it was classed into three grades, and the levy on *ding* would not be too unbearable if grading of *ding* into the nine tax classes was continued. Some regulations would also be needed to make the merchants contribute to corvée. He did not explain what he had in mind, but it would presumably have been commutation of assets other than land either to *ding* or to *mou* of land. When grading of *ding* was to be retained, the tax classes would still have to be assessed, so this system does not appear to have been any great improvement on its predecessor. The only simplification was the abolition of the *men*-silver. However the improvements must have been noticeable, as Yu said that if such a system was introduced, then the inhabitants of all the districts of Shandong could obtain the benefit of the Single Whip without excessive hardship.

The Single Whip did not solve all the problems in the tax and corvée system. Yu stated (and this was also mentioned in other sources concerning the Single Whip in Shandong),[27] that the whole question of the Single Whip was related to the larger question of 'government by man' or 'government by law'. The Single Whip was obviously an attempt to stress 'government by law', but this could not be complete, since the officials still had to be allowed to make adjustments to regulations and registers in order to avoid malpractices. This presumably meant that adjustments were to be made in response to changing conditions and certainly required a certain degree of 'government by man'.

One problem that could not be completely solved by the Single Whip involved the agents for the corvée. There were corvée services of varying urgency, and different dates for the collection of the corvée silver. If the silver was not received on time, then the officials or the agents who were responsible for the corvée work had to borrow from money lenders, and a great deal of the silver collected to pay for the corvée services would have to be used towards paying interest on such loans. The result was that the agents did not receive sufficient compensation for their efforts, so that the hardship of the corvée heads now fell solely on them. Yu Shenxing did not give details about who were conscripted as agents. He only said that corvée heads and agents had previously been selected among the people according to convenience, and that the agents were 'idle people'. Originally their services cannot have been regarded as corvée, because they were to receive full compensation, but if both before and after the Single Whip reform they had to waive some of this compensation, then a new kind of corvée service had apparently been created.

Yu Shenxing ended his letter to Song Yingchang by refuting the charge by the opponents of the Single Whip that it was not in accordance with the ancient laws of the dynasty. He claimed – with justification – that the Single Whip did not abrogate the original laws of the dynasty, as there had already been successive changes. More important is his point that the Single Whip followed the spirit of the early laws. In these, the people were divided into tax classes because the lawmakers wanted to create equality between them, and this was precisely the goal of the Single Whip as he saw it.[28]

THE SINGLE WHIP IN LICHENG AND ZHANGQIU

1. Licheng District

The 1640 edition of the Licheng gazetteer enumerated ten points which, according to its compilers, were the advantages of the Single Whip in that district. These ten points have a more general interest as they are similar to ten points paraphrased by Kataoka from the 1589 edition of the gazetteer for Anqiu District in Qingzhou Prefecture.[29] This use of ten specific points indicates that they had obtained a certain degree of acceptance where the Single Whip had been adopted.

The Licheng gazetteer began the Single Whip section by stating that laws were only changed if they resulted in 'a hundred benefits'. Of the laws for taxes and corvée none were better than the Single Whip, which had ten advantages. Such statements can have been used in the gazetteer to emphasize the advantages of the Single Whip but may also indicate that in the view of the compilers reforms ought to bring considerable benefits if the laws were to be changed. In other words, we are left with an impression that a certain degree of conservatism prevailed with regard to the fiscal system. This conservatism is of course also seen in the rather slow introduction of the Single Whip reforms in the sixteenth century.

According to the gazetteer, the ten advantages of the Single Whip were:

1. Hardship and ease were distributed equally upon the ten *jia* in each *lijia*, so that the levies upon *ding* and taxes were equal and households liable to corvée did not suffer excessively.
2. Households with privileged exemptions from taxes and corvée could not shift excessive burden upon other households since they could not get exemptions beyond the authorized amount.
3. The silver was paid to the officials and there was no possibility of extortion.
4. People were not forced to sell some of their property in order to make up deficits in the collected taxes and corvée. In this way they avoided ruin.
5. All the various corvée items such as silver and labour corvée and public and private expenses for the officials were amalgamated, so that one person did not have to be corvée head for several different items.
6. The distinction between corvée heads and assistant households was abolished, so that rich and poor became equally taxed.
7. A system was introduced for the payment of salaries and allowed no room for graft.

8. People hired to perform corvée work were paid by the officials and did not have to demand or exact further payments from the people.
9. The rich could not evade their responsibilities and the poor did not suffer from illegal extra burdens.
10. With fixed figures for the silver to be paid for each item, the registers were clear and provided no opportunities for manipulations.

Because of these ten advantages the people respected the Single Whip as they 'respected fortune-tellers', and they loved the men who had introduced the Single Whip as they 'loved their ancestors'. The Single Whip in Licheng may have been a good system but apparently was not good enough. After it had been in operation for some time it fell into confusion. In addition the Single Whip did not possess sufficient flexibility to meet new demands. Later, when the need arose to increase the levies considerably to cover the costs of military expenditure, *dahu* had to be re-introduced. No date is given for this change but it may have been as late as the 1630s.[30]

2. Zhangqiu District

The Single Whip was introduced into Zhangqiu in 1586 or 1587 by Magistrate Mao Guojin.[31] Zhangqiu is singled out for special treatment here because the 1596 edition of the district gazetteer contains one whole chapter in twenty-six pages under the heading: Single Whip. This edition was compiled by Magistrate Dong Fuheng, who held office from 1593 to c. 1598.[32] The chapter on the Single Whip is obviously written by Dong himself; he referred in the personal form 'I' to decisions which he had to take in the aftermath of the introduction of the Single Whip and which are described below. Given the sparse amount of information on the Single Whip and the subbureaucratic government system in most gazetteers, an extensive discussion of this chapter seems justified, particularly in view of the important qualifications of the author. Zhangqiu was also one of the larger districts in Jinan Prefecture – the largest in terms of number of *lijia* – and its location immediately east of the provincial capital made it a fairly average district compared with the busy west and the more desolate northeast.

Only a little information is available on the *lijia* and fiscal system in Zhangqiu before the Single Whip. Savings in the *lijia* corvée (*sheng lijia*) were made around 1560, as mentioned in the biography of Magistrate Dong Wenshen. Subsequent magistrates also made alterations in the tax system to the benefit of the people.[33] Details of these are not given, but they must have incorporated some of the measures ordered by the provincial government during this period, perhaps including a codification of the equal and *lijia* corvée.

By 1586 the subbureaucratic government system for assessment and collection of taxes and corvée in Zhangqiu comprised c. 1,352 persons. These included c. 116 *dahu* in charge of the tax chests, 10 chests for taxes, 10 for corvée and 6 for horse-payment money (*majia*). The number of *dahu* at each chest is not specified, but a simple calculation would indicate that there were 6 *dahu* per *majia* chest and probably 4 at each of tax and corvée chest. In addition to the *dahu* each *lijia* had one tax-pressing *li*-leader and one tax-assessing *li*-registrar, i.e. 103 of each. Each *jia* also had one tax-pressing *zongcui*, i.e. 1,030 in all. The services were assessed to 12 taels for the *dahu*, 5 taels for the *li*-leaders, 10 taels for the *li*-registrars, and 5 taels for the *zongcui*. The total annual assessment was thus 8,087 taels. Dong Fuheng wrote that these were the expenses (*feiyin*) for these services, but he did not make it clear whether the silver was actually received by the district administration and later paid out, or whether it was regarded as part of the household corvée, which was then deducted from their corvée payments. He also appears not to have been too accurate in his adding of the figures. He gave the total number of persons as 1,700 and the cost as 8,000–9,000 taels per year. The reason for this lack of precision cannot be ascertained; we can only note that he was writing about things which had existed before his time in the district.[34]

After the introduction of the second Single Whip, Mao Guojin had the ten advantages of this policy engraved upon a tablet, but Dong Fuheng does not list them all. He only outlines the three main points:

1. The equal corvée was not assessed.
2. The *lijia* [corvée] was not established.
3. Corvée heads were not conscripted.

The taxes and corvée were in the Single Whip levied upon land and *ding*.[35] The land was divided into three grades, so we must assume that Zhangqiu was one of the districts in which a complete Single Whip was not feasible but where it could be used with some modifications, as suggested by Yu Shenxing. Examples of such modifications must therefore have already been in operation when he made his suggestion in 1592. Dong Fuheng eulogized the Single Whip, saying that the people were happy and returned to the land even if the levies of taxes and corvée for the whole district had not been reduced and there had been no increase in acreage in 1586.[36]

The registered acreage had, however, increased by about 30% following the re-measurement of land in 1581. The last recorded figure

140

was 10,567 *qing* in 1529, and in 1581 the acreage was 13,678 *qing* divided into upper, middle and lower land. The registered acreage in 1369 had been 10,379 *qing*.[37] The reason for the 1581 increase could be either that land which had been brought under cultivation during the intervening 200 years had been left unregistered until now, or that a new standard of measurement had been adopted. In the latter case the land hardest hit by the re-measurement was that to which a generous measurement had previously been applied and which was probably owned by the more wealthy and privileged landowners. No matter what the reason was, the levy on a *mou* of registered land was reduced in 1581 by c. 25%, and this was probably to the advantage of the marginal taxpayers, so this reform would already have encouraged such people to return to the land.

The above information is supplied by Dong Fuheng at the end of the chapter, but he seems to have overlooked it in his initial eulogy of the Single Whip, in which he wrote that the acreage had for several decades been over 13,000 *qing*. A remeasurement of land could have taken place between 1529 and 1581, but this seems unlikely. He rather overstressed the case for the Single Whip and, after all, the fifteen years between 1581 and 1596 were almost 'several decades'.

Minor adjustments to the acreage were made in 1587, so the total in that year was 13,666 *qing* divided into:

first grade land	7,236.97 *qing*
second grade land	2,846.59 *qing*
third grade land	3,582.95 *qing*

The *ding* in the district numbered 57,126, of which 1,185 were exempted from corvée by privilege, so the taxable *ding* totalled 55,941. Among these 46,339 belonged to landholding households, while 9,602 belonged to landless households. In addition, the returned households had 1,415 persons.[38]

For the collection of taxes and corvée all positions in the subbureaucratic government system were abolished except thirty-seven chest heads to supervise the reception at the tax chests. They received a monthly salary from a small levy upon the tax payments. Mao Guojin fixed this levy at one *wen* (0.001 tael) per 0.035 *dan* of grain in tax payment. His successor Zhang Qicheng continued this practice and made it an integral part of the regular tax payment, not just a surcharge.[39]

In 1593 the district received an order from the governor to abolish the chest heads and instead to conscript *li*-leaders to receive taxes.[40] This order met with considerable opposition in the district and ways were found to circumvent it. Before describing how this happened we must examine the terminology for the title of the governor used in this chapter of the gazetteer. The term used is *junmen*, which in the Ming dynasty was used for the commander of the training divisions in Peking and possibly also for other trusted senior military commanders. Cartier describes this office as that of a supra-provincial official in charge of land taxes for coastal defences.[41] In the Qing dynasty the *junmen* was the epistolary title for the provincial military commander-in-chief.[42]

In Shandong in the 1590s the title must have been used for the provincial governor. Two officials with the surnames Sun and Zheng are given this title. The successor to Song Yingchang as governor was Sun Kuang, and his successor was Zheng Rubi. Between them they held the governorship from 1592 until 1595–1596.[43] The coincidence of surnames proves beyond reasonable doubt that the title *junmen* must have referred to the governor. The question here is why this title was used consistently by Dong Fuheng instead of the usual *xunfu*. I suggest that the reason was that the governor was acting in a capacity connected with the military emergency in the north, over which Song Yingchang had been appointed supreme administrator.

If this suggestion is correct, then the use of this title indicates that the governor's interest in the administration of tax collection was connected with raising funds to meet military expenditures, a role similar to that described by Cartier. This need for additional funds is clear, since Dong Fuheng, when he was enumerating the taxes, stated that orders had recently been received to collect 2,176 taels in military-supply silver in addition to normal taxes.[44] The logical conclusion must be that the governor did not regard the tax collecting institutions under the Single Whip as adequate when urgent additional levies had to be made. The *lijia* system, or similar institutions, were more suited for that purpose, because there were in them a relatively small – but not too small – number of people from whom extra levies could be extorted quickly; these people were then left with the task of recouping at least some of the money from the rest of the population. This seems to be in accordance with the re-introduction of the *dahu* in Licheng District.

The 1593 order of the governor also indicates that he did not expect that the *lijia* system had been completely abolished after the introduction of the Single Whip system. Probably the *lijia* still existed in connection with the compilation of the Yellow Registers, while its tax collecting function had been discontinued following the introduction of the Single Whip.

RECEPTION HEADS

1. Zhangqiu District

The order of Zhangqiu in 1593 to abolish the chest heads could not be neglected by the district authorities, but they were under some pressure from the local people to find ways of circumventing it. The order was even followed by a further order from the regional inspector to recover the money which had been paid to the chest heads.[45] This could indicate that the original reform in Zhangqiu had not obtained approval from the provincial administration, but no positive evidence for this effect is available. However, the interest of the regional inspector left the local officials in no doubt that they had to take action in accordance with the order of the provincial administration.

When the order to abolish the chest heads was received in the district, Dong Fuheng had only occupied the position of magistrate for a short period. He consulted the inhabitants and found that they did not want to have the *li*-leaders conscripted to collect taxes. They were afraid that this would be similar to the re-introduction of the *dahu* and thus of the financial strain on the households who had to perform such duties.[46] The people he consulted were the elders and possibly the 'élite' (the text is slightly damaged here), and they were probably the people who would be hardest hit if such tax-collecting corvée were re-introduced. They regarded the Single Whip, which had abolished all such duties, as a blessing or 'like receiving the well-counselled instructions of the Sage'[47] and thought of the officials who had introduced the Single Whip as their 'father and mother'.[48] The exact words here may be an exaggeration, but as the work was published in the district at that time, they must have reflected the sentiment among the people, at least the influential people who had been consulted by the magistrate.

A compromise was needed and was found by replacing the chest heads with reception heads (*shoutou*). This modification of the governor's order received sufficient approval from higher authorities to keep the local officials free of any accusation of disobedience.[49] Dong Fuheng quotes extensively from three submissions made to the provincial authorities. Final approval was only received after the third submission. The governor had already changed from Sun Kuang to Zheng Rubi before the first submission, which declared – perhaps a little flatteringly – that in Zheng's view policies should be adapted to local customs and not be enforced slavishly. Both the governor and the regional inspector were of the opinion that they could not go against the wishes of the people, but on the other hand they could not go against the order of the governor. So the stage was set for a compromise. Unfortunately the text describing the compromise is ambiguous. It reads as follows:

> When among the incumbent *li*-leaders each *lijia* has to select a single energetic and duly qualified person to be conscripted as reception head – with this to be regarded as a corvée service for the year, and with the received tax to be the responsibility of the private family – then nothing must prevent a suitable compromise if there are small *lijia* or small *jia* which are poor and cannot be charged with this service. Such a compromise will be that one or two persons are conscripted from the larger *lijia* or larger *jia*, while the smaller *lijia* and *jia* are ordered either to pay a salary acting as joint-service households (*penghu*), or to deliver personally, or to hire privately. In general, payments will be made daily according to the registers and will be deposited in the treasury every day. The officials will not have to pay salaries and the people will not have to manage directly. In this way neither rich nor poor households will be ruined and the sufferings of the former *dahu* will not exist. The title of the present chest heads will be abolished and their wages will be saved. Extreme malpractices will be impossible. This will be convenient to the officials and not troublesome to the people. It will be in accordance with the new policy of the governor and not against what the influential men (*shifu*) of the whole district have recommended. This is a law which can operate for a long time with neither public nor private fraud.[50]

This text from the first submission does not clearly define the persons to be appointed as *li*-leaders for tax collection. Each *lijia* had only one incumbent *li*-leader, so the selection of a person of good standing from among the incumbent *li*-leaders within the *lijia* is difficult to explain. We must leave this problem unsolved and ascribe it to an ambiguity in the text which may have been a result of condensing the original submission. The proposal, however, accepts the connection between the *lijia* and the tax collection. In the stronger *lijia* one or two households would be in charge, while in the weaker *lijia* several ways were proposed to avoid one single household being held responsible for the tax of the whole *lijia* or even one *jia*.

The argument that the weaker *lijia* could not be expected to select one or two households is not immediately easy to understand. A weak *lijia* would only own relatively small amounts of property and have few *ding*, so it would have to pay correspondingly less in taxes and corvée. However, since this argument was used, it must have carried some weight. One explanation could be that when the service had to be performed in a rotation there were insufficient numbers of affluent people in these *lijia* who could guarantee the tax collection with their own assets. Another explanation could be that the people expected impositions on the *lijia* that would not be distributed according to the respective strength of each *lijia*. The people of the district feared that the reform would not only ruin the *li*-leaders but would also be a heavy burden upon the whole *lijia*[51] They obviously tried to avoid the use of the *lijia* for collecting taxes and corvée, either because they were afraid that the *lijia* organization was incapable of this service or because they feared that any relationship between the *lijia* and the collection of taxes might stimulate a notion among higher officials that extra levies could easily be imposed upon the *lijia*.

The second submission is mainly concerned with a detailed description of the advantages of the Single Whip and the disadvantages of the new policy but offers no specific proposals. However, in the third submission the district officials allowed themselves to deviate from the principle of a direct connection between the *lijia* and tax collection. They stated that in the view of the local people reception heads should be selected from among the *gongtong, gongzheng*, and elders (*laoren*).[52] The *gongtong* are not mentioned in other parts of the district gazetteer, but the *gongzheng* were part of the non-fiscal subbureaucratic government structure in 1596. The district was divided into thirty granary divisions (*she*) each with one granary for the prevention of famines. A *gongzheng* was in charge of such a granary, and he also had certain functions in the supervision of the *xiangyue* and *baojia* (see Ch. VI below). The title of *gongzheng* appears to have been used for persons who performed the duties of elders. Kuribayashi quotes a case from the fifteenth century in Taizhou Prefecture, Zhejiang, where the *lilaoren* had ceased to function and had been replaced by *gongzheng*.[53] In Jinan Prefecture *gongzheng* had participated in a remeasurement of land in Lijin District c. 1572 where they received the results of the remeasurement and made a register, which was sent to the district administration.[54] In Binzhou Subprefecture *gongzheng-laoren* had been ordered to supervise the *dahu* after a reform of 1582, so their presence in the prefecture was not unusual.[55]

The number of people selected among the *gongtong, gongzheng* and elders in Zhangqiu as reception heads was to be thirty-seven, i.e. the same number as the chest heads they had to replace. Payment of a salary was considered, but this was rejected as it would be against the order of the governor. The solution was to distribute the 462.5 taels per year paid to the reception heads on all the *lijia* in the district according to *ding* and land, so they would be paid, but not directly by the officials.[56] The chest heads had only supervised the reception of taxes at the tax chest, and the following day the money was transferred to the district treasury, so they did not actually handle the money. The reception heads would have had greater responsibility in handling taxes if the order of the governor had been fully applied. However, the fact that the number of chest heads and reception heads was the same and that they received the same remuneration indicates that the duties of the reception heads were not

145

considerably different from those of the chest heads. The only significant difference I can find is that the reception heads were not hired by the officials. They were formally selected among the people as a kind of corvée, and in this respect they were in compliance with the governor's order. Governor Sun Kuang had apparently also objected to the long-term service of the chest heads and preferred a rotational service of the *li*-leaders. As we do not know the terms of service of the *gongtong*, *gongzheng* and elders, not to speak of that of those selected as reception heads, we cannot determine whether or not the order was complied with in this respect.

2. Tangyi District, Dongchang Prefecture

The detailed description given above of the introduction of the reception heads in Zhangqiu was necessary not because the change from chest heads to reception heads resulted in any great changes in the actual tax collection procedures of the district but because the change may have had some consequences outside Zhangqiu. One such example may be the introduction of reception heads in Tangyi District in 1608. This may not have been a direct result of the Zhangqiu experience, since reception heads might have been introduced simultaneously in other districts. In that case the submissions from Zhangqiu must have been at least noteworthy contributions to official discussion of the reception heads. The method introduced in Tangyi District possibly sheds some further light on the role of the reception heads.

The Tangyi description was written by one of the compilers of the 1708 district gazetteer, Liu Qi, so its source value is less than that of the Zhangqiu description. It is, however, part of a major treatise on the *lijia* system included in the gazetteer. This treatise was also included in at least two general works on administration during the Qing dynasty,[58] so we must assume that their compilers regarded Liu Qi as one of the more informed observers of the *lijia* system during the early Qing period and also that this treatise was based upon serious study in local archives. The relevant text seems to be a more or less verbatim quotation from a submission of Magistrate Wang Yingqian to higher authorities.

The reception heads in Tangyi are not referred to in connection with a Single Whip reform. Liu Qi arranged the discussion of them under the tax captains (*liangzhang*), and he referred to Wang's submission as a proposal to replace the *dahu* and end their suffering. Tax chests were in existence, so the tax was probably managed by 'combined reception and separate forwarding'. This method had imposed considerable hardship as a result of cheating at the various stages of the collection and forwarding. The hardship was considered so severe by the people that they used every kind of manipulation to conceal property in order to avoid the service, and the people of modest means (*xiaomin*) regarded conscription as *dahu* as equivalent to 'being thrown into the tiger's den.'

The Single Whip was, however, introduced in 1608, so the reform of the *dahu* was undertaken at the same time.[59] Wang Yingqian proposed and apparently obtained permission to abolish the *dahu* and replace them with reception heads. Ten of these were conscripted to receive silver and seventeen to receive taxes in rice and grain. The hardship on the *dahu* had mainly been caused by the forwarding; this was now completely abolished, because the reception heads only received, while all forwarding was to be handled by the officials. The reception heads were conscripted according to the *lijia*, apparently one for each of the seventeen *lijia* in the district. This method of conscription would only have provided the seventeen reception heads for taxes in kind; how the ten conscripted to receive silver were selected is not specified. Within each *lijia* the service was rotated among the *jia*, so that each *jia* served one year in a ten-year rotation. One of the advantages of such an arrangement was that the *lijia* assessment only had to be made every ten years instead of the five-year assessments which had previously been applied. No further explanation of this previous system of assessment was given by Wang Yingqian, but perhaps the *lijia* corvée had at some time been changed from service for one year in ten to service for six months in five years. Such an arrangement might have served to alleviate some of the burdens on the *lijia*, but, as we can see, this would also put additional pressure on the district administration for the assessment work.

The regulations for the reception heads allowed for some flexibility. Some *jia* could be economically so strong as to justify a conscription of two or more reception heads, while other *jia* could be so weak that it would be unfair to ask for even one reception head. It is not clear whether adjustments were made between the *jia* within a *lijia* or between the incumbent *jia* of different *lijia*. Such adjustments were further justified, since the reception heads received a certain renumeration. This was to be paid by the whole district but no indication is given as to how the funds were collected and disbursed.

Wang continued by saying that he had already selected twenty-seven reception heads and also two granary men (*cangfu*), who presumably worked at the district granary to receive the taxes from the reception heads. He extended certain privileged exemptions from taxes and corvée to these households for ten years, and this made these positions so attractive that households apparently competed for them.[60]

Kuribayashi has already described the reception heads to some extent. His conclusion is that they were probably successors to the *li*-leaders.[61] From my description they seem rather to have been successors to the *dahu*, either directly as in Tangyi District or indirectly as in Zhangqiu. This conclusion is further supported, since *shoutou dahu* are already mentioned for 1571 in the *SDJHL*.[62]

In Tangyi District the major reform was the abolition of the forwarding service of the *dahu*, and perhaps the payment of the reception heads. The method of conscription may have been the same as that used previously for the *dahu*. Of particular interest is the fact that the reception heads were conscripted on the basis of the *lijia*, but probably in varying numbers according to the strength of each *lijia*.

THE SINGLE WHIP IN OTHER JINAN DISTRICTS

This section will give short descriptions of the Single Whip in other districts for which details are available. Occasionally hints are given about the fate of the *lijia* or about administrative processes which either directly or indirectly must have influenced the subbureaucratic government system. The picture cannot be complete, since information is not provided for all the districts. However, the Single Whip appears from the following description to have been so widely accepted as to suggest that it was introduced in most if not all districts of the prefecture.

In Binzhou Subprefecture a reform of the *dahu* was introduced which resembles similar reforms under the Single Whip. The subprefecture had c. 90 *dahu* who had each collected c. 500 taels of silver and had suffered greatly from this service. In 1582 Magistrate Ai Mei ordered that the *dahu* would only have to weigh and receive the taxes and act under supervision of the *gongzheng-laoren*. The collection was to be checked each day in the yamen, and on the last day the chief officer (*shouling-guan*) was ordered to manage the forwarding. The expenses of the forwarding were to be covered from the collected surplus in the tax and was explicitly not to be demanded from the *dahu*. The *shipai* had previously been middlemen between the taxpayers and the *dahu* and had misappropriated considerable sums. Ai Mei now ordered that the *dahu* of each *lijia* should collect the tax and the taxpayers should hand their tax directly to the *dahu*.

The details of the previous forwarding service of the *dahu* are not available because of textual damage, so we cannot establish whether this forwarding could have had an influence on the relationship between the

148

dahu and the *lijia*. The connection between the two is clear from 1582, although no order was given to reduce the number of *dahu* to correspond to the seventy-eight *lijia* in the subprefecture. This would hardly have mattered, since the *lijia* from which more than one *dahu* had been conscripted would have been the economically more powerful, and with higher tax payments they could probably have used more than one *dahu*. I suggest that with the termination of the forwarding duties of the *dahu* the connection between them and the *lijia* became closer when the question of granary rates or matching the collections for deliveries to specific granaries no longer existed. When the *dahu* were only receiving the taxes, the *lijia* were probably still administratively and geographically the most convenient units from which to collect.[63]

Another district where the Single Whip is not specifically mentioned but where similar reforms were carried out was Shanghe. Beginning in the Longqing period the *lijia* [corvée] was abolished, and all corvée levied in silver according to land and *ding*. The payments were fixed and graded. But not all services could be included in this corvée regulation, since from time to time artisans had to be conscripted to repair the yamen offices and also temporary levies in support of other districts (*xieji*) could not be regularized.[64]

Yangxin District introduced the Single Whip for taxes and corvée in 1582,[65] and Taian Subprefecture introduced it in early Wanli.[66] In Pingyan District the *li*-leaders, *shipai* and *li*-registrars were abolished in 1587. The *li*-elders were retained in order to preserve some traditional subdivisions (*dutu*).[67] The Single Whip was introduced in Zhanhua District in 1588, but the gazetteer gives no information on the organizational changes involved.[68] In Xincheng the population figures were revised in 1578 and tax classes were abolished.[69] This would seem to have been part of a Single Whip reform, but the gazetteer only used this term for reforms introduced by Magistrate Zhao Wenbing, who held office between 1586 and 1589. In this reform the equal corvée was no longer to be assessed and the *dahu* were abolished. Tax payments were divided into ten installments to be paid in the first ten months of each year. The amount in each installment was further decided according to the harvest time. For an annual payment of one tael of silver 0.2 tael was paid in the fifth and the tenth months, while the remaining 0.6 tael was divided equally over the other eight months.[70]

Putai District amalgamated the levy of equal corvée with *lijia* corvée and other levies in 1587.[71] In Qidong the Single Whip was introduced between 1589 and 1595, and the services as *li*-leaders and other services where the households were conscripted to corvée (probably the *shipai*, here called *paijia*) were abolished.[72] Laiwu District apparently received orders shortly before 1595 to introduce the Single Whip, whereby the corvée duties of the *li*-leaders, etc., were abolished and collection organized by the officials.[73] In Qingcheng the final consolidation of taxes and of corvée to be levied on land was probably in 1596, and this apparently met with some opposition, which had died down when the gazetteer was compiled in 1612.[74] The *lijia* corvée had, however, disappeared soon after 1575, when Magistrate Li Jigao shortly after his arrival in 1574 economized on excessive expenditures, reassessed the corvée, abolished the *lijia* [corvée] and discontinued rotational services.[75]

The Single Whip in Zichuan District was introduced by 1602,[76] and in Deping it was introduced in 1604. In this latter district the people claimed that they had suffered under the former tax system, and after deliberations a decision was made to introduce the Single Whip. This was then approved by the higher authorities from prefect to governor. The main problem in Deping was to equalize the corvée, which was done by abolishing the tax classes and having only two rates, one for *ding* with land and one for those without land. Another major problem was the forwarding of taxes and corvée, which had hitherto been performed by forwarding households (*jiehu*). They had previously served one year in three, but this had developed into annual service. The proposal was now made to introduce a ten-year rotation where each *lijia* would rotate the service among its *jia*, but with provisions that the stronger *jia* could serve for two years while the weaker *jia* could serve jointly. This was approved by the 'élite' and the elders and was then put up as a petition. The way this service was conscripted resembles the method used for the reception heads. However, there is no indication that they were paid for their service and their function was apparently also different.[77] Finally the Single Whip was introduced at some unspecified time during the Ming Dynasty in Lingnan District, but no details are available.[78]

The sources for this survey have been rather disappointing. However, sufficient information has been unearthed to indicate that the *lijia* corvée was abolished under the Single Whip and also that most of the other functions of the *lijia* were no longer performed. The bureaucracy still had a tendency to prefer to use the *lijia* organization for tax collection – and perhaps in Deping forwarding was also imposed upon the *lijia*. But with the·provisions for modifications according to the strength of each *lijia* or each *jia*, these services must be regarded as fundamentally different from the original *lijia* corvée. My impression is that when a rotational service was desirable – and this could be the case for tax collectors to prevent them from continuous frauds – then the *lijia* might as well be used, since it was already in existence and had been so since the founding of the dynasty. Continued reliance upon the *lijia* also had the advantage that the officials – at least to a certain extent – still only had to manage the relatively larger units instead of households; finally the *lijia* would have continued to be a convenient instrument for the emergency – or irregular – levies.

FISCAL CHANGES

1. Corvée

The reform of the corvée in the Wanli period was mainly concerned with the collection of levies from the people and perhaps also the further commutation to silver payments. For the collection from the households we have details from Putai District after it had been consolidated in 1587. We also have figures for the equal corvée in 1565. However, a direct comparison of the figures is impossible, since the 1587 figures contain several items that were not included in the equal corvée of 1565. These items included *lijia* contributions (*lijia-gongfei*), horse-price silver, levies of straw or fodder (*caoliao*), salt tax and some forwarding charges. The equal corvée had in 1565 been assessed every three years, but this had changed to every five years after orders to that effect had been received during the Wanli period. The triennial assessments in 1565 do not correspond to the biennial assessments of which there was so much evidence in the *SDJHL*. The explanation may be that local variations were allowed at that time, but the discrepancy may also be the result of a misprint. The figures for Putai District in 1587 are probably rather unique for the prefecture, as they still include a levy of *men*-silver after consolidation, and this was not normal in the Single Whip. The figures given are in taels of silver.[79]

| | 1565 | | 1587 | |
Tax Class	*men*	*ding*	*men*	*ding*
1	4.0	0.7	16.1	4.15
2	3.0	0.6	12.5	3.59
3	2.0	0.5	11.7	3.09
4	1.0	0.4	8.9	2.59
5	0.9	0.3	7.16	1.80
6	0.7	0.2	5.92	1.26
7	0.4	0.2	2.515	1.06
8	0.1	0.15	0.535	0.532
9	–	0.07	–	0.36

Details for the number of households in each tax class in Putai are not recorded. In Binzhou the figures of households and *ding* in each tax class were as follows.[80]

Tax Class	Households	Ding	Ding/Households
1	8	20	2.5
2	26	68	2.6
3	50	161	3.2
4	87	262	3.0
5	168	433	2.5
6	562	1,282	2.3
7	2,021	4,621	2.3
8	6,090	13,833	2.3
9	7,630	16,744	2.2

No gazetteers other than that of Putai give figures for the levy of corvée on each tax class, not even those compiled during the Wanli period. They usually enumerate in detail all the different corvée items to be levied in the district. This may indicate that the compilers of the gazetteers and also the district officials were more interested in having the correct figures for the district levies – which had to be supplied to higher authorities and also for use in the districts itself – than they were in the problem of allocating the levies on the taxpayers. From the point of view of the government the quotas to be filled by the districts were probably more important than the way they were collected. The government was not, however, disinterested in collection and delivery procedures; after all the reforms that had taken place from 1550 and perhaps also before were mainly aimed at equalizing the burdens upon the taxpayers. But the underlying argument for this, as put directly by Ge Shouli, appears to be the concern for maintaining a constant flow of funds to the central and local government as much as a concern for the livelihood of the individual taxpayer.

In the gazetteers compiled during the Wanli period the most important *lijia* corvée, such as *qingfu*, *baifu* and *lijia* horses, are not mentioned in the sections on corvée in Dezhou, Qidong, Zhanhua, and Zichuan.[81] In Binzhou, Shanghe and Wuding these services are listed as part of the equal corvée,[82] and in Qingcheng, Taian and Zhangqiu they are listed as separate items of *lijia* corvée.[83] Putai District did not list the corvée items, but the *lijia* silver was incorporated in the general levy. In the Pingyuan gazetteer the section on corvée is illegible, so the categorization of the *lijia* corvée cannot be determined.[84] In Wuding and Qingcheng special categories of statutory contributions (*ezhi* or *eban-*

gongfei) and miscellaneous contributions (*zazhi* or *zaban-gongfei*) are listed. These categories included various small levies for ceremonial and administrative expenses in the subprefecture or district. Their nature is that of the original levies on the *lijia* for local expenses. They had not been consolidated in the *SDJHL*, but their listing in these gazetteers indicates that they had continued to be levied at least in some and perhaps in all subprefectures and districts. The gazetteers give no indication whether or not these contributions were still levied on the *lijia*. These levies also existed in Zhangqiu as special categories but were included in the overall Single Whip together with the equal corvée and the *lijia* corvée.

The levies for each item of corvée did not change significantly during this period. A comparison between the 1583 Binzhou gazetteer and the *SDJHL* shows that the total levy of silver corvée was reduced from 5,825.1 taels to 5,142.1 taels. The reduction was due to the omission of three items and variations in some other items which are accounted for in the gazetteer. The figures for the labour corvée correspond to the *datao* figures in the *SDJHL*, which indicates that these figures included both the original silver valuations and the surcharge. The labour corvée in Binzhou was in 1583 still organized so that wealthy and honest households collected the silver and then paid for the corvée work, so the corvée heads must still have been in existence.[85]

2. Remeasurement of land

In 1580:11:10 the emperor authorized a measurement of all land in the empire to be based on the experience of a remeasurement in Fujian Province during the preceding two years. This was – as far as is known – the only order of the kind issued during the dynasty.[86] All the districts in Jinan Prefecture apparently obeyed this order at least to the extent that in districts for which information is available the figures for acreage from the Wanli period are used – sometimes with modification – as the basis for future tax assessment.

Many districts had reported at least one measurement of the land in the sixteenth century, so for them a remeasurement was not a completely new thing. During the remeasurement in Shanghe District the *mou* of 240 *bu* had been used, but the unit of measurement had been the 'large foot' (*dachi*), which was about one and a half times the size of the official foot. During the measurement of 1581 the official measurement instrument (*guancha*) was to be used, and the result was an acreage about double the previous figure (16,324.98 *qing* to 7,938.52 *qing*). In the new measurement the land was classed in three grades, the middle grade being one and one-third times the size of the upper grade, and the lower grade twice the size of the upper grade. As a result of the fiscal acreage was 10,216.13 *qing*.

In Lijin District the land had been measured in 1571. Each person measured his own land according to the standard laid down by the magistrate and sent the results to the *gongzheng*, who in turn informed the yamen. The results are somewhat puzzling. The original acreage had been 3,747.72 *qing*, as given in the introduction to the section on land in the 1673 gazetteer. In the same section the 1572 acreage is given as 3,345.59 *qing*, while in the essay on the equalization of land under Magistrate Jia Guangda in 1571 the acreage is given as 2,073.17 *qing*, or if calculated strictly according to 240 *bu* per *mou*, 2.354.59 *qing*. The acreage after the remeasurement in 1571 was 4,644.52 *qing*, which is very close to double the 1571 figure, so it was probably a result of applying the official measure rather than the traditional larger foot, as in Shanghe. In the Chongzhen period the acreage in Lijin was reduced by about 600 *qing*. This Chongzhen figure was split into three grades.[88] This division may go back to 1581; the reason for its omission may have been that the compilers of the 1673 gazetteer did not feel any need to include such information for the earlier period.

The participation of the people in the measurement of their own land was apparently a common practice in the prefecture. In Zichuan District the 'élite' and elders welcomed the remeasurement, because fields had hitherto been measured unequally. Moreover they proposed that one or perhaps several persons should be selected to be in charge of the measurement. The magistrate Wang Jiuyi firmly rejected this proposal. Instead he distributed measuresticks among the people (*baixing*), and they could themselves select persons to undertake the measurement. The magistrate would take no part in this selection. All the land that had not formerly been registered was to be newly listed in the registers, presumably together with the land that had been listed previously. The registers were to be handed over to the *lizheng*, who in this district had some functions at the relief granaries and were probably equivalent to the *gongzheng*. The magistrate then examined a sample of the fields in a way which even a modern statistician would not entirely disapprove. He had an arrow shot from a bow and where it landed he would check the measurement. The people – according to the biography of Wang Jiuyi – were astounded and all went to the place where the arrow had landed and said: 'The magistrate has arrived'. In this way there was no cheating, with the result that the registered acreage exceeded that of the previous registers. The increase was from 5,635.68 to 6,671,95 *qing*, and after

1581 the land was divided into four grades. This story was probably written about twenty years after the event, so the details may not be completely reliable but the general outline is probably correct.[89] This suggests that Wang did not want to entrust the measurement to the 'élite' or the subbureaucratic government organization, either of which would have been the natural choice if he himself had to make the selection. Such people were only used for the collection of the registers. Some of the landowners may have been forced to rely on literate people to fill in their register entry, but the magistrate at least tried to eliminate any cheating by such people with his personal checking of samples.

In Qingcheng District the acreage was increased from 2,364 *qing* to 3,039 *qing*. The reason was that the old *mou* had been 304 *bu*, while the new *mou* was 240 *bu*. In 1594 the general administration circuit intendant of Jinan, Wang Yingjiao, had apparently heard that all land in Qingcheng had not been measured, and he ordered that an additional measurement be undertaken before a certain date. The magistrate protested vigorously, since the land of Qingcheng was not extensive and there was no possibility of concealment. He succeeded in not having to undertake a new measurement.[90]

Most districts reported that the land had been classed in several grades in 1581 or at least in the Wanli period. The only districts for which information is available and which did not report grading of land were Changqing, Licheng and Taian.[91] The Taian gazetteer states that the tax was collected according to a uniform levy. Licheng District reported in the Qing dynasty that the land was classified in five 'metallic' grades which may go back to the middle of the sixteenth century. So in most districts the conditions were such that a graded corvée levy could be imposed on the land. This was clear in Putai District, where in the Wanli period *lijia* silver was levied on land at 0.003 tael per *mou* on first-grade land, 0.002 tael on second grade, and 0.001 tael on third grade.[92] In Leling District taxes and some corvée were levied on land and both were assessed according to the land grading.[93]

NOTES TO CHAPTER V

1. *SL* 1570:8:*bingwu*.
2. *SDJHL* 5/26–27. I have previously suggested the possibility that all land in a *lijia* (*she*) was to have the same granary rate. This is however an overextension of the sources. See Littrup (Single Whip), p. 91.
3. *DMB* pp. 898–902.
4. *GDSGWJ* 10/25.
5. *Ibid.* 14/24.

6. *Mingshi* 112/3471, 214/5667.
7. *DMB* pp. 54–55.
8. *SDJHL* 9/69–70.
9. Littrup (Single Whip), pp. 93–95.
10. *DMHD* 20/15.
11. *DMB* pp. 1440–1441. The claim that Wang was the first to use the term Single Whip in a publication raises the question whether he interpolated the term into the *SDJHL* documents. The term was, however, used about Shandong by Ge Shouli in his letter to Liu Cai c. 1557 and was used about other provinces in documents from 1531 onwards. Liang Fangzhong «Mingdai yitiaobianfa nianbiao», *Lingnan Xuebao* 12.1 (1952), 19
12. *GDSGWJ* 14/40.
13. *Ibid.* 14/46.
14. *Mingshi* gives the date for the empire-wide introduction of the Single Whip as 1581 but it appears to have been a more gradual process. Wada (1957), p. 218.
15. *DMB*, p. 1441.
16. Kuribayashi (1971), pp. 146–147.
17. *Ibid.* p. 150.
18. *DMHD* 20/15.
19. *DMB*, pp. 1614–1615.
21. *DMB*, p. 832.
22. *Guchengshanguan wenji* 34/15.
23. *SL* 1577:1:*xinhai*.
24. Bai Dong was appointed magistrate of Donga in the Longqing period and continued in Wanli. *Yanzhou fuzhi* 1685/11/66. He was appointed circuit intendant in 1591 and relieved the same year. *Ibid.* 11/17; Huang, p. 97.
25. *Guchengshanguan wenji* 34/15.
26. *Ibid.* 13/33.
27. *Zhangqiu xianzhi* 1596/12/63.
28. *Guchengshanguan wenji* 34/15–20.
29. Kataoka, pp. 153–154.
30. *Licheng xianzhi* 1640/5/40–41.
31. *Zhangqiu xianzhi* 1596/21/75.
32. *Ibid.* 1596/10/28, 1691/4/9.
33. *Ibid.* 1596/21/74; *Jinan fuzhi* 1839/36/11.
34. *Zhangqiu xianzhi* 1596/12/68–70.
35. *Ibid.* 12/64.
36. *Ibid.* 12/63.
37. *Ibid.* 12/78.
38. *Ibid.* 12/81–82.
39. *Ibid.* 12/65.
40. *Ibid.* 12/65–66.
41. Cartier, p. 54.
42. H. S. Brunnert and V. V. Hagelstrom, *Present day Political Organization of China* (Shanghai, 1912), p. 337.
43. *Jinan fuzhi* 1839/25/3.
44. *Zhangqiu xianzhi* 1596/12/87.
45. *Ibid.* 12/67.
46. *Ibid.* 12/65–66.
47. Quotation from the *Shujing.* James Legge, *The Chinese Classics*, 3 vols. (Hongkong-London, 1865), III, pt. 1, p. 163.
48. *Zhangqiu xianzhi* 1596/12/70.

49. *Ibid.* 12/65.
50. *Ibid.* 12/66–67.
51. *Ibid.* 12/68.
52. *Ibid.* 12/72.
53. Kuribayashi (1971), p. 252.
54. *Lijin xianzhi* 1673/10/27.
55. *Binzhou zhi* 1583/2/51.
56. *Zhanqiu xianzhi* 1596/12/72–73.
57. *Ibid.* 12/67.
58. *Huangchao jingshi wenbian* 74/1–2 and *Qingchao lunce leibian. Zhengzhilun* ch. 4. The latter is quoted in Liang (1957), p. 104.
59. *Tangyi xianzhi* 1710/4/7.
60. *Ibid.* 2/11–12.
61. Kuribayashi (1971), pp. 175–176.
62. *SDJHL* 4/34.
63. *Binzhou zhi* 1583/2/50–51.
64. *Shanghe xianzhi* 1586/3/6.
65. *Yangxin xianzhi* 1682/3/8.
66. *Taian zhouzhi* 1670/2/8.
67. *Pingyuan xianzhi* 1590/1/20.
68. *Zhanhua xianzhi* 1619/3/55.
69. *Xincheng xianzhi* 1693/3/2.
70. *Ibid.* 12/17.
71. *Putai xianzhi* 1592/4/2.
72. *Qidong xianzhi* 1685/4/16.
73. *Laiwu xianzhi* 1673/4/7, 7/20.
74. *Qingcheng xianzhi* 1617/1/15.
75. *Ibid.* 1617/1/15.
76. *Zichuan xianzhi* 1602/15/1.
77. *Deping xianzhi* 1796/3/2, 10/40–42.
78. *Lingxian zhi* 1845/7/1.
79. *Putai xianzhi* 1592/4/2–3.
80. *Binzhou zhi* 1583/2/38.
81. *Dezhou zhi* 1576/4/2–3; *Qidong xianzhi* 1617/15/5; *Zhanhua xianzhi* 1617/3/6; *Zichuan xianzhi* 1602/16/2–3.
82. *Binzhou zhi* 1582/2/50; *Shanghe xianzhi* 1586/3/28; *Wuding zhouzhi* 1588/5/5.
83. *Qingcheng xianzhi* 1612/1/26–27; *Taian zhouzhi* 1670 (1603)/2/12; *Zhangqiu xianzhi* 1596/12/26.
84. *Pingyuan xianzhi* 1590/1/20.
85. *SDJHL* 5/6; *Binzhou zhi* 1583/2/48–49.
86. *SL* 1580:11:*bingzi*; Huang, p. 300.
87. *Shanghe xianzhi* 1586/3/1–2.
88. *Lijin xianzhi* 1673/4/2, 10/27.
89. *Zichuan xianzhi* 1602/10/1, 27/10–11.
90. *Qingcheng xianzhi* 1612/1/14–15.
91. *Licheng xianzhi* 1640/5/2; *Taian zhouzhi* 1670 (1603)/2/8; *Changqing xianzhi* 1845/5/4.
92. *Putai xianzhi* 1591/3/10.
93. *Leling xianzhi* 1762/2/50.

VI. Other subbureaucratic government institutions c. 1550–1600

INTRODUCTION

This chapter will describe the other subbureaucratic government institutions known to have existed in Jinan Prefecture around 1550–1600. A short description of the fate of the institutions introduced early in the dynasty will be followed by a longer description of the institutions established during the sixteenth century to serve some of the same non-fiscal purposes; finally the welfare organizations, primarily the welfare granaries, will be dealt with at some length. The sources are the local gazetteers, but for the function of some of the institutions other sources have been used to provide further insights. Some of these other sources can be related to Jinan Prefecture. As was the case with sources for the *lijia* system, the gazetteers compiled during or immediately after the period give more information than those compiled during the Qing dynasty. However the Qing gazetteers show slightly more interest in the non-fiscal subbureaucratic government system of the Ming than in its *lijia* system. One reason for this may be that the Qing compilers regarded the non-fiscal subbureaucratic government system of their dynasty as a continuation from the Ming, while the Qing fiscal subbureaucratic government system was created from scratch after the great economic upheavals during the dynastic transition. Another reason may be that the non-fiscal system was in some cases tied to buildings or at least to the land on which permanent or temporary constructions had been erected. As the gazetteers often record the history of buildings and other permanent structures, including major repairs and final or temporary abolition, some information is provided in this way.

ALTARS AND PAVILIONS

Altars for the 'five soil and five grain' spirits (*lishe*) were established in Changshan District in 1369, one in each *li*. Sacrifices to the soil and grain spirits of the *li* were performed in spring and autumn followed by communal wine-drinking and pledge-reading (*xiangyue*). The altar for the unconsoled spirits (*xiangli*) was identical to the *lishe* altar and ceremonies were performed three times a year at the *Qingming* festival, in the middle of the seventh month, and at the beginning of the tenth month. These ceremonies were performed by the *li*-elders (*lijialao*) and other local elders. The dating of the terms of *xiangyue* and *lijialao* in the district gazetteer may be doubtful, but there seems to be no reason to doubt that the altars and the ceremonies were introduced at the level of the *li* in early Ming. They had all been abolished by 1716.[1]

Information on the altars at the subbureaucratic government level is only available for the *xiangli* altars in a few other districts. In Haifeng District one altar had been established in each *li* and sacrifices were performed at the same time as those at the district *xiangli* altar. These altars were under direction of the *li*-leader (*lizhang*).[2] In Lijin District there had been over forty altars, one in each *li* (the district had thirty-four and later forty *lijia*).[3] Pingyuan had forty-six altars, one in each *li* (forty-six *lijia*).[4] Qidong apparently had one in each *lijia*, and in 1685 the land on which they had been erected still existed in fourteen places.[5] All these altars had been abolished at the time the gazetteers were compiled; only the Pingyuan gazetteer was compiled before 1600.

In Deping District there had been altars in each subdistrict. They had been confiscated (*qinmo*) in the Jiajing period to settle people on the land.[6] Zichuan District also had altars in each subdistrict, and they had been abolished by 1602.[7] The general impression from these examples is that the altars had probably existed in all districts at the beginning of the dynasty, and at least in some cases either in the *lijia* or in units that were later directly absorbed in the *lijia* system. We cannot determine how long they survived, but the fact that they are referred to in relatively few gazetteers suggests that the decline of this institution had started early in the dynasty.

At the district level the altars survived longer. The district altar in Changshan had been repaired in 1483,[8] and the Qidong altar had been relocated in 1486.[9] The most conspicuous example of such survivals is the relocation of the Binzhou Subprefecture altar in 1583 recorded in the gazetteer of this year together with information on the ceremonies performed at it.[10] So ceremonies for the unconsoled spirits were performed in this subprefecture in late Ming and presumably also in the other subprefectures and districts of Jinan.

Shengming and *Jingshan* pavilions are only referred to at the district level. Many Qing gazetteers reported that they had been abolished, although in Qidong proposals were made to re-introduce them in 1685.[11] These pavilions are reported in Pingyuan around 1500,[12] and they had been repaired in Lijin District c. 1552.[13] In Dezhou Subprefecture they were rebuilt between 1573 and 1576.[14] The latter example indicates that they still served some purpose in that subprefecture, either as meeting places or for posting notices of good or bad behaviour. In the latter role they may have been connected with the subbureaucratic government system, since in the *xiangyue* system records of the behaviour of the people were sent to the district yamen. The pavilions may also have been retained and repaired to show reverence for the decisions of the founding emperor and as a constant reminder to the people that their behaviour was the object of public scrutiny.

BAOJIA AND XIANGYUE

1. Origin of the *baojia*

With the erosion of the non-fiscal duties of the *li*-elders, in Shandong as well as in other parts of the empire various policies were adopted in the sixteenth century to create new organizations for the non-fiscal duties of the subbureaucratic government system. The most famous of these organizations were the *baojia* and *xiangyue*, which are closely connected with the names of Wang Yangming (Wang Shouren)[15] and Lü Kun.[16]

The first operation of the *baojia* system in the Ming dynasty was probably during the Zhengtong period, when it was used as a security organization in mining areas of Fujian Province. Watch towers were constructed by these *baojia* and *jia*-leaders were appointed among the wealthy households. The large-scale application of the *baojia* began, however, in 1517, when Wang Yangming became governor of Nangan (the border area of Jiangxi, Fujian and Guangdong Provinces), which suffered greatly from banditry. Immediately after arriving he took steps to suppress robbers within the city by promulgating the 'ten-family-card' system (*shijiapaifa*), which was later called the *baojia* system. Ten households were grouped together and their names written upon a card which was circulated every day among the members of the group. Each day between five and seven p.m. a member of the household on duty was to carry the card round to the other households and – with their knowledge – they would note any changes in the composition of the household or any other noteworthy matters. If anything suspicious was discovered, the officials were to be informed. If anything was concealed, then all the ten households were considered quilty when this was discovered.[16]

The explicit mutual responsibility of the·households in security matters under Wang Yangming's system is quite different from the subbureaucratic government system of the early years of the dynasty. The Precepts of Popular Instruction did not spell out any mutual responsibility. They only alluded to this when they said that the people should not harbour criminals, since this could be harmful to relatives and neighbours. These people would certainly have been implicated if the sheltering of criminals was discovered.[17] The reason for this difference in emphasis may be that the Precepts of Popular Instruction were promulgated while the dynasty was still relatively new. At that time there may have been a feeling among the lawmakers that the people after long years of unrest were more inclined to be law-abiding. The situation facing Wang Yangming was completely different. He was appointed governor to a border area between three provinces with the specific purpose of bringing lawlessness under control, and for this purpose mutual responsibility between households was doubtless a useful instrument.

The original *baojia* system of Wang Yangming was only concerned with mutual surveillance by the households. No police action was expected from the 'ten-family-card' units and no leader was selected. Wang Yangming's reason for this was that he did not want to promote any of the households in these small units to a position where they enjoyed advantages over the others.[18] This attitude probably reflects some aspect of the social structure at that time. For the surveillance of the households relatively small groups were most suitable, but on the other hand such groups were too small for leaders to be designated if social harmony was to be maintained.

With no leadership in the 'ten-family-card' units, other leaders were needed to mobilize the population in case of bandit alarms. For this purpose watch-chiefs were established in the villages. The watch-chiefs were not to be concerned with disputes in the villages but only with the command of the villagers during bandit alarms. An elaborate system was set up to warn the villagers and also to secure communication between villages during alarms.[19]

The 'ten-family-card' system was not widely adopted in China during the Ming dynasty. It was used in some areas during military emergencies. As a durable subbureaucratic government institution it already proved inadequate in the Nangan area during Wang Yangming's time. When the only function was to watch the households and report on irregularities, there was a tendency among the officials and the people to stress the formalities of this watching while neglecting its real purpose. To overcome this problem the educational element of subbureaucratic government was emphasized, and Wang Yangming did this by combining the *baojia* with the *xiangyue*.[20]

11 – Subbureaucratic government . . .

2. Xiangyue

The *baojia* system of the Ming dynasty is generally supposed to be a continuation of similar systems which began during the Song period on the model of Wang Anshi, although the Song systems did have leaders of the ten-family groups.[21] The Song dynasty roots of the Ming *xiangyue* are even more evident; at first the Ming *xiangyue* copied those of the Lü family (*Lüshi-xiangyue*), which had been further refined by Zhu Xi during southern Song.

The *xiangyue*, or pledge groups, were first proposed in the Ming dynasty in 1388, when a Hanlin bachelor Xie Jin proposed that, since new educational laws were not ready, the Household Rules of the Zheng family ought to be adopted as the regulations for families, and the '*Xiangyue* of the Lü family' should be adopted for conciliation between neighbours. This proposal came at a time when the 'elders' were not formally established in their community role. It was not accepted and became irrelevant on the establishement of the *li*-elders between 1394 and 1398.

Following the weakening or breakdown of the community functions of the *li*-elders in the fifteenth century, local experiments were made with the *xiangyue*. The first records are from Chaozhou Prefecture, Guangdong Province, in c. 1440, when the prefect ordered the villagers to erect pavilions in which pledge-group directors (*yuezheng*) and recorders (*yueshi*) chosen from the people were to carry out the *xiangyue* system. Other local records mention the system over the next eighty years. However, the initiative taken by Wang Yangming appears to have been the decisive step for a more widespread application of this method of subbureaucratic government. This may have been because of his high reputation but also because social conditions were ripe for this kind of experiment.[22] One noticeable factor in the development of the *baojia* and *xiangyue* is that they – like the Single Whip – were instituted on the initiative of local officials. This stands in sharp contrast to the policy of the Hongwu period when, perhaps following local experiments, detailed centralized regulations were enforced for subbureaucratic government.

The *xiangyue* of Wang Yangming in Nangan was primarily intended to regulate the activities between the people within the *xiangyue*. The size of the *xiangyue* was not defined, so the village was probably the unit. Each *xiangyue* was to have one *yue*-leader (*yuezhang*) and two deputies (*yuefu*). They were to be elderly persons respected by the people of the *xiangyue*. In addition four directors (*yuezheng*), four advisers (*zhiyue*), four recorders (*yueshi*) and two ritualists (*yuezan*) were selected. These were all to possess the personal virtues necessary for carrying out their functions. Each *xiangyue* was to keep three registers. The recorders were to list the names of all the members of the *xiangyue* in one register together with their daily activities. The other two registers were used to record the behaviour of the members, one for good and commendable actions and one for misdeeds. The *yue*-leader was to be responsible for these registers. All good deeds were to be recorded in clear and definite language, while misdeeds were to be described more cautiously, not condemning the members too hastily, so as to give them a chance to reform. The *xiangyue* were to meet each month at a suitable place, e.g. a temple with sufficient space and within convenient distance for all the members. Modest refreshments of food and drink were to be served, for which the members were to pay 0.03 tael.

The *xiangyue* was responsible for assistance to members who were in any difficulties; if they failed in this duty the whole *xiangyue* would be guilty of neglect. At the time of tax collection the *xiangyue* was to make sure that no member absented himself before the taxes had been paid, so that the other members would not have to make up the deficit. It had a strong responsibility to ensure that no member of the community suffered from excessive economic strain, for example to ensure that moneylenders did not charge excessive interest or harshly insist on loan repayments. This provision was evidently intended to prevent members of the *xiangyue* from being driven to unlawful actions out of economic necessity. Membership of the *xiangyue* was to be open to reformed bandits but at the same time the *xiangyue* were to ensure that such persons did not engage in dubious activities or practise extortions. Finally the *xiangyue* were responsible for seeing that marriage and funeral ceremonies were conducted with due regard for the financial capabilities of the households.[23]

The educational functions of the early *xiangyue* followed the Four Pledges of the *Lüshi-xiangyue*. These were: Mutual encouragement in worthy endeavours, Mutual restraint of misconduct, Ceremonialization of every social intercourse, and Mutual help in misfortune. When this form of *xiangyue* was amended by Zhu Xi, he gave elaborate explanations for situations covered by each of these pledges.[24]

The break with the *xiangyue* tradition of the Lü family began probably in 1529, when the Six Maxims of the Hongwu emperor began to replace the Four Pledges. In the same year subbureaucratic government of the *xiangyue* type was adopted as official policy. On 1529:3:9 the Left vice-minister of War Wang Tingxiang[25] complained that there had recently been famines in all provinces and as a remedy he proposed that welfare granaries (*yicang*) should be established in each *lishe*, because the relief granaries in subprefectures and districts were insufficient. He

163

suggested that in the villages 200–300 families should form one association (*hui*), and that each month the members of these associations should pay an amount of grain to the granary according to their tax class. One virtuous man was to be selected as head (*shetou*) and another was to keep the books as deputy. In years of bad harvests the grain was to be distributed first to the middle and lower tax-classes and then to the upper tax-classes. Only the latter were to repay the grain. The distribution was to be made according to the wishes of the people without interference from the officials, but records were kept for their inspection. This measure would create sufficient social stability, so that both the *baojia* and the *xiangyue* could function and thus contribute to control over the population.[26]

The Ministry of Revenue ordered these proposals to be implemented, but some changes were made, either immediately in the ministerial order or later in the actual introduction. These changes are recorded in the *DMHD, Ming huiyao* and *Guochao dianhui*. The latter states that the granary association was to hold monthly meetings under the direction of a *she*-director (*shezheng*). During these meetings the Precepts of Population instruction were read and the people were commended or admonished for their behaviour.[27] In the *DMHD* the *she*-head (*shetou*) presided together with the *she*-director over these meetings to be held at the beginning of each month. If any of the members failed to comply, then in serious cases they were reported to the officials and in minor cases were to pay a fine to the welfare granary.[28] With regard to the size of the granary associations the sources are in disagreement. The *Guochao dianhui* follows the *SL* and gives the size as 200–300 families, while both the *DMHD* and the *MHY* give the size as 20–30.[29] Which of the four sources is the most reliable is impossible to say. There may be errors in printing, which were then perpetuated in the two traditions. Hoshi Ayao puts forward the explanation that the *SL* tradition was mostly concerned with the establishment of subbureaucratic government in principle, while the *DMHD* tradition recorded actual implementation.[30] This explanation may be correct, since groups of 30–50 households have often been regarded as the most convenient size for effective subbureaucratic government.

The situation in Zhangqiu District in the Wan-li period may help to shed some further light on the origin of this discrepancy. Zhangqiu had 103 *lijia*. For welfare granaries the district was divided into 30 *she*, each with one granary under the supervision of a *gongzheng*. The *gongzheng* also supervised 410 *xiangyue*, which each had officers to conduct ceremonies and keep records. So each granary association was on average based upon three and a half *lijia* or perhaps, given the

164

uncertainty of the *lijia* households registration, between 300 and 600 households. This would leave each *xiangyue* with perhaps 30–50 households.[31] The *DMHD* gives 30–50 families as the size of the granary associations but does not clarify whether each association was to have one granary or whether each association was simply to be the basis for the monthly or bi-monthly meetings at which the members contributed the grain to be stored in the welfare granary. In the latter case a granary might have been established for several associations. Whatever the explanation is, we have to accept that two traditions apparently existed from 1529 with regard to the size of granary associations. This may have left some discretion to the local officials in the implementation of the policy and may be the explanation for the situation in Zhangqiu.

From 1529 the *baojia* and *xiangyue* together with the welfare granaries were part of central government policy, but they were apparently not introduced extensively during the Jiajing period. Most local sources only report them in the Longqing and Wanli periods, and this is definitely true for Jinan Prefecture. According to Sakai Tadao, the *Lüshi-xiangyue* continued in the Jiajing period, but from the later years of the reign the Precepts of Popular Instruction and the Six Maxims became predominant.[32]

3. The *xiangjia* of Lü Kun

One of the better known systems of *xiangyue* and *baojia* in the Wanli period was that devised and introduced in 1592 by Lü Kun while he was governor of Shanxi Province. One of the reasons this system is well-known is because Lü Kun's description of it was included in his *Shizhenglu, (SZL)*, which was used during the Qing dynasty as a guide to local administration. However, regardless of how widely Lü Kun's system was applied in the Ming dynasty, it must be taken into consideration here, since Lü Kun had been administration circuit intendant in Jinan Prefecture from 1587 to 1589, immediately before his transfer to Shanxi first as surveillance commissioner and later as governor. So local development in Jinan could have been influenced by his ideas or these ideas could have been influenced by his experience in Jinan, or, most likely, a mixture of the two.

Lü Kun's system was an amalgamation of the *xiangyue* and *baojia*. This system was based upon a *li* which had to have 100 families. Whether in practice the *li* corresponded to the *lijia* is doubtful, but it was important that the member families of the *xiangjia* (as it was abbreviated) should all be mutual neighbours with no members of other *xiangjia* interspersed among them[33] Each *xiangjia* would have one director (*yuezheng*), one deputy (*yuefu*), one instructor (*yuejiang*) and one recorder (*yueshi*). The first two were the leaders of the *xiangyue* and the two latter were in charge of administrative and educational duties. The families were divided into groups of ten called *jia*. These ten families would select one *jia*-leader (*jiazhang*).[34] The basic mutual surveillance unit to which a family belonged was the 'four neighbours' (*silin*), a system which has a long tradition in Chinese history. If any member of the *xiangjia* did anything wrong, then the neighbours on the four sides were to admonish him; if he did not repent, they would report this to the *jia*-leader, who would report to the *yue*-director to have it recorded in the Book of Misdeeds. If a member did anything meritorious, then the neighbours were to report it in the same fashion, and it would be entered in the Book of Merits.[35]

Guidelines regulated the relationship between the government officials and the officers of the *xiangjia*, so that officials or other government personnel could not harass the members of the *xiangjia*. It was in particular forbidden to ask the officers of the *xiangjia* to perform any outside services.[36] Each *xiangyue* was to hold two meetings per month, on the second and the sixteenth, in a building large enough to accommodate all 100 members. This could be a temple, a public building or a private home. During the meeting a tablet with the Six Maxims was to be displayed at one end of the room with the officers of the *xiangyue* seated on each side, while the other members sat in rows along each side of the hall. There would be singing during the meeting, and the *jia*-leaders were to step forward and report on good and bad behaviour. The members concerned were to be praised or admonished, and their deeds were to be entered in the appropriate book.[37]

Some flexibility was allowed in the organization of the *xiangjia*. First of all, if men suitable for the four positions could not be found within one *xiangjia*, then four persons would be selected from another *xiangjia*, so that 200 families formed two *xiangjia*, each with four officers with the appropriate qualifications. If the number of families was not 100 or 200, then an official was to re-arrange the *xiangjia*, but some flexibility was allowed, and it was not permitted to include in a *xiangjia* families who lived at a distance too great for a convenient performance of the duties.[38]

The officials in subprefectures and districts were to personally examine the books of merits and misdeeds. If the officials discovered that the *xiangyue* officers or the 'four neighbours' had not reported as was their duty, then these would be severely censured and punished. Sub-bureaucratic government institutions were also to participate in this general surveillance of the *xiangyue*. At the subprefecture or district town as well as in each subdistrict, two wealthy and honest persons were to be appointed as *gongzheng* with the duty of administering the *xiangyue* within their area. Lü Kun commenced his section on the *gongzheng* with a description of the decline of the *laoren*. The latter had previously assisted the administration in the subprefectures and districts, but by this time they had been degraded to mere tax collectors in the *lijia*, yamen runners, etc. So in his view the *gongzheng* were successors to the 'elders' (*laoren*). However, he does not say whether the *laoren* were *li*-elders or some other elders at the subdistrict level. He says that at the beginning of the dynasty two *laoren* were appointed to the *Shenming* and *Jingshan* pavilions, which could have been established at *lijia* (or *li*), subdistrict and/or district levels. From the context it is, however, clear that he was thinking of levels below the districts, i.e. subdistricts or *lijia*.[39]

The members of the *xiangyue* were first of all landowners and houseowners in the area. 'Élite families' (*jinshen*), which must refer to those with a ranking official in the family, and families with licentiates or bachelors did not have to enrol in the *xiangyue*. 'Mean' people such as entertainers (*yuehu*),[40] domestic servants (*jianu*), hired labourers (*yonggong*) and tenants were not allowed to join the *xiangyue*. Together with temporary visitors they were under the control of landowners or houseowners. All other labourers who performed duties that had formerly been provided as corvée, such as artisans, cooks, runners, etc., were allowed to join the *xiangyue* if they had originally been registered in the district or subprefecture or had been residents for a long time, and if they took the pledge of the members of the *xiangyue*.[41]

The *xiangyue* had certain judicial powers in petty cases which were not subject to heavy punishment, such as the cangue or banishment, and for which no formal accusation had been made to the district officials. Any misconduct was of course entered in the Book of Misdeeds, which each month was examined by the officials so they could monitor improper activities and the way in which the *xiangyue* dealt with them. The punishments allowed for the *xiangyue* were reprimand and exclusion from the community. A sign written in large characters was to be nailed to the left side of the offender's gate giving his name and the activities of which he was guilty, such as unfilial behaviour, deceit, theft, gamling, etc. The offender was to attend the meetings of the *xiangyue* to hear the Precepts, but otherwise the people in his neighbourhood were to have no dealings with him. Only when the other members of the *xiangyue* were convinced that the offender had sincerely repented were they to give a bond of joint responsibility and guarantee that he had reformed. The sign would then be removed from his gate.[42]

The surety function of these subbureaucratic government units was to be under the direction of a *bao*-director (*baozheng*) if the *xiangyue* had 100 households. If there were 150 households a deputy (*baofu*) was also appointed.[43] These officers were systematically to investigate the coming and going of the people of the *xiangyue* as well as other people from the district and those who were under the control of landowners or houseowners. They were to report to the officials on robbery and with the assistance of the other members of the *xiangyue* provide protection for those who had been robbed. Each *xiangjia* was to employ an instructor to drill the men between eighteen and sixty years (*sui*) of age in the use of weapons, and the members were to keep the weapons at home ready for use. In order to perform their duties the *bao*-director and his deputy were to be physically strong men from wealthy families.[44]

4. *Xiangyue* and *baojia* in Jinan Prefecture.

Both *xiangyue* and *baojia* are reported in many districts of the prefecture, so they were apparently widespread in the period. The *xiangyue* is treated most frequently in the gazetteers, at least in terms of separate headings. In some of these cases they are combined with the *baojia*. Indirect evidence for the widespread use of *baojia* is provided by Song Yingchang, who had extensive administrative experience in Shandong, including surveillance commissioner c. 1565, prefect of Jinan c. 1580 and governor c. 1590–1592.[45] As Vice-minister of War he wrote in a despatch to the governor of 1593:1:10 that he was afraid the conscription of able-bodied men (*zhuangding*) from the *baojia* of each circuit could not continue.[46] This was a function that could previously have been demanded from the *lijia*, so it is possible that Song for defence purposes renamed the *lijia* as *baojia*. This would correspond to a development in Boping District, Dongchang Prefecture, where in 1586 the *lijia* had been changed to *baojia* and the *xiangshe* to *xiangyue*.[47]

The first reference to the *baojia* in Jinan Prefecture is in Putai District. Under the heading of defence in the 1592 gazetteer it is reported that the *baojia* were introduced in 1566. They did not, however, last long and were re-introduced in 1588 with 102 *baojia*. These were identical to the *xiangyue*.[48] The *baojia* was also reported without reference to the *xiangyue* in Binzhou Subprefecture in early Wanli. The 1583 gazetteer mentions in a general description of the *lijia* system and the elders that the *baojia* had spread to this subprefecture. The result had been a constant improvement in bandit prevention and in settling vagrants.[49] The *baojia* system must have been in operation a few years before 1583, but perhaps in view of the experience of Putai not for long. Under the heading 'subdistricts and small towns' (*xiangzhen*) in the same gazetteer it is stated that the small towns were places where people lived together for more convenient defence and trade, and that the *baojia* system had recently brought about more law-abiding conduct in the subdistricts and small towns. In 1583 the subprefecture had 16 of these small towns,[50] and there were probably 173 *baojia*.[51]

The *xiangyue* have been found in almost half of the districts and subprefectures of Jinan. Their introduction in Zichuan is directly connected with the name of Lü Kun,[52] and he must have exercised direct or indirect influence on their introduction in many of the other districts, since this usually took place in the period 1587–1596. The course of this introduction was as follows:[53]

District or Subprefecture	Year of Introduction	Number of *xiangyue*	Number of *lijia*
Xingcheng	1586–1589		
Pingyuan	1587	155	46
Putai	1588	102	59
Wuding	(*xiangyue* pavilions mentioned in 1588 gazetteer)		
Zichuan	(introduced by Lü Kun)	93	63
Linyi	1590	83	32
Laiwu	1592–1596		
Qingcheng	1592–1596		
Zhangqiu	before 1596	410	103
Xintai	mentioned 1615		
Lingxian	before 1618		
Qidong	(apparently in existence but source unreliable)		
Taian	(possibly in existence)		

The *xiangyue* were introduced into Pingyuan in 1587 after the circuit intendants in the [Jinan] administrative circuit (Lü Kun?) and the Wu-De surveillance circuit had investigated the conditions in the district and had obtained the permission of the governor and the regional inspector. The district was divided into 155 *xiangyue*, each with one *yue*-director, one deputy, one instructor and one recorder. The *xiangyue* were to hold two monthly meetings where the Six Maxims were read out and explained, together with the summary of the Ming code and a chart giving examples of filial behaviour. After this, good and bad behaviour was to be recorded in the respective registers. The seal-holding official in the district would choose the most spectacular incidents from these registers and record them in district registers which each season were sent to the circuits for inspection.[54]

The officers in the *xiangyue* in Pingyuan correspond to the system of Lü Kun. Variations are, however, recorded in contemporary sources. The *xiangyue* of Putai had one ritualist (*yuezan*) in addition to the director, the deputy, the instructor and the recorder. In Zhangqiu each *xiangyue* had one recorder, one master (*shuai*) and one instructor. The 398 *baojia* of Zhangqiu had *jia*-leaders and *xiaojia* as officers. The families were divided into groups of ten called *pai* for the purpose of defence. The *xiangyue* were for education and the *gongzheng* were in addition deputed by the officials to settle minor matters such as arrears in payment of debts or disputes over fields and houses.[56]

In Xincheng the *xiangyue* and *baojia* were introduced by Magistrate Zhao Wenbing between 1586 and 1589. The functions of the two organizations were as usual. However, the *xiangyue* together with the *difang* had to report on thieves in the village.[57] This appears to be a new function for the *xiangyue*, and at the same time the *difang* or 'local constable' is introduced. In the Qing dynasty the *difang* was a part of the subbureaucratic government system and had largely the same functions as provided in the *baojia* system.[58] The *xiangyue* in Xincheng also became part of the taxation system. In cases of arrears in tax payments the runners (*muzaoli*) would order [officers of] the *xiangyue* to go to the gate of each offender and to draw up registers stipulating time-limits for payments to facilitate investigations. If anybody had not paid within these time-limits, then the yamen police (*kuaishou*) was sent out to compel them to pay. The *xiangyue* were not directly involved in the money transactions as had been the case with the *lijia*, and in the commemoration eulogy for the magistrate this was praised as benevolent to the people.[59]

Participation in tax collection procedures was not among the normal duties of the *xiangyue*, so we are left to wonder whether in spite of this eulogy such involvement would not in the long run lead to misuse of the *xiangyue*.

The information given in the gazetteers on the *baojia* and *xiangyue* in Jinan Prefecture is generally short but appears to be reliable, because much of it is in contemporary sources. Lü Kun was no doubt instrumental in developing this aspect of subbureaucratic government in the prefecture, but he was probably not the only influence. It is furthermore worth noting that, although the provincial authorities were apparently consulted on the introduction of the *xiangyue* and *baojia*, they did not enforce a uniform system.

Together with the introduction of the *xiangyue* and *baojia* attempts were also made during this period to revive the local *she*-schools (*shexue*). These schools were a heritage from the Yuan dynasty, and in the Ming they were ordered to be introduced all over the empire in 1375, with one school for each fifty families. This was probably part of the government's general policy to regulate life in the villages after the pacification of the empire. If any schools were established pursuant to this order, they did not fare too well, probably because the officials interfered with their operation in improper ways. When a new order to establish *she*-schools went out in 1383, the officials were forbidden to meddle with the affairs of the schools. The *lijia* was probably the basis for these schools, which were then under total subbureaucratic government control. The purpose of the schools was primarily moral education and dissemination of government orders to the villages, and it is unlikely that they were used to any great extent as prepatory schools for further education. Instruction was mainly in the Great Proclamation of the Hongwu emperor (*Da-Gao*), the Ming Code, and in some places also in some of the classics. The lifespan of most if not all of these *she*-schools was apparently not long. This is perhaps easy to understand, since the schools demanded money expenditure or at least some effort both by the students and the communities responsible for the operation of the schools. There is evidence that many families did not want or could not afford to have their sons go to classes.[60]

The nature of the *she*-schools changed during the fifteenth century. The general tendency became to have only one or a limited number of schools in each district functioning as a kind of elementary school for boys whose family could not afford private tutors. In 1436 these schools came under full official control, and this seems to have been the policy for the rest of the dynasty. At the same time the officials were ordered to promote the brightest students from these *she*-schools to the Confucian school (*ruxue*).[61] Several orders from the government to establish *she*-schools during the fifteenth century are recorded in Jinan gazetteers, so we also have to question whether these *she*-schools operated effectively for any length of time.[62]

She-schools were probably established during the Hongwu period in each *li* (or *lijia*) in the districts of Jinan Prefecture. The 1533 edition of the Shandong provincial gazetteer still reported *she*-schools in each *li* in nineteen subprefectures and districts. Three of these also had a *she*-school in the district town. The remaining districts only reported one *she*-school, and these were all, with the exception of Zhangqiu, in the district

171

town.[63] We cannot be sure that the schools actually operated in 1533, but the gazetteer shows that they had been established at some time, and that in 1533 remains of the schools such as land, buildings or a tablet still existed. The schools had probably been initiated in the Hongwu period, although the evidence is not conclusive. Three Jinan gazetteers recorded that the schools had been ordered to be established during this period, but all three are Qing editions, so they may have relied on central government sources for this information.[64] In Changqing District the *she*-schools were established in each *li* at the beginning of the Hongzhi period, but this does not preclude the establishment of similar schools earlier.[65]

The tendency in the sixteenth century to have only one *she*-school in a district is clear in Zhanhua, where the *she*-school was rebuilt c. 1556 for forty to fifty students aged thirteen to fourteen years. They studied ceremonies and certain unspecified books, were examined twice a month in the *Minglun* Hall, and could advance to the Confucian school.[66]

In the Wanli period increasing attention was paid to the *she*-schools when Lü Kun was circuit intendant, so it is reasonable to assume that this was connected with his initiatives for subbureaucratic government. In the *SZL* he has a section on the revival of the *she*-schools. He prescribed that the teachers in the *she*-schools were to be chosen from men above the age of forty who were honest and interested in learning, although previous education was not required. These men were instructed in the *Xiaoxue* and *Xiaojing* and in writing and pronunciation. If after one year they were proficient in these subjects, they were to be appointed teachers in the *she*-schools. Four schools were established in the district town and one for each 200 families in the countryside. The *jia*-leader was to select a number of students between the age of eight and sixteen to attend school from the tenth month to the third month of the following year. Lü Kun continued his instructions with detailed regulations for the conduct of the students in the schools.[67]

In Jinan the establishment of *she*-schools along the lines described by Lü Kun was concentrated in the period 1587–1591. Linyi established 83 schools connected with the *xiangyue* and the *she*-granaries. Pingyuan had 40 schools and Zhangqiu more than 10, while in Putai there were 75 schools with a total of 800 students. Leling considered the re-establishment of the old *she*-schools in 1591, but the result is unclear.[68] It is possible that similar *she*-schools were established in other districts during this period. Such an assumption may be supported by the fact that in three of the above cases the gazetteers were compiled in the years immediately following the establishment of the schools. However, some of the other gazetteers record establishment of schools in the period after

172

1600, so if any noticeable activity had taken place during the 1588–1591 period in districts where such records exist, it would most likely have been noted in these gazetteers. A tentative conclusion must therefore be that the *she*-schools of the kind prescribed by Lü Kun were not established in a majority of the subprefectures and districts of Jinan.

The *she*-schools established after 1600 were on a less ambitious scale than those of the previous period. Only Lingxian is recorded to have set up a considerable number, i.e. twenty. Deping established one *she*-school in c. 1605, Xintai two schools in 1613, and Yangxin rebuilt eight schools in the same year.[64]

The expenses of the *she*-schools were to some degree the responsibility of the subbureacratic government system but also involved official funds and control. In Putai the schools were supported with grain from the welfare granaries, and in Linyi they were closely connected with such granaries and the *xiangyue*. In Pingyuan a fee was probably paid by students from well-to-do families, while the fees for poors students were paid by giving the teachers land that had belonged to absconders. The school in Deping was supported by a plot of school-land. School-land is also reported in other districts, but in most cases the income from such land went towards supporting academies (*shuyuan*), so we cannot assume that the *she*-schools were usually endowed with such funds. Finally the *she*-school in Lingxian was supported from official funds.[70]

The revival of the *she*-schools as part of the subbureaucratic government system was clearly a policy in the prefecture during the Wanli period, but serious efforts were concentrated in the short period c. 1587–1591. As they only appear to have been introduced in relatively few districts, where they were probably short-lived, this policy cannot be described as successful.

WELFARE GRANARIES

1. Background

Together with the general interest in the 1580s in subbureaucratic government institutions such as the *xiangyue* came a new wave of initiatives for the re-introduction of welfare granaries in Jinan Prefecture. These granaries were established at the subprefecture and district levels as well as at the subdistrict and lower divisional levels. The main purpose of these granaries was to store grain or other foodstuffs in abundant years to prepare for lean years, so that famines could be eliminated or at least alleviated. To prepare for effective famine relief the element of distance was very important in the organization of the granaries. They had to be located so that the people to whom grain was distributed did not have to travel long distances, which could exhaust them in their undernourished state.[71] As the people first affected by famines were those who did not have the capability to store grain in good years, the granary organization also had an element of social welfare policy.

Welfare granaries have a long tradition in Chinese history, and in the Ming they were instituted shortly after the founding of the dynasty. The first empire-wide order seems to have been the instruction of 1377 to establish ever-normal granaries (*changpingcang*) in all districts. These granaries were not primarily welfare granaries. Their main function was to keep the price of staple foods relatively even. In good years the officials were to buy grain and then re-sell it in bad years.[72] Indirectly this served the interests of the poor, but an element of economic policy was also involved and these granaries could be viewed as part of the general policy for agricultural recovery.

The early ever-normal granaries were not effective for famine relief, either because they were not established at all or because they were inadequate as a relief measure. After a famine in Shandong in 1388 an order was issued to the Ministry of Revenue that it should make funds available for the purchase of grain. In the districts this grain was to be stored in four granaries built in places with high population concentration, so that people with surplus grain could conveniently sell to these granaries. The official was to lock up the granaries when the grain had been received and put them under the guard of rich people. Grain was only distributed in bad years as a relief measure, so these granaries appear to have been the first real welfare granaries for emergency situations.[73]

The granaries ordered in 1388 were probably identical to the so-called emergency granaries (*yubeicang*). In the 1583 edition of the Binzhou gazetteer it is stated that in the past each subdistrict had an emergency granary, which had been instituted in the Hongwu period.[74] In Wuding Subprefecture there had also been emergency granaries in each subdistrict, and these had been abolished in 1440. That subprefecture also has records of ever-normal granaries which had been abolished by 1588, probably some time previously, since the ground was now used for a horse market.[75] References to emergency granaries are given in the gazetteers of other districts, but no details are available, except that they had been abolished by the time when the gazetteers were compiled during the Qing dynasty. With a view to the method of compilation of the gazetteers we can however assume that these granaries had existed in many if not all districts during the Hongwu period. As pointed out by Shimizu Taiji, there is no reason to believe that these granaries were only established on the order of the central government, since the people were probably anxious to establish some kind of relief granaries that could then later be formalized and regularized by the government. Such a time could have been that of the government order of 1388.[76]

During the Hongwu period the emergency granaries were to some extent under the administration of subbureaucratic government, as the distribution of the grain was determined by the magistrate in consultation with the elders. This element of subbureaucratic government may have been a weakness in the system, as several instances of mismanagement of the granaries were reported to the central government. The problem was that wealthy households, some of whom had to guard the granaries, could illegally borrow grain without returning it.[77] The supervision of the officials was apparently not sufficiently strict at this time to ensure that such malpractices in the subbureaucratic government system could not occur. No order to abolish these granaries was issued as a result of these complaints. After all the general policy of the government at that time was to make use of subbureaucratic government of institutions outside the immediate vicinity of the yamen as was seen with the *lijia* and the *li*-elders.

Even with such records of mismanagement the emergency granaries may have served their purpose for some years, but they would probably have broken down sooner or later as did the other non-fiscal subbureaucratic government institutions. Such a process may for the emergency granaries in Shandong and surrounding provinces have been accelerated by the civil war from 1399 to 1402. Orders were issued in 1403 and 1404 to distribute grain from official granaries, so the emergency granaries were clearly not able to cope with the misery in these provinces caused by the war.[78] But that was probably beyond their expected capability. However, the emergency granaries were apparently not effectively restored until the Zhengtong period, at which time they came under stronger official management and were mostly relocated in the cities. High officials were sent out to the different parts of the empire in 1440 to implement a relief policy along these lines.[79] This coincides with the abolition of the subdistrict emergency granaries in Wuding. The subprefectural town still had an emergency granary in 1588.[85]

The strengthening of official control over the granaries did not mean that the subbureaucratic government element was completely removed. But the administrative procedures for supervision were elaborated, and the mere relocation of the granaries to the vicinity of the yamen would have shifted the balance greatly towards official control. The government paid regular attention to the administration of the granaries in the years following 1440,[81] but no details have been found for Jinan Prefecture. An emergency granary was established in Qidong District shortly after 1512,[82] probably in response to needs that had arisen after the large bandit incursions of the preceding years. This granary may also have been built as a replacement for one which had been destroyed by the bandits, so no supposition can be made that the granary did not exist before that time.

The emergency granary under official control was not without its problems. Dishonest officials could oppress the people by demanding grain in excess of the normal tax paid to these granaries. Even if this did not happen, the people could easily have regarded the granaries as potential means of oppression. This would weaken their basis of support, and according to the *Guochao dianhui* most of the emergency granaries had been abolished in Shandong by 1540.[83] This is consistent with the lack of information on the granaries during this period in the gazetteers and is to some extent confirmed by the *SDJHL*. Between the years 1559 and 1565 several instances were recorded where the weigher corvée (*douji*) at the emergency granaries was reduced; in 1559 among other places in Qidong, in 1563 in Binzhou, and in 1565 in Yanzhou Prefecture.[84] These reductions may indicate that the granaries had not been entirely abolished, but they are no proof of this, since the corvée services could have continued as a source of revenue after the actual work at the granaries had been discontinued. But they are a good indication that the granary organization was now in decline. However, the emergency granary in Changqing District was extended both in the Jiajing and Longqing periods, so this decline cannot have been universal.[85]

The response in the sixteenth century to this decline of the emergency granaries was a revival of other forms of granaries, notably those under subbureaucratic government control. The decisive change in government policy was probably the approval of Wang Tingxiang's memorial in 1529 concerning granaries and their accompanying association (*hui* or *she*). *She*-granaries had existed in some parts of the empire from the beginning of the dynasty. They are reported to have existed during the Hongwu period in Dengzhou Prefecture, Shandong, and in other parts during the fifteenth century. A major consideration in the establishment of *she*-granaries – often referred to as *she*-granaries of Zhu Xi – was that they were spread more widely over the subprefecture or district than were the emergency granaries and thus more accessible for people in need.[86]

The Zhu Xi method for the *she*-granaries had been codified in 1181, when he was circuit intendant for grain, tea and salt administration in the eastern circuit of Liangzhe. In his method the people were each year registered in the *baojia*, and grain could only be distributed to members of these *baojia*. The officers of the *baojia* were responsible for assessing the amount of grain to be distributed to each member and for identifying them during the distribution. The granaries were at the level of the subdistricts (*xiang*) and the actual distribution was under supervision of a reliable official sent out by the district administration. Grain was normally distributed as loans in the spring before the new harvest, and these loans had to be repaid during the autumn with an interest of 3% to cover wastage and administration expenses.[87]

The granaries proposed in 1529 by Wang Tingxiang were called *yicang*, but they must have been what was normally termed *shecang* in the Ming dynasty. This confusion stems from changes in the use of the term *yicang*. In the Sui and early Tang dynasties this term was used for welfare granaries at levels below the district, while in later Tang and Song it was used for welfare granaries established in district towns. These were more similar to the emergency granaries of the Ming after 1440. The confusion in Ming is evident, as one source mentions *yubeiyicang*, while another source states that the *yicang* were also called *shecang*. Hoshi Ayao concludes that the *yicang* of the Ming were really either emergency granaries or *she*-granaries and dismisses them as a separate category.[88] I generally agree with this conclusion but, as will be seen later, the term *yicang* was used in Jinan Prefecture during the Wanli period for some special granaries.

2. Granaries in the Wanli period

The year 1529 is taken by Hoshi Ayao to be the turning point in government policy towards granaries, but from his own work – mostly with government sources but also some gazetteers – he also concludes that this policy did not have any widespread effect before the end of the Jiajing period. This is certainly supported by the evidence in Jinan Prefecture, where the only development between 1529 and the Wanli period was the previously mentioned extension of the emergency granary in Changqing District.

Considerable granary activity in the districts of the prefecture is reported from 1576 and for the rest of the Wanli period with regard to *yubeicang, changpingcang, shecang, yicang* and *baochicang*. In Hoshi's opinion the emergency granaries were not part of the policy to establish granaries in the Longqing and Wanli periods. They are, however,

177

reported in Jinan, and their nature is worth exploring. Binzhou, which in the Hongwu period had one emergency granary in each subdistrict, had later changed this to one granary to the north of the subprefectural city with four storehouses, which could hold 8,000 *dan* of grain. In 1582 a further ten granaries were built for the storage of over 3,000 *dan* of grain. The grain for these granaries was provided partly from purchase in years of good harvests and partly from fines paid instead of punishments.[89] In this way more grain was accumulated than ever before. The year 1583 was one of bad harvest, and grain was needed for relief. Apparently this was provided in the form of loans to the inhabitants of the subprefecture which had to be repaid with a small interest.[90] This function of the emergency granaries with several smaller granaries perhaps spread over the subprefectures seems to be following the practice of the *she*-granaries, and they should perhaps be regarded as the same. But no information is given about any subbureaucratic government participation and as this appears to have been an essential part of the *she*-granaries, it is perhaps appropriate to describe them as emergency granaries.

An emergency granary is reported in Dezhou Subprefecture in 1576. In Putai District the emergency granary was rebuilt in 1574 and enlarged in 1589. The granary in Qingcheng was renovated and enlarged in 1576; the same happend to the Pingyuan granary in 1582 and 1588.[91] According to the 1586 edition of the Shanghe gazetteer, the emergency granary was expanded in that year with two new granaries close to the district administrative buildings, but in the 1836 edition the events of 1586 are described as the establishment of an ever-normal granary, so there is some confusion as to the nature of these granaries.[92] In Jiyang District emergency and *baochi*-granaries were probably built in 1602, and the emergency granary in Xintai was restored in 1613 as part of a general policy in the district for building granaries.[93] The evidence presented here cannot be regarded as conclusive. The term *yubeicang* clearly survived in the prefecture during the Wanli period, but the nature of the granaries may have changed. In the two most informative cases – Binzhou and Shanghe – the gazetteers were compiled the same year or the year after the activities concerning the granaries took place. This could indicate that the officials and compilers of the gazetteer had not yet made up their minds as to what name the granary should rightly be called in view of the general granary policy. So the contention of Hoshi Ayao may be correct in spite of the survival of the term *yubeicang*.

Ever-normal granaries are, besides Shanghe, also reported in Changqing District in 1592, but no details are given. They are also mentioned in 1587 in Xingcheng, but the terminology used in this district is confusing, since the function of the granary is closely connected with the *xiangyue* and lending of grain. This ever-normal granary is described in a commemoration tablet for Magistrate Zhao Wenbing, who established the granary, but in the same edition of the gazetteer the name *baochi* is used for the granary established in 1587. So a description of this particular institution properly belongs to the section below.

3. *Xiangyue* and granaries

The *she*-granaries in Jinan were in all recorded instances established at least after 1583 and probably after 1587. This of course indicates that Lü Kun was influential in introducing the granary organization in connection with the *xiangyue*, so it is reasonable to describe what he had to say about granary administration.

The *SZL* does not contain any section entirely devoted to the *she*-granaries. Regulations for such local granaries and the involvement of the *xiangyue* in relief works are included in a lengthy instruction of management of grain storage – including directions for construction of ventilation for the storehouses, for the measurement utensils to be used, and prohibitions against the use of open fire for lights. No less than 10,000 *dan* of grain was to be stored in the district town and no less than 500 *dan* in each market town in the four subdistricts. The grain was procured from four sources: payments in lieu of punishments, fines, purchases, and inducements to donate grain. It was apparently loaned to the people in the spring and returned in the autumn. The interest rate is not stated. The rate in private loans of a similar kind could be as high as 50% or 100%, so the official interest rates were probably considerably less. The high interest on private loans did not prevent these loans from being repaid, while this was not done with the official loans. This was a problem of enforcing the repayment, so Lü Kun ordered that the officials who were in charge of the granaries could not be relieved of their duties until all grain had been returned.

For storage of grain among the people, in addition to that held in the granaries described above, Lü Kun encouraged the formation of association granaries (*huicang*). The association was to meet twice a month, and the members were to deposit an amount of grain according to their wealth. During the twenty-four annual meetings the rich were to deposit twenty-four *dan* of grain and the poor no less than 2.4 *dan* This grain was stored at a place large enough to hold all the grain. The aim of the association granary was not primarily relief for the poor. The intention was that households which had surplus grain to store should do so under mutual supervision, which would help to promote such storage better than if they had been left to store grain privately. The contents of the association granaries were to be reported to the officials, and if they were not properly stocked, the officials were to reprimand the administrators of the granaries, who were to be wealthy and honest local men.[94]

The *xiangyue* was the administrative unit for the distribution of grain. Each *xiangyue* was to draw up a register in which the people entitled to receive grain were divided into four groups according to their wealth. The conditions or the amount to be loaned to the members of each group were different (from poor to rich: *jie, fang, di, she*). The officials were to calculate the amount of grain needed for each group and regulate the amount to be loaned to each group according to the stocks; the households were then issued certificates stipulating the amount they could borrow. The people were to mutually guarantee the transactions; the basic group was to be ten people with different surnames. If such groups did not function properly, then the *jia*-leader and *yue*-director would guarantee and make up any arrears in repayments. The grain was issued, apparently from the district or subdistrict granaries, according to the nature of the loans in the following order: *she, fang, jie,* and *di*. The maximum number of persons to receive grain each day was 500.[95]

The clear intention of this organization was to secure an adequate supply of grain for all the inhabitants, no matter what the size of the harvest and without depending too much on the storage capabilities of individual households. In really bad years this organization was not, however, adequate to cater for the poorest members of the community. To relieve their plight Lü Kun ordered the distribution of rice gruel in the same way as when he served in Shandong. The gruel was to be provided either from private charity – for which some official pressure was applied – or from the public granaries. In the villages the grain for the gruel was to be provided from the *she*-granary. The gruel was to be distributed both to inhabitants of the district and to vagrants. It was to be cooked at as many places as possible in the districts, preferably in every village, but at least so that no one would have to go more than ten *li* to be served. Lü Kun gave directions for the establishment of facilities to prepare the gruel which were to be managed by the stronger of those asking to be fed, a form of subbureaucratic government. Management included registrars to keep records of all the people to whom food was distributed.[96]

180

4. *She*-granaries in Jinan

The *she*-granaries in Jinan were in some cases called *yi*-granaries, a fact that supports the view of Hoshi Ayao. According to the founder of the *yi*-granaries in Xintai District, Magistrate Wang Yingxiu, these granaries followed the tradition of the Sui and Tang dynasties, so he failed to notice the change in terminology of later Tang and Song. The *yi*-granaries were introduced in 1618, and the people of Xintai District willingly provided the grain for them, since public funds were made available to pay for it. From the people's point of view they could then use the grain, which they would in any case prefer to store as collateral for loans from the district treasury. There was, however, resistance among the elders and the *yue*-leaders to building storage granaries. They suggested that the grain should be distributed for storage among the people, but this was rejected by Wang Yingxiu. The twenty-five *bao*, which in Xintai were equal to the *lijia*, were divided into five areas (*qu*), each with five *bao*. The district town had one granary for the ten *bao* closest to the town, and three granaries were established outside for the *bao* along the southeastern road, the southwestern road, and the northwestern road respectively.[97]

Storage in private houses was, however, practised in some districts. *Yi*-granaries were established in Zhanhua District in 1588, but with no fixed buildings. In the district town the grain was stored in public buildings, while in the villages it was stored in the private homes where this was most convenient. The total amount of stored grain was at the outset of 1588, or shortly after, over 1,000 *dan*.[98] Zichuan District established *baochi*-granaries in 1591 by borrowing 2,070 *dan* of grain from the emergency granary to be the basic stock of the new granary system. Each of the *xiangxue* directors was ordered to store twenty-two *dan* or a total of 2,046 *dan*. It is not clear whether this was in addition to the grain borrowed from the emergency granary. The figures are so suspiciously close to each other as to suggest that it was the same grain. However, the district town had a *baochi*-granary administered by four elders as part of this system. The total storage was in 1603 – at least on the books – 11,358.5 *dan*. The real figure may have been lower, because there had been considerable cheating.[99]

It is possible that *she*-granaries were constructed in each *xiangyue* in some districts, but the evidence is inconclusive. *She*-granaries were, according to the 1837 edition of the Linyi gazetteer, established in 1590 at eighty-three places in conjunction with the *xiangyue*.[100] The 1673 Lijin gazetteer reported that there had been six *baochi*-granaries in the district town and fifty-three in the *xiang*. This may refer to the Wanli period.[101] The information from these two districts does not allow us to make any estimate as to the construction of granaries in the *xiangyue*. The impression I get from reading Lü Kun is that the subbureaucratic government participation in his general welfare system was as much a question of the organization as of the actual provision of storage room, although he does mention that the *she*-granaries needed supervision by officials to check the presence of the stock.[102]

The operation of the granaries in Xincheng District may have been organized along the lines suggested by Lü Kun. In 1587 Magistrate Zhao Wenbing established an ever-normal granary to store over 10,400 *dan* of grain. The grain was sold in bad years to reduce the price and then bought in good years to increase the price. This information is included in the commemoration tablet for Zhao Wenbing as the introduction to one of its ten sections. The section then continues in small type: 'Stored grain and established *yue*' and goes on to describe the distribution of grain in spring, its return in autumn with an interest of 20%, and how the amount loaned to a person should be according to his wealth, so there would be no problems with repayment.[103] The granary established at Xincheng in 1587 is referred to in the section on granaries of the same edition as a *baochi*-granary.[104] This term was apparently then used for an ever-normal granary which at the same time functioned as a central storage for the grain distributed and collected annually through the *xiangyue*. This system appears to have been identical with the one used in Zichuan, with one *baochi*-granary and additional storage in each *xiangyue*.

The most common system seems to have been that described in Xintai, and the fact that it was adopted in that district in 1618 suggests that it was regarded as the most effective. A few granaries spread over the district would to some extent have solved the problem of distance without sacrificing the benefits of effective control, which would have been difficult to exercise over granaries in each *xiangyue*. In Pingyin District one *yi*-granary was established in 1585 in the district town, and *she*-granaries were established in 1589 in three market towns (*dian*).[105] Ten *she*-granaries were established in Putai District in 1590, and they were followed in 1591 by a *yi*-granary. An example of the location of a *she*-granary in that district is Yizi [*xiang*]-*yue* in Liting village on the eastern road. So they were out in the villages, but with several *xiangyue* per granary. The functional difference between the *yi*-granary and *she*-granaries in Putai was that the *yi*-granary was established with over 1,000 *dan* of grain to assist poor scholars who could not pass the provincial examination, to support respectable young people of good family (*fushimin*) while they grew up, and to pay for marriage and funeral expenses. This function of the *yi*-granary arouses the suspicion that it may have been privately established for the benefit of the offspring of well-established households, but it was in fact established by the magistrate, so it was part of the official system. The *she*-granaries, each with over 1,000 *dan*, were to assist when there was a grain shortage and also in the education of youngsters in the *she*.[106]

Zhangqiu District was divided into thirty *she*, each with a *baochi*-granary, which in 1596 was to hold no less than 400–500 *dan* of grain. The grain was distributed in spring and returned in autumn, and the granaries were under the control of the *gongzheng*.[107] The section on granaries in the 1596 gazetteer also lists over thirty *yi*-granaries which had been established in 1589 for relief purposes.[108] The coincidence of these numbers suggests that the two kinds of granaries were based upon the same organization and may even to some extent have used common facilities, but a distinction was made between them from an institutional and functional point of view. *Baochi*-granaries were finally established in Jiyang District in 1602, but no details are provided.[109]

The welfare granaries established in Jinan during this period were clearly under the management of subbureaucratic government, often as an integral part of the *xiangyue* and *baojia* system. Officials were, however, definitely involved in the establishment of the granaries and probably also in supervising them. The granaries were subject to abuse and neglect from both sides. There are several recorded instances where the stock of the granaries was not maintained because people did not repay the loans or the grain was improperly loaned to wealthy households who also defaulted. The clerks and other personnel in the yamen also used the stock of the granaries for their own personal benefit.[110] Such dishonesty contributed to the decline of the welfare granaries, probably accompanying a decline in the role of the *xiangyue*.

The fate of the relief granary systems during the Ming dynasty seems to have been that they functioned relatively well in a locality only for relatively short periods, as shown by the constant reorganizations ordered by the government and recorded in local gazetteers. This may, however, be deceptive, since we are dealing with time-spans that might have appeared to be long in the lives of contemporaries. Even modern societies cannot really complain if some measures to prevent excessive misery among the people can work effectively only for a decade or two before they have to be adjusted or re-invigorated. In the Chinese society of the sixteenth century it was not a bad achievement that these relief organizations could have been instituted with some degree of uniformity and within a relatively short period of time, as was apparently the case in Jinan. It would rather have been a surprise if they had lasted for very long.

1. *Changshan xianzhi* 1716/2/11.
2. *Haifeng xianzhi* 1670/5/9.
3. *Lijin xianzhi* 1673/3/2.
4. *Pingyuan xianzhi* 1590/1/23.
5. *Qidong xianzhi* 1617/7/2, 1685/2/12–23.
6. *Deping xianzhi* 1796/2/11.
7. *Zichuan xianzhi* 1602/8/2.
8. *Changshan xianzhi* 1714/2/11.
9. *Qidong xianzhi* 1617/2/1–2.
10. *Binzhou zhi* 1583/2/16.
11. *Qidong xianzhi* 1685/2/3.
12. *Pingyuan xianzhi* 1590/2/23.
13. *Lijin xianzhi* 1673/10/26.
14. *Dezhou zhi* 1576/2/1.
15. *DMB*, pp. 1408–1416.
16. Wada (1939), pp. 121–122; Elmquist, pp. 241, 301–303.
17. Elmquist, p. 287.
18. *Ibid.* p. 250.
19. *Ibid.* pp. 305–306.
20. *Ibid.* p. 242; Wada (1939), p. 122; Sakai Tadao, «Mindai zen shoki no hōkōsei ni tsuite», in *Shimizu hakase tsuitō kinen Mindaishi ronsō,* (Tokyo, 1962), p. 604.
21. Elmquist, p. 81.
22. *Ibid.* pp. 240–241; Wada (1939), p. 120–121.
23. Elmquist, pp. 308–315.
24. *Ibid.* pp. 89–95.
25. *DMB*, pp. 1431–1434. Wang had been Right administration commissioner of Shandong in 1524.
26. *SL* 1529:3:*jiazheng.*
27. *Guochao dianhui* 101/13.
28. *DMHD* 20/23.
29. *DMHD* 22/51; *Ming huiyao (MHY)* 56/1077.
30. Hoshi Ayao, «Mindai no yosō to shasō», *Tōyōshi Kenkyū* 18 (1959), 133.
31. *Zhangqiu xianzhi* 1596/14/97.
32. Sakai Tadao, *Chūgoku zensho no kenkyū,* (Tokyo, 1951), 44.
33. *SZL* 5/4.
34. *Ibid.* 5/2.
35. *Ibid.* 5/3.
36. *Ibid.* 5/4.
37. *Ibid.* 5/4–5, 14.
38. *Ibid.* 5/5.
39. *Ibid.* 5/6–7.
40. T'ung-tsu Ch'ü, *Law and Society in Traditional China*, (Paris–La Haye, 1965), p. 129–130.
41. *SZL* 5/2, 8, 10.
42. *Ibid.* 5/10.
43. *Ibid.* 5/12. In Elmquist's translation, if there were 150 households an additional *baozheng* and one *baofu* were to be appointed. This is however a misinterpretation. Elmquist, p. 326.
44. *SZL* 5/12–13.

45. *Jinan fuzhi* 1839/25/3, 26/4, 27/5.
46. *Jinglüe fuguo yaobian* 5/21.
47. Kuribayashi (1971), p. 286.
48. *Putai xianzhi* 1592/2/57, 4/6.
49. *Binzhou zhi* 1583/2/42.
50. *Ibid.* 1/34–36.
51. *Ibid.* 1701/1/7.,
52. *Zichuan xianzhi* 1602/19/2.
53. *Xincheng xianzhi* 1693/12/17; *Pingyuan xianzhi* 1590/1/27; *Putai xianzhi* 1592/4/5; *Wuding zhouzhi* 1588/4/7; *Zichuan xianzhi* 1602/19/2; *Linyi xianzhi* 1837/4/13; *Laiwu xianzhi* 1673/5/25; *Qingcheng xianzhi* 1612/1/40; *Zhangqiu xianzhi* 1596/14/97; *Xintai xianzhi* 1659/6/25; *Lingxian zhi* 1845/16/29; *Qidong xianzhi* 1685/2/36; *Taian zhouzhi* 1671/2/8.
54. *Pingyuan xianzhi* 1590/1/27, 1749/4/10.
55. *Putai xianzhi* 1592/4/5.
56. *Zhangqiu xianzhi* 1596/14/97.
57. *Xincheng xianzhi* 1673/12/17.
58. Ch'ü (1962), p. 3; Hsiao, p. 63.
59. *Xincheng xianzhi* 1673/12/18.
60. *SL* 1375:1:*dinghai*, 1381:10:*gengsi*; Wang Lanyin, «Mindai zhi shexue», *Shida yuekan* 21 (1935), 44, 25 (1936), 110; Igarashi Seiji, «Minsho ni okeru shagaku settei o megoru shojijō ni tsuite», in *Yamazaki sensei taikan kinen Tōyōshigaku ronsō*, (Tokyo, 1967), pp. 16–23; Tilemann Grimm, *Erziehung und Politik im konfuzianischen China der Ming Zeit (1368–1644)*, (Hamburg, 1960), pp. 139–144.
61. *DMHD* 78/23; Wang (1935), pp. 54–80, (1936), pp. 84–110; Igarashi, p. 14.
62. *Linyi xianzhi* 1837/4/12; *Changqing xianzhi* 1835/8/8.
63. *Shandong tongzhi* 1533/16/2–7.
64. *Binzhou zhi* 1701/2/60; *Leling xianzhi* 1762/3/32; *Linyi xianzhi* 1837/4/13.
65. *Changqing xianzhi* 1835/8/8. The dating to the Hongzhi period may be an unlikely but not impossible error for the Hongwu period. For one example of such an error see Ch. II note 53.
66. *Zhanhua xianzhi* 1619/2/35.
67. *SZL* 3/7 ff.
68. *Pingyuan xianzhi* 1590/7/26; *Putai xianzhi* 1592/4/5; *Zhangqiu xianzhi* 1596/21/74; *Leling xianzhi* 1762/3/32; *Linyi xianzhi* 1837/4/13.
69. *Lingxian zhi* 1845/16/28; *Deping xianzhi* 1796/2/7, 5/10; *Xintai xianzhi* 1659/2/3; *Yangxin xianzhi* 1682/2/11, 10/19.
70. See notes 68 and 69 above.
71. Hoshi (1959), p. 129.
72. Hoshi Ayayo, *Mindai sōun no kenkyū* (Tokyo, 1963), p. 453.
73. *Ibid.* p. 454.
74. *Binzhou zhi* 1583/1/27.
75. *Wuding zhouzhi* 1588/4/5.
76. Hoshi (1963), p. 454.
77. *Ibid.* p. 464.
78. *Ibid.* p. 456–457.
79. *Ibid.* p. 462.
80. *Wuding zhouzhi* 1588/4/5.
81. Hoshi (1963), p. 467.
82. *Qidong xianzhi* 1617/3/5.
83. Hoshi (1963), p. 469.

84. *SDJHL* 8/14, 41, 57.
85. *Changqing xianzhi* 1835/3/12.
86. Hoshi (1963), pp. 471–472.
87. Elmquist, pp. 95 ff.
88. Hoshi (1963), pp. 478 ff.
89. Huang, p. 249.
90. *Binzhou zhi* 1583/1/27.
91. *Dezhou zhi* 1576/2/2; *Putai xianzhi* 1592/4/8; *Pingyuan xianzhi* 1590/1/6; *Qingcheng xianzhi* 1612/1/7.
92. *Shanghe xianzhi* 1586/2/12, 1836/3/25.
93. *Jiyang xianzhi* 1765/2/8; *Xintai xianzhi* 1659/2/3.
94. *SZL* 2/12–15.
95. *Ibid.* 2/25–26.
96. *Ibid.* 2/41–46.
97. *Xintai xianzhi* 1659/6/24–25.
98. *Zhanhua xianzhi* 1619/2/27.
99. *Zichuan xianzhi* 1602/19/1.
100. *Linyi xianzhi* 1839/3/16.
101. *Lijin xianzhi* 1673/2/4.
102. *SZL* 2/30.
103. *Xincheng xianzhi* 1693/12/17. The tablet was composed at the initiative of elders, *yue*-leaders and deputies, 200 in all.
104. *Ibid.* 2/6.
105. *Pingyuan xianzhi* 1590/1/7.
106. *Putai xianzhi* 1592/4/8, 11/16.
107. *Zhangqiu xianzhi* 1596/14/47.
108. *Ibid.* 21/74.
109. *Jiyang xianzhi* 1679/2/8.
110. *Zichuan xianzhi* 1602/19/2; *Xincheng xianzhi* 1693/12/17.

VII. Conclusions

In the investigation of the subbureaucratic government system of the Ming dynasty I have concentrated on the developments that took place in Shandong Province, with particular reference to Jinan Prefecture in the second half of the sixteenth century. The official subbureaucratic government involved participation by the people in the process of government at the lowest level, supplying a contact between the bureaucracy and each household and also regulating minor disputes that might arise between the households. The system was established by the government – central or local – and was employed by the officials as a part of the administrative processs for the levy of taxes and corvée and for control of the populace. This study clearly shows that such an official subbureaucratic government system still existed in Shandong in the sixteenth century, and that the officials still regarded it as an integral and active element in the administration of the province.

Unofficial subbureaucratic government institutions or «local self-government» has not been the object of the investigation. This does not mean that such unofficial systems or organizations did not exist. On the contrary all evidence on the history of Chinese society almost up to the present day indicates that such organizations existed at least for religious purposes, and the Jinan gazetteers amply verify that religion was a part of daily life in the sixteenth century. However, little evidence has been found that they actually performed duties of the subbureaucratic government such as mutual assistance and settlement of disputes. This probably happened, but the sources – written and compiled by and for officials and other educated people – are not very informative. The indications are that such unofficial subbureaucratic government activities, at least those conducted under the leadership of commoners, were not approved by the officials, because they might be an obstacle to the government's control over the population.

The official subbureaucratic government system of the Ming dynasty was from the establishment of the *lijia* system in 1381 heavily oriented towards fiscal functions. The basic unit, the *lijia*, was established strictly according to the number of households, without any provisions for modification according to settlement patterns. The intention was no doubt to have units of comparable economic strength in order to equalize the corvée burdens. The households were too small for this purpose as the division into tax classes shows. The administrative work of the bureaucracy was probably also reduced by inserting the *lijia* between the households and the local yamen as a unit for collection of taxes and corvée. The *lijia* was also used as the unit for population registration by means of the Yellow Registers, and the accuracy of the population figures obtained in the last two decades of the fourteenth century was probably unsurpassed for 400 years.

Some scholars have suggested that this accuracy in population figures was already lost under the Hongwu emperor by giving increasing priority to the fiscal aspect of such registration, and also that the *lijia* tended to become more a territorial unit rather than one based upon the number of households, as a result of policies introduced by this emperor. This study contends that these suggestions are certainly applicable to later developments, but they cannot be ascribed to policies deliberately introduced by the founding emperor. The Yellow Registers were from the outset fiscal in nature, and the procedural changes in the registration must be seen as corrections to weaknesses and misunderstandings in the original procedures. The policy that the *lijia* should be kept within the boundaries of the subdistrict can be seen as a concession to traditional administrative and settlement patterns, but it did not in itself indicate a basic change in the policy of organizing the *lijia* according to the number of households. In my view all this was part of a prospective continuous process of amending the subbureaucratic government regulations whenever inadequacies were revealed in the existing laws. The reason why this process did not continue was in the first instance the death of Zhu Yuanzhang and the ensuing civil war, which interrupted the administration for several years, and later the result of a lack of interest on the part of the emperors and their advisers in subbureaucratic government. Perhaps the fact that corrections in the *lijia* and Yellow Registers were only to be made every ten years contributed to the discontinuance of this process, since it only gave the founding emperor one occasion on which to issue supplementary regulations.

1. Fiscal duties

The *lijia* was organized with ten *li*-leaders, each serving one year in a decennial rotation, and 100 *jia*-heads divided into ten *jia*. This study shows that each *li*-leader was permanently attached to one *jia*. During the year of incumbency he was assisted by the *jia* in carrying out his duties as *li*-leader, and during the years of non-incumbency he acted as leader of the *jia* for the purpose of collecting taxes and equal corvée and for registration work. The *jia*-heads – despite the deceptive terminology – did not exercise any supervisory power over other *jia*-heads. Their position towards households in the *lijia* that were not members of the official *lijia* structure, a situation that must have existed in many of the larger *lijia* in the sixteenth century, has not been clarified. During this period the *lijia* was still regarded as the unit for the levy of certain items of corvée, at least in the sense that some of these were levied upon the districts according to the number of *lijia*. All the evidence shows, however, that the officials were fully aware of the discrepancies in the economic power of the *lijia*, and that most, if not all, levies within the districts were probably made according to the respective strength of the *lijia*.

Besides the incumbent and non-incumbent *li*-leaders, the fiscal officers of the subbureaucratic government system of all subprefectures and districts included the *li*-registrars and the *dahu*. The *li*-registrars were apparently permanent positions in each *lijia*, but we have no information about the terms of service of the individual *li*-registrars. For the origin and function of the *dahu* in Shandong Province I suggest that they were conscripted on the basis of the *lijia*. When they were first introduced, perhaps late in the fifteenth century, each *dahu* was to collect from several *lijia* a limited amount of tax, all with the same granary rate, and forward it to the designated granary. At that time *dahu* may only have been conscripted for taxes to more distant granaries, either from the stronger *lijia* or jointly from two or more *lijia*. Each *dahu* then relieved several *li*-leaders of one of their more onerous burden. When more *dahu* were needed, they were drafted from most or all of the *lijia* in a district but still with due consideration for the strength of the *lijia*, at least in the allocation of the duties. The stronger *lijia* could also be asked to furnish more than one *dahu*. When the forwarding duties of the subbureaucratic government system were abolished, the *dahu* may have become more directly linked with their own *lijia* or perhaps other divisions such as the *she* in Zhangqiu District. In this case the *dahu* would appear to perform the tax collection part of the duties of their own *li*-leader, perhaps in the larger *lijia* with several *dahu* working together. If the above interpretation of the origin and function of the *dahu* is correct, then the conclusion must be that they gradually took over more and more of the work of the *li*-leaders, since these were no longer able to perform all their duties. Other economicaly strong households were needed to perform some of the heavier duties. These households were the *dahu* or literally 'large households'.

Corvée heads who were responsible for each item of corvée still performed in the form of labour should perhaps also be recognized as part of the subbureaucratic government system. The *li*-leaders, *dahu* and corvée heads all had the responsibility of making up deficits in payments of taxes and corvée. Afterwards they could attempt to recoup at least some of it from the assisting households or the other members of the *lijia*. Most of the reforms carried out in the second half of the sixteenth century aimed at eliminating these services, and this appears to have been effected in most districts for most services by the end of the century. This followed official deliberations – which must have been fairly common during the period – as to the continuous involvement of the *lijia* and other subbureaucratic officers in these processes. Perhaps there were also considerations of the capacity of the bureaucracy to take over these duties. This transfer of duties from subbureaucratic government to the bureaucracy was done in order to avoid households from being ruined and also to prevent them from using their posts for their own personal benefit. Such a transfer of duties to the bureaucracy was greatly facilitated by the increasing commutation of taxes, and in this period particularly corvée, to silver payments. The officers of the *lijia* are the only recorded middlemen between the taxpayers and the receiving tax agencies. Unofficial middlemen may have existed, but they have not been recorded in these official writings. Their absence indicates that the *lijia* system at least brought such middlemen under official scrutiny, even if control was not always effective.

Corvée items for which no other budgetary allowances existed were still levied upon the *lijia*. This was to a certain degree eliminated with the consolidation of the *lijia* corvée in the late 1560s, but my impression is that even thereafter the officials regarded the *lijia* as a legitimate and convenient source for emergency and irregular levies, and that they were reluctant to see this function of the *lijia* disappear. But the case of the reception heads in Zhangqiu in the 1590s shows that the officials were under strong pressure from the people, at least those heeded by the local officials, to completely abolish the offices of the *lijia* in order to avoid the ruin of households which could follow from these duties. This appears to have been successful to some extent, but some *dahu* were reintroduced during the emergencies in the first half of the seventeenth century.

2. Non-fiscal duties

The non-fiscal duties of the subbureaucratic government system were from 1381 connected with the *lijia*. From the 1390s they were under the direction of the *li*-elders, whose positions were more or less permanent and not rotational like those of the *li*-leaders. The prestige and function of the *li*-leaders seems to have declined rapidly. They still existed in Shandong in the second half of the sixteenth century, but they seem to have been used mainly for fiscal duties, even to the extent of performing corvée as door-men.

During this period their non-fiscal functions were to some extent performed by *gongzheng*. These *gongzheng* were responsible for welfare granaries and supervised the educational function of the *xiangyue*, but they also performed fiscal duties such as receiving returns from land registrations, and they could be drafted as reception heads. The officials apparently allowed local litigation to be settled without the assistance of any official subbureaucratic government officer as long as the decisions were recorded in the district yamen. From the 1580s educational, judicial, and security functions were performed through the officially instituted *baojia* and *xiangyue*, with mutual responsibility for the behaviour of the members. These organizations, which seem to have been widespread in Jinan Prefecture, also assisted in the collection and distribution of grain from the various welfare granaries, and in the establishment of local schools. The direct purpose of these organizations was no doubt to prevent social unrest and perhaps to force, in an official setting, a contact between the different social strata. They may also have served to counteract a closure of the local community which in malignant form could result in xenophobic local chauvinism. I have not been able to ascertain the success of these organizations. My impression is that they may have operated with some success for a period of a few years, but they were certainly not enduring.

3. Subbureaucratic government and late Ming society

Subbureaucratic government depended upon the willingness and ability of the members and particularly the leaders to perform their duties. To get effective operation the leaders moreover needed to be reasonably honest people with a certain standing in the community. In the subbureaucratic government system of the Ming dynasty such persons were defined in terms of taxable property. This seems to have been the weakness of the *lijia* system. The élite households of the officials and examination graduates were normally not conscripted to service in the *lijia*. Their numbers increased considerably during the Ming dynasty and, as many of them were landowners, the basis for the conscription of the *li*-leaders and other officers of the subbureaucratic government system was eroded. They had furthermore by statute or customary rights exemptions from some taxes and corvée, so that they could avoid the heavy corvée as corvée heads.

Commoners with large landholdings were then the designated leaders in the subbureaucratic government system. They were classified into the upper tax classes according to property and number of male adults. The households in these tax classes not only had to serve as *li*-leaders but also as *dahu* and corvée heads for equal corvée and horse administration. All this amounted to heavy progressive taxation on these households and, as could be expected, tax evasion became the norm. The powerful households among the commoners were in the best position to manipulate themselves into lower tax classes, with the result that the households registered in the upper tax classes, i.e. those who were conscripted as *li*-leaders, were no longer the wealthiest – but probably not the poorest either.

Progressive taxation was obviously an important concern of the officials during this period, indeed the purpose of the Single Whip policy was to eliminate such progression, first by abolishing the granary rates and later by abolishing or at least diminishing reliance upon the households and tax classes for the levy of corvée. The burden of corvée may also have been alleviated when corvée items were shuffled between the different forms of levy, such as equal corvée and *lijia* corvée, and also when assessment periods were shortened, so that migrations and fluctuations in the fortune of the individual household could be registered much earlier than had been the case in the decennial registrations of the Yellow Registers.

The subbureaucratic government system of the Ming dynasty could not be maintained when the leadership of the organizations was affected by heavy progressive taxation. But even after at least some of the problems with this progressions were solved, the government did not try to reinvigorate the subbureaucratic government system. Following the Single Whip and the commutation of taxes and corvée to silver payments, the bureaucracy took over a good part of the fiscal duties of the subbureaucratic government system. Attempts were made by local officials to create organizations for the non-fiscal duties, but if they were effective they were certainly not lasting. If these or similar official subbureaucratic government organizations should have functioned for a long time, they would have needed an effective leadership. The 'élite' could, on the basis of official positions, degrees, and property, have provided such leadership, but the government was apparently not prepared to order it to assume such official leadership, either because it was not able to or did not want to do so. This may have paved the road for the more informal power of the 'élite' in local society which became prominent in the Qing dynasty.

Appendix I

Lijia in Jinan Prefecture

	Early Ming	Jia-jing[1]	Late Ming	Notes
Binzhou	78	78	78	1583/1/7, 1/35
Changqing	41	44		1835/1/2
Changshan		63		
Deping	40?	41		1796/2/14
Dezhou	20?	34		1576/1/?
Feicheng		32		
Haifeng	25	43	43	1670/2/10
Jiyang		40		
Laiwu	30	40	42	1673/2/16
Leling	56	56	56	1762/1/65
Licheng	98	98		1640/3/16
Lijin	34	40	40	1673/4/1
Linyi		32		
Lingxian	32	32	32	1673/3/1
Pingyuan	46	46	46	1590/1/20
Putai	63	59	59	1592/5/4
Qidong	46	55	55	1685/1/6, 1617/6/1–2
Qihe		27		
Qingcheng	33	33	33	1612/1/33
Shanghe	58	68	68	1586/1/2
Taian	97	97		1671/1/1
Wuding	114	98	98	1588/2/1
Xingcheng	42	45	45	1693/1/3
Xintai[2]	21	21	25	1784/2/1, 1659/1/7
Yangxin		70	70	*Wuding zhouzhi* 1588/15/1
Yucheng		56		
Zhanhua	48	24	24	1619/1/4
Zhangqiu	103	103	103	1596/1/4–5, 14/96
Zichuan	60	63	60	1602/1/2
Zouping		57		

1. *Houhuzhi* 2/52.
2. The *lijia* in Xintai was called *bao*. In 1556 the 21 *bao* were combined to 5 *bao* on the initiative of a local man. They were divided again in early Wanli into 21 *bao* and four more *bao* were added in 1582. *Xintai xianshi* 1784/2/1, 16/6.

Appendix II

Commutation of Transferred Revenue Summer Taxes in Taels[1]

	I	II	III	IV	V	VI	VII	VIII	IX
Licheng	1.2	1.6	0.75	1.0					
Zhangqiu	1.2	1.6	0.75		0.8				
Qihe	1.2	1.6	0.75		0.8				
Changqing	1.2	1.6	0.75		0.8				
Linyi		1.6		1.0	0.8	1.1	1.0	0.8	
Zichuan	1.2	1.6	0.7(5)		0.8				
Yucheng	1.2	1.6			0.8			0.8	
Changshan	1.2				0.8				
Zouping			0.75		0.8		1.0	0.8	
Feicheng	1.2		0.75		0.8				
Xincheng		1.6		1.0	0.8				
Qidong	1.2							0.8	
Jiyang	1.2				0.8				
Lingxian								0.8	
Wuding	1.2	1.6	0.75		0.8		1.0		
Yangxin	1.2			1.0	0.8			0.8	1.4
Shanghe	1.2				0.8			0.8	
Haifeng			0.75	1.0					
Leling	1.2				0.8			0.8	
Dezhou	1.2				0.8				
Deping	1.2							0.8	
Pingyuan	1.2		1.0	0.8	1.1		0.8		
Taian	1.2		0.75		0.8				
Xintai			0.75		0.8				
Laiwu			0.75						1.4
Binzhou				1.0		1.1		0.8	
Putai			0.7(5)		0.8				
Zhanhua			0.7(5)		0.8				
Lijin				1.0				0.8	
Qingcheng	1.2		0.75		0.8				

I: Three granaries in Baoan Subprefecture in northwestern Beizhili.
II: Pasturage Granary probably in northern Beizhili.
III: Guangying Granary in Baoding Prefecture in southern Beizhili.
IV: Gusheng Horse Administration Granaries in northeastern Beizhili.
V: Dezhou Granary in northern Jinan Prefecture.
VI: Office of Provisions (Jiucumianju), Peking.
VII: Court of Imperial Entertainment, Peking.
VIII: Tianjin Granary in eastern Beizhili.
IX: Xunxiang Battalion in Beizhili.

1. *SDJHL* 1/1-46.

Appendix III

Population figures

	Households	*Ding*	Persons	Source
Jinan (1533)	239,143		2,102,935	[1]
Binzhou (1583)	16,641	37,912		1583/2/38
Changqing (Ming)		48,335		1845/5/2
Changshan				
Deping (1556)	6,977			1796/3/2
Deping (1587)	14,286			1796/3/2
Dezhou (1573)	8,887		50,130	1576/2/1
Feicheng				
Haifeng (1581)		22,690		1670/8/1
Jiyang (Wanli)		39,802		1765/3/1
Laiwu (1596)	5,829		51,861	1673/4/1
Leling (Longqing)	14,492		23,699	1762/2/42
(Wanli)	24,514		31,779	1762/2/42
Licheng (1640)		70,722		1640/5/2
Lijin (1572)	6,500	25,333		1673/4/1
(1596)	21,233	23,274		1673/4/1
Linyi				
Lingxian				
Pingyuan (1541)	5,535		51,638	1590/1/18
Putai (1567)	8,335	10,850		1592/4/1
(c. 1586)	14,654	14,675		1592/4/1
Qidong (1551)	11,340		101,290	1617/15/4
Qihe				
Qingcheng (1612)		22,681		1612/1/11
Shanghe (1587)	11,314		123,986	1586/3/3
Taian (1603)		71,325		1671/2/8
Wuding (1588)		62,770	132,650	1588/5/1
Xingcheng (1543)	6,372		53,230	1693/3/2
(1578)		13,751		1693/3/2
Xintai (Wanli)		10,182		1659/3/1
Yangxin (1597)	11,546	38,871		1682/3/4
Yucheng (late Ming)		55,368		1808/5/1
Zhanhua				
Zhangqiu (c. 1530)	13,170			1596/3/9
Zichuan (1553)	11,051		107,770	1602/12/1
(1602)	9,804			1602/12/1
Zouping (Jiajing)	8,235		men 45,783	1660/3/1
			women 22,647	
(1609)		19,077		1660/3/1

[1] *Shandong tongzhi* 1533/8/20.

Appendix III (cont.)

A definite estimate of the population figure for Jinan Prefecture in the period 1550–1600 cannot be made on the basis of these figures. However, in the fifteen subprefectures and districts for which households figures are available the average number of households is over 12,000. This suggests that the average number of households per district in the whole prefecture may have been well over ten thousands. With an average size of the households at eight to ten persons the total population of the prefecture may have been three millions or more. This figure is not incompatible with the 1533 figure, for which there may have been some under-registration.

Appendix IV

Taxes and corvée in Jinan Prefecture 1571

	Summer taxes[1] dan of xiaomai	Autumn taxes[1] dan of sumi	Transf. summer taxes[1] taels	Transf. autumn taxes[1] taels	Horse fodder[1] taels	Salt tax[1] taels	Equal corvée[2] taels	Lijia[3] taels	Postal service[4] taels	Horse delivery[5] taels
Binzhou	13,287	30,992	3,085	14,314	2,715	804	7,042	1,017	3,523	2,952
Changqing	9,225	21,526	3,237	16,330	1,956	286	6,421	3,620	2,170	2,016
Changshan	9,245	21,573	2,872	16,124	1,477	378	5,086	2,323	2,070	2,976
Deping	6,162	14,379	1,535	9,109	1,564	294	5,501	1,017	1,386	1,872
Dezhou	5,186	12,101	1,790	9,631	1,191	232	7,066	2,481	1,197	1,536
Feicheng	4,043	9,435	1,348	7,417	941	101	6,567	3,343	954	1,464
Haifeng	5,287	12,337	1,114	5,113	891	296	3,127	1,017	945	1,824
Jiyang	10,610	24,758	3,076	17,593	1,360	520	5,943	2,323	1,566	2,544
Laiwu	5,471	12,767	1,234	8,826	1,053	362	5,647	1,427	1,640	480
Leling	9,181	21,424	2,104	12,077	1,403	456	4,633	1,017	2,034	1,992
Licheng	13,633	31,904	4,396	18,887	2,237	496	9,152	7,420	2,448	1,488
Lijin	6,015	14,035	1,262	7,229	875	296	3,147	1,017	1,162	1,464
Linyi	6,621	15,450	1,888	11,467	1,000	170	4,824	1,619	1,519	1,464
Lingxian	5,486	12,801	1,826	8,920	996	119	4,489	1,348	1,246	1,968
Pingyuan	8,059	18,806	2,626	14,924	1,467	312	5,873	3,343	2,137	
Putai	8,752	20,426	1,804	9,002	1,664	577	3,756	1,017	1,750	2,256
Qidong	9,112	21,262	2,672	16,404	1,676	244	5,097	1,017	2,016	2,544
Qihe	7,391	17,246	2,213	12,817	799	193	3,595	3,406	1,659	1,272
Qingcheng	3,850	8,985	1,358	7,890	993	388	4,138	1,017	886	1,536
Shanghe	12,992	30,315	2,974	19,076	2,057	710	6,225	1,017	2,200	2,880
Taian	9,607	22,417	3,025	14,291	2,416	1,186	8,764	3,447	2,657	4,224
Wuding	16,302	38,038	4,376	23,608	2,973	1,138	8,796	2,370	2,983	4,944
Xingcheng	7,195	16,789	1,589	10,833	931	330	3,138	1,017	580	1,920
Xintai	4,086	9,536	816	4,912	386	262	2,982	1,258	816	
Yangxin	11,059	25,804	3,504	15,743	2,575	910	6,255	1,017	2,484	2,952
Yucheng	7,042	16,433	2,144	12,359	1,728	402	5,441	3,343	1,662	2,400
Zhanhua	5,793	13,517	1,095	5,655	840	194	2,621	1,017	966	1,056
Zhangqiu	16,961	39,576	5,818	29,118	2,772	900	9,238	2,483	3,717	4,464
Zichuan	8,114	18,934	2,316	12,082	1,885	295	5,090	1,017	1,528	2,592
Zouping	10,042	22,801	2,983	16,030	1,038	500	4,894	2,483	1,995	2,592

[1] *SDJHL*, 1/1–48   [2] *Ibid.*, 5/1–30   [3] *Ibid.*, 10/1–8   [4] *Ibid.*, 11/1–8   [5] *Ibid.* 12/1–8.

Appendix V

The history of subbureaucratic government institutions.[1]

In the *Zhouli*[2] the *xiangshi, suishi, zhouzhang, dangzheng, zushi, lizai, bishi, lüshi, lüxu* and *bizhang* were in charge of collecting taxes from the six *xiang*. In Qin and Han ten *li* formed one *ting* and the *ting* had a leader. Ten *ting* formed one *xiang* and the *xiang* had a *sanlao*, a *sefu*, and a *youjiao*. The *sanlao* was in charge of education, the *sefu* handled litigations and collected taxes, and the *youjiao* apprehended thieves.

In the Tang dynasty 500 families formed one *xiang* and there was appointed a *xiangzheng*. One hundred families formed one *li*, and a *lizhang* was appointed. They administered the population, gave advice about planting and cultivation and about mournings, and they investigated bad conduct. Those who lived in the towns were called *fangzheng*. They were in charge of the gate of the *fang*, kept the keys and controlled villainous behaviour. In the countryside they were called *cunzheng* and their responsibilities were similar to the *fangzheng*.

The Song used *lizheng, huzhang*, and *xiangshushou* to levy and collect taxes and *qizhang* and *zhuangding* to pursue and apprehend thieves. Later there were three groups of corvée *yaqian, chengfu, renli, shouli, sancong*, and *zhihou*[3]. The *yaqian* corvée, which was levied upon the rural households, was the heaviest. People performing this corvée were either in charge of granaries or treasuries or transported goods to the granaries, often to the extent that they ruined themselves. So in the Huangyou period (1049–1503) it was prohibited to use households serving in the *xiang* for the *yaqian* corvée, and orders were given to hire people to do this work. In the Xining period (1068–1077) there was also the *baojia* method, and in the Baoqing period (1225–1227) there was the *yiyi* method.

The Yuan dynasty established *fangzheng* in the *fang*, *lizheng* in the *li*, and *zhushou* in the *du*. Without assistance they pressed for payment of the taxes, and they summoned and escorted the people to public works.

In this dynasty the Yellow Registers for taxes and corvée were first compiled in 1381. One hundred and ten households formed one *tu* [*lijia*]. The ten households with most taxable property were chosen to be *li*-leaders (*lizhang*) and the other one hundred households became *jia*-heads (*jiashou*). They served in rotation over ten years. They pressed for the payment of taxes and other public expenses and administered public affairs. They were like the *ligui* and *tingzhang* of Qin and Han and the *fangzheng* and *lizheng* of Tang, Song, and Yuan. Virtuous old men in the *fang* and *li* were selected as elders (*laoren*). They were issued with the

Precepts of Popular Instruction (*Jiaomin pangwen*) and supervised public morals and litigations. They were like the so-called *sanlao*.

Tax-captains (*liangzhang*) were appointed to exact the two kinds of taxes; they were like the so-called *sefu*. The *zongjia* and *xiaojia* investigated irregular events; they were like the so-called *youjiao*. These were the regular ten-year-corvée services.

At present all public expenses for sacrifices and worship are paid in addition to the land tax. Al these items are called *lijia*, because they are provided by the *lijia* of the entire district. There are also miscellaneous corvées in the ten years. They are called 'labour corvée' (*lichai*) and 'silver corvée' (*yinchai*). They are all levied from the *lijia*, from the adult males (*ding*) and from the fields. There are also militia (*minbing*) and postal horses (*fuma*). The *fuma* are substitutes for postal services in kind. For highly frequented water and land transport stations there are levies for mutual assistance (*xieji*).[4] The levy of these services is equally distributed among the *li*-leaders, the *ding* and taxable property, but there are not sufficient of these to satisfy the needs of the whole country. The levies are increased year after year. How can there be a limit on *ding* and fields?

1. The following translation is part of the essay «Jiangxi chaiyi shiyi», which was included in the *Tushubian* by Zhang Huang in 1613. The text used here was included in the *Babian jingshi leizuan* (1626, photographic reprint Taipei, 1966), 35/16. The author and the date of the essay is not given but from internal evidence it was probably written at the beginning of the sixteenth century.
2. There has been some doubt whether the *Zhou Li* was actually compiled before the Han dynasty. In the opinion of Karlgren it was compiled during the Zhou, so the institutions described here probably refer to that period, although they may be somewhat idealized. Shimizu, p. 14; Bernhard Karlgren, «The Early History of the Chou Li and Tso Chuan texts», *BMFEA* 3, (1931), 7–8, 58.
3. The corvée services of the early Song can be divided into four groups: 1. The *yaqian* in charge of public goods, 2. the *lizheng*, *huzhang*, and *xiangshushou* in charge of taxation, 3. the *qizhang*, *gongshou*, and *zhuangding* for apprehending thieves, and 4. *chengfu*, *renli*, *shouli*, *sancong*, etc., who provided services for the officials. Li Jian-nong, p. 226.
4. *Xieji* was used when one district or province assisted the postal system in another district or province. *SDJHL* 9/41.

Glossary
TERMS AND TITLES
(with the most important reference)

201

Proper names

207

208

Bibliography

JINAN GAZETTEERS

Binzhou zhi 濱州志 1583

Binzhou zhi 濱州志 1701

Changqing xianzhi 長清縣志 1833-35

Changshan xianzhi 長山縣志 1716

Deping xianzhi 德平縣志 1796

Dezhou zhi 德州志 1576

Dezhou zhi 德州志 1673

Feicheng xianzhi 肥城縣志 1672

Haifeng xianzhi 海豐縣志 1670

Jinan fuzhi 濟南府志 1692

Jinan fuzhi 濟南府志 1839

Jiyang xianzhi 濟陽縣志 1765

Laiwu xianzhi 萊蕪縣志 1673

Leling xianzhi 樂陵縣志 1762

Licheng xianzhi 歷城縣志 1640

Lijin xianzhi 利津縣志 1673

Linyi xianzhi 臨邑縣志 1837

Lingxian zhi 陵縣志 1673

Lingxian zhi 陵縣志 1845

Pingyuan xianzhi 平原縣志 1590

Pingyuan xianzhi 平原縣志 1749

Putai xianzhi 蒲臺縣志 1592

Putai xianzhi 蒲臺縣志 1763

Qidong xianzhi 齊東縣志 1617

Qidong xianzhi 齊東縣志 1685

Qihe xianzhi 齊河縣志 1673

Qingcheng xianzhi 青城縣志 1612

Shanghe xianzhi 商河縣志 1586

Shanghe xianzhi 商河縣志 1836

Taian zhouzhi 泰安州志 1670 (1603)

Taian fuzhi 泰安府志 1760

Wuding zhouzhi 武定州志 1588

Wuding fuzhi 武定府志 1759

Xincheng xianzhi 新城縣志 1693

Xintai xianzhi 新泰縣志 1659

Xintai xianzhi 新泰縣志 1785

Yangxin xianzhi 陽信縣志 1682

Yucheng xianzhi 禹城縣志 1808

Zhanhua xianzhi 霑化縣志 1619

Zhangqiu xianzhi 章邱縣志 1596

Zhangqiu xianzhi 章邱縣志 1691

Zichuan xianzhi 淄川縣志 1602

Zichuan xianzhi 淄川縣志 1687

Zouping xianzhi 鄒平縣志 1660

OTHER SOURCES

Babian jingshi leizuan 八編經世類纂 (1626. Taipei
1966 reprint).

Baoding fuzhi 保定府志 1607.

210

Da-Ming huidian 大明會典 (1587. Taipei 1963 reprint).

Daxue yanyibu 大學衍義補 (1487. Taipei 1976 reprint).

Ge Duansugong wenji 葛端肅公文集 (1582). By Ge Shouli.

Guchengshanguan wenji 穀城山館文集 (1607). By Yu Shen-xing.

Guochao dianhui 國朝典彙 (1601. Taipei 1965 reprint).

Houhuzhi 後湖志 (1611).

Huangchao jingshi wenbian 皇朝經世文編 (1887).

Huangming zhishu 皇明制書 (1579. Taipei reprint n.d.).

Jinglüe fuguo yaobian 經略復國要編 (Taipei reprint of Wanli edition). By Song Yingchang.

Li Kaixian ji 李開先集 (Preface 1556. Shanghai 1959 edition).

Ming huiyao 明會要 (1887. Taipei 1963 edition).

Minglü jijie fuli 明律集解附例 (1610. Taipei reprint of 1908 reprint).

Ming shi 明史 (1736. Peking 1974 edition).

Ming shilu 明實錄 (Taipei 1963–1968 reprint).

Qingchao lunce leibian. Zhengzhilun 清朝論策類編 政治論 (Quoted in Liang, 1957).

Shandong jinghuilu 山東經會錄 (1571).

Shandong tongzhi 山東通志 (1533).

Shandong tongzhi 山東通志 (1678).

Shandong tongzhi 山東通志 (1911).

Shizhenglu 實政錄 (1593. 1871 edition). By Lü Kun.

Tangyi xianzhi 堂邑縣志 (1710).

Tushubian 圖書編 (1613. Quoted from Babian jingshi leizuan).

Modern Secondary Literature

Atwell, William S., "Notes on Silver, Foreign Trade, and the Late Ming Economy", *Ch'ing-shih wen-t'i* 3.8 (1977), 1-33.

Beattie, Hilary J., *Land and Lineage in China. A Study of T'ung-ch'eng County, Anhwei, in the Ming and Ch'ing Dynasties*, (Cambridge, 1979).

Brunnert, H.S., and V.V. Hagelstrom, *Present Day Political Organization of China*, (Shanghai, 1912).

Bryant, Daniel, "A DMB Chronology", *Ming Studies* 8 (1979), 27-40.

Cartier, Michel et Pierre-Étienne Will, "Démographie et institutions en Chine: Contribution a l'analyse des recensements de l'époque impériale (2 ap. J.-C. - 1750)", *Annales de Démographie Historique* (1971), 165-235.

Cartier, Michel, *Une Réforme Locale en Chine au XVIe Siècle. Hai Rui à Chun'an 1558-1562*, (Paris - La Haye, 1973).

Chang, George Jer-lang, "The Village Elder System of the Early Ming Dynasty", *Ming Studies* 7 (1978), 53-72.

Ch'ü T'ung-tsu, *Law and Society in Traditional China*, (Paris-La Haye, 1965).

Ch'ü T'ung-tsu, *Local Government in China under the Ch'ing*, (Cambridge, Mass., 1962).

Elmquist, Paul Oscar, *Rural Control in Early Modern China* (Ph.D. thesis, Harvard University, 1963).

Farmer, Edward L., *Early Ming Government. The Evolution of Dual Capitals*, (Cambridge, Mass., 1976).

Franke, Wolfgang, *An Introduction to the Sources of Ming History*, (Kuala Lumpur-Singapore, 1968).

Franke, Wolfgang, "Material aus Gesammelten Shcriften (*pieh-chi*) als Quelle für Lokalgeschichte. Bemerkungen zu einer Untersuchung von Michel Cartier", *OE* 21 (1974), 191-198.

Franke, Wolfgang, "Zur Grundsteuer in China während der Ming Dynastie", *Zeitschrift für vergleichende Rechtswissenschaft* 56 (1953), 93-103.

Friese, Heinz, *Das Dienstleistungs-System der Ming Zeit (1368-1644)*, (Hamburg, 1959).

Goodrich, L. Carrington, and Chaoying Fang, eds., *Dictionary of Ming Biography*, 2 vols., (New York and London, 1976).

Grimm, Tilemann, *Erziehung und Politik im konfuzianischen China der Ming Zeit (1368-1644)*, (Hamburg, 1960).

Handlin, Joanna F., "Lü K'un Compromises with the Common People", *Ming Studies* 1 (1975), 79-94.

Ho, Ping-ti, *The Ladder of Success in Imperial China, Aspects of Social Mobility, 1368-1911*, (New York and London, 1962).

Ho, Ping-ti, *Studies on the Population of China 1368-1953*, (Cambridge, Mass., 1959).

Hosack, Robert E., *Shantung: An Interpretation of a Chinese Province*, (Ph.D. thesis, Duke University, 1951).

Hoshi Ayao 星斌夫 , "Mindai no yobisō to shasō", 明代の 預備倉と社倉 , *Tōyōshi kenkyū* 18 (1959), 117-137.

Hoshi Ayao 星斌夫 , *Mindai sōun no kenkyū* 明代漕運 の研究 , (Tokyo, 1963).

Hsiao Kung-chuan, *Rural China. Imperial Control in the Nineteenth Century*, (Seattle, 1960).

Huang, Ray, *Taxation and Governmental Finance in Sixteenth-Century Ming China*, (Cambridge, 1974).

Hucker, Charles O., *The Censorial System of Ming China*, (Stanford, 1966).

Hucker, Charles O., "Governmental Organization of the Ming Dynasty", *HJAS* 21 (1958), 1-66.

Hucker, Charles O., *The Ming Dynasty: Its Origins and Evolving Institutions*, (Ann Arbor, 1978).

Igarashi Seiji 五十嵐正一 "Minsho ni okeru shagaku settei o meguru shojijō ni tsuite" 明初における 社学設定 をめぐる 諸事情について , in *Yamazaki sensei taikan kinen Tōyōshigaku ronsō*, (Tokyo, 1967), pp. 13-26.

Iwami Hiroshi 岩見宏 , "Kasei nenkan no rikisa ni tsuite" 嘉靖年間の力差について , in *Tamura hakase shōju tōyōshi ronsō*, (Kyoto, 1958), pp. 39-56.

Iwami Hiroshi 岩見宏 , "'Santō keikairoku' ni tsuite" 山東 経会禄について , in *Shimizu hakase tsuitō kinen Mindaishi ronsō*, (Tokyo, 1962), pp.197-220.

Karlgren, Bernhard, "The Early History of the Chou Li and Tso Chuan Texts", *BMFEA* 3 (1931), 1-59.

Kataoka Shibako 片岡芝子 "Kahoku no tochi shoyū to ichijō benpō 華北の 土地 所有と 一條鞭法 in *Shimizu hakase tsuitō kinen Mindaishi ronsō*, (Tokyo, 1962), pp.139-163.

213

Kawakatsu Mamoru 川勝守 , "Mindai no kishōku ni tsuite"
明代の寄莊戸に ついて , *Tōyōshi Kenkyū* 33.3
(1974), 48-71.

Kawakatsu Mamoru 川勝守 , "Mindai rikō hensei no henshitsukatei -- Oyama Masaaki-shi no 'sekiko no igi' ron no hihan"
明代の里甲編成の 変質過程——小山正明氏の「析戸の意義」
論の 批判—— *Shien* 112 (1975),
521-542.

Kōno Mitsuhiro 河野通博 , "Shindai Santōshō no kansei
rikujō kōtsūro" 清代 山東省の 官制陸上交通路
Shirin 33.3 (1950), 317-336.

Philip A. Kuhn, "Local Self-Government under the Republic. Problems of Control, Autonomy and Mobilization", in Frederic Wakeman, Jr. and Carolyn Grant, eds., *Conflict and Control in Late
Imperial China*, (Berkeley, 1975), pp. 257-298.

Kuribayashi Nobuo 栗林宣夫 , "Mindai kōki no nōson to rikōsei" 明代後期の 農村と里甲制 , *Tōyō shi-
gaku ronshū* (1955), 365-400.

Kuribayashi Nobuo 栗林宣夫 , *Rikōsei no kenkyū* 里甲
制の研究 , (Tokyo, 1971).

Legge, James, *The Chinese Classics*, 3 vols., (Hongkong-London,
1865).

Lidai yudi yangetu 歷代與地沿革圖 , (Taipei, 1975).

Li Guang-bi 李光璧 , *Mingchao shilüe* 明朝史略 ,
(Wuhan, 1957).

Li Jiannong 李劍農 , *Song-Yuan-Ming jingji shigao* 宋元
明經濟史稿 , (Peking, 1957).

Liang Fangzhong 梁方仲 , *Mingdai liangzhang zhidu* 明代
粮長制度 , (Shanghai, 1957).

Liang Fangzhong 梁方仲 , "Mingdai yitiaobianfa nianbiao",
明代一條鞭法年表 , *Lingnan xuebao* 12.1 (1952),
15-49.

Littrup, Leif, "The Early Single Whip in Shandong, 1550-1570",
Papers on Far Eastern History 15 (1977), 63-95.

Littrup, Leif, "The Yellow Registers of the Ming Dynasty - Translation from the Wan-li Da-Ming Hui-dian", *Papers on Far Eastern
History* 16 (1977), 67-106.

McKnight, Brian E., *Village and Bureaucracy in Southern Sung China*, (Chicago, 1971).

Mori Masao 森正夫 , Nihon no Min Shin shidaishi kenkyū ni
okeru gōshinron ni tsuite 日本の 明清時代史 研究における
郷紳論に ついて , *Rekishi hyoron* 308 (1975),
40-60; 312 (1976), 74-84; 314 (1976), 113-128.

214

Nishijima Sadao 西嶋定生 , "Mindai ni okeru momen no fukyū ni tsuite" 明代に於ける木棉の普及に就いて
    Shigaku Zasshi 57 (1948), 193-314, 275-304.

Obata Tatsuo 小田龍雄 , "Kōnan ni okeru rikō no hensei
ni tsuite" 江南における里甲の編成について
    Shirin 39.2 (1956), 89-123.

Oyama Masaaki 小山正明 , "Fueki seido no henkaku" 賦役
制度の変革 , in *Higashi-Ajia sekai no tenkai*, v.2
= *Iwanami kōza sekai rekishi*, v. 12, (Tokyo, 1971), pp.313-345.

Oyama Masaaki 小山正明 , "Mindai ni okeru zeiryō no kachō
to kosoku to no kankei" 明代における税粮の科徴と戸則
との関係 , *Bunka kagaku kiyō* 7
(1965), 41-74.

Perkins, Dwight D., *Agricultural Development in China, 1368-1968*,
(Chicago, 1969).

Sakai Tadao 酒井忠夫 , *Chūgoku zensho no kenkyū* 中國
善書の研究 , (Tokyo, 1961).

Sakai Tadao 酒井忠夫 "Mindai zen shoki no hōkōsei ni
tsuite" 明代前中期の保甲制について ,
in *Shimizu hakase tsuitō kinen Mindaishi ronsō*, (Tokyo, 1962),
pp. 577-610.

Schurmann, Herbert Franz, *Economic Structure of the Yüan Dynasty*,
(Cambridge, Mass., 1956).

Shimizu Morimitsu 清水盛光 , "Chūgoku no gōson tōchi to
sonraku" 中國の郷村統治と村落 , in *Shakai
kōseishi taikei* 社會構成史体系 , v. 2, pt. 2,
(Tokyo, 1949).

Skinner, G. William, "Chinese Peasants and the Closed Community:
An Open and Shut Case", *Comparative Studies in Society and History* 13 (1971), 270-281.

Skinner, G. William, "Marketing and Social Structure in Rural
China", *JAS* 24 (1964), 3-43.

Skinner, G. William, "Urban Development in Imperial China", in
G.William Skinner, ed., *The City in Late Imperial China*, (Stanford, 1977), pp.3-31.

Tani Mitsutaka 谷光隆 , *Mindai basei no kenkyū* 明代馬政
の研究 , (Kyōto, 1972).

Taniguchi Kikuo 谷口規矩雄 , "Mindai Kahoku ni okeru
ginsa seiritsu no ichi kenkyū - Santō no mongin seiritsu o chūshin ni shite" 明代華北における銀差成立の一研究
——山東の門銀成立を中心にして *Tōyōshi Kenkyū* 20.3
(1961), 1-33.

Taniguchi Kikuo 谷口規矩雄 , "Mindai Kahoku no daiko
ni tsuite" 明代華北の実戸について
    Tōyōshi Kenkyū 27 (1969), 474-505.

Taniguchi Kikuo 谷口規矩雄 , "Kuribayashi Nobuo, Rikōsei no kenkyū" 栗林宣夫；里甲制の研究
Tōyōshi Kenkyū 31.2 (1972), 116-121.

Taylor, Romein, "Ming T'ai-tsu and the Gods of the Walls and
Moats", *Ming Studies* 4 (1977), 31-49.

Thorp, James, *Geography of the Soils of China*, (Nanking, 1936).

The Times Atlas of China, (London, 1974).

Tsurumi Naohiro 鶴見尚弘 , "Kyū Chūgoku ni okeru
kyōdōtai no shomondai" 旧中国における共同体の 諸
問題 , *Shichō* (New Series) 4(1978), 63-86.

Tsurumi Naohiro 鶴見尚弘 , "Mindai ni okeru goson shi-
hai" 明代における鄉村支配 , in *Higashi-*
Ajia sekai no tenkai, v.2, = *Iwanami kōza sekai rekishi*, v.12,
(Tokyo, 1971), pp.57-92.

Tsurumi Naohiro 鶴見尚弘 , "Mindai no kireiko ni tsuite"
明代の 畸零戸に ついて , *Tōyō gakuhō* 47.3 (1964),
35-64.

Twitchet, D.C., *Financial Administration under the T'ang Dynasty*,
(Cambridge, 1963).

Wada Sei 和田清 , *Minshi Shokkashi yakuchū* 明史食貨志
譯註 , 2 vols., (Tokyo, 1957).

Wada Sei 和田清 , *Shina chihō jichi hattatsushi* 支那地方
自治發達史 , (Tokyo, 1939, reprinted Tokyo 1975
as *Chūgoku chihō*...).

Wang Lanyin 王蘭蔭 , "Mingdai zhi shexue" 明代之社
學 , *Shida yuekan* 21 (1935), 42-102, 25 (1936), 63-129.

Watt, John R., *The District Magistrate in Late Imperial China*,
(New York and London, 1972).

Wei Qingyuan 韋慶遠 , *Mingdai huangce zhidu* 明代黃册
制度 , (Peking, 1961).

Wiens, Mi Chu, "Changes in the Fiscal and Rural Control Systems
in the Fourteenth and Fifteenth Centuries", *Ming Studies* 3
(1976), 53-69.

Wu Chengluo 吳承洛 , *Zhongguo duliangheng shi* 中國
度量衡史 , (1937, Shanghai 1957).

Yamane Yukio 山根幸夫 , "Jūgo jūroku seiki Chūgoku ni
okeru fueki rōdōsei no kaikaku" 十五・十六世紀中國に
おける 賦役勞働制の改革 , *Shigaku zasshi*
60.11 (1951), 43-68.

Yamane Yukio 山根幸夫 , "Kahoku no byōkai" 寧北の廟会
, *Shiron* 17 (1967), 1-22.

Yamane Yukio 山根幸夫 , "Mindai richō no shokuseki ni
kansuru ichi kōsatsu" 明代里長の 職責に 関する一考察
, *Tōhōgaku* 3 (1952), 79-87.

216

Yamane Yukio 山根幸夫 , *Mindai yōeki seido no tenkai*
明代徭役制度の展開 , (Tokyo, 1966).

Yamane Yukio 山根幸夫 , "Min Shin jidai Kahoku ni okeru
teikishi" 明清時華北に ろける 定期市
Shiron 8 (1960), 493-504.

Yamane Yukio 山根幸夫 , "Min Shinsho no Kahoku no shishu
to shinshi-gomin" 明清初の華北の 市集と 紳士・豪民
, in *Nakayama Hachirō kyōju shōju kinen
Min Shin shi ronshū*, (Tokyo, 1977), pp. 303-332.

Yang, C.K., *Religion in Chinese Society*, (Berkeley and Los Angeles, 1961).

Zuo Yunpeng 左云鹏 ,"Mingdai yaoyi zhidu sanlun" 明代徭役
制度散论 , *Zhongguoshi yanjiu* 1980.2, 16-26.

Index

218